Social Security in the Balkans – Volume 2

Studies in
Critical Social Sciences

Series Editor
David Fasenfest (*Wayne State University*)

Editorial Board
Eduardo Bonilla-Silva (*Duke University*)
Chris Chase-Dunn (*University of California-Riverside*)
William Carroll (*University of Victoria*)
Raewyn Connell (*University of Sydney*)
Kimberlé W. Crenshaw (*University of California, LA,* and *Columbia University*)
Raju Das (*York University*)
Heidi Gottfried (*Wayne State University*)
Karin Gottschall (*University of Bremen*)
Alfredo Saad-Filho (*King's College London*)
Chizuko Ueno (*University of Tokyo*)
Sylvia Walby (*Lancaster University*)

VOLUME 196

The titles published in this series are listed at *brill.com/scss*

Social Security in the Balkans
Volume 2

*An Overview of Social Policy in the Republics
of North Macedonia and Montenegro*

Edited by

Marzena Żakowska
Dorota Domalewska

BRILL

LEIDEN | BOSTON

Cover illustration: Courtesy of Arkadiusz Kupiec, 2020, arway.waw.pl and Freepik.

Library of Congress Cataloging-in-Publication Data

Names: Żakowska, Marzena, editor. | Domalewska, Dorota, editor.
Title: Social security in the Balkans. Volume 2, An overview of social
　policy in the republics of North Macedonia and Montenegro / edited by
　Marzena Żakowska, Dorota Domalewska.
Other titles: Overview of social policy in Croatia, Albania, Bosnia and
　Herzegovina, Greece, Romania and Bulgaria
Description: Leiden ; Boston : Brill, [2022] | Series: Studies in critical
　social sciences, 1573-4234 ; volume 196 | Includes index.
Identifiers: LCCN 2021048710 (print) | LCCN 2021048711 (ebook) |
　ISBN 9789004306882 (hardback) | ISBN 9789004306899 (ebook)
Subjects: LCSH: Social security–Balkan Peninsula. | Public welfare–Balkan
　Peninsula.
Classification: LCC HD7211 .S64 2022 (print) | LCC HD7211 (ebook) |
　DDC 362.9496–dc23/eng/20211006
LC record available at https://lccn.loc.gov/2021048710
LC ebook record available at https://lccn.loc.gov/2021048711

Typeface for the Latin, Greek, and Cyrillic scripts: "Brill". See and download: brill.com/brill-typeface.

ISSN 1573-4234
ISBN 978-90-04-30688-2 (hardback)
ISBN 978-90-04-30689-9 (e-book)

Copyright 2022 by Marzena Żakowska and Dorota Domalewska. Published by Koninklijke Brill NV, Leiden, The Netherlands.
Koninklijke Brill NV incorporates the imprints Brill, Brill Nijhoff, Brill Hotei, Brill Schöningh, Brill Fink, Brill mentis, Vandenhoeck & Ruprecht, Böhlau Verlag and V&R Unipress.
Koninklijke Brill NV reserves the right to protect this publication against unauthorized use. Requests for re-use and/or translations must be addressed to Koninklijke Brill NV via brill.com or copyright.com.

This book is printed on acid-free paper and produced in a sustainable manner.

Contents

Acknowledgements VII
List of Figures and Tables VIII
Abbreviations X
Notes on Contributors XI
Abstracts XVI

Social Policy in the Republic of North Macedonia and the Republic of Montenegro: Developments and Challenges   1
   Marzena Żakowska and Dorota Domalewska

PART 1
Social Security in the Republic of North Macedonia

1 The Social Security Policy of the Republic of North Macedonia: Reform Process, Opportunities and Perspectives   13
   Katerina Veljanovska Blazhevska

2 Health, Pensions and Disability Insurance in the Republic of North Macedonia   34
   Afet Mamuti

3 Poverty as a Social Phenomenon in the Republic of North Macedonia   62
   Kire Sharlamanov and Katerina Mitevska Petrusheva

4 Unemployment in the Republic of North Macedonia: Characteristics and Perspectives   84
   Kire Sharlamanov and Katerina Mitevska Petrusheva

PART 2
Social Security in the Republic of Montenegro

5 Pension System and Reforms in Montenegro   109
   Maja Baćović

6   The Public Health Care Sector in Post-transition Montenegro   152
     Natalija Perišić

7   Social Protection System in Montenegro   171
     Marzena Żakowska and Tomasz Ferfecki

8   Unemployment and Emigration as a (Main) Challenge for the Social Security System and Stability of a Multiethnic State: The Case of Montenegro   197
     Agata Domachowska

    Index   223

Acknowledgements

The inspiration for writing this three-volume book was the experience gained during research begun by Marzena Żakowska in the Balkans in 2014. However, it could not have been written without the help of many people whom we wish to thank profusely.

Our gratitude goes to Professor Cezary Smuniewski for his encouragement to start the project and his guidance and constructive comments during the development process. We would like to thank Professor Jarosław Gryz and Professor Mark Juszczak for their insightful discussions during the research. We acknowledge the funding received from the War Studies University, Warsaw, Poland. Our thanks go out for the support we received from Professor Col. Tadeusz Zieliński, Professor Col. Andrzej Soboń, and Professor Jarosław Solarz, who authorized the project and offered us thoughtful advice. We owe thanks to Tomasz Żornaczuk from the Polish Institute of International Affairs and Marta Szpala from the Center for Eastern Studies for their valuable counsel.

We are thankful to Professor Ilona Urych, Col (res) Doctor Lech Drab, Doctor Adam Szynal and Shkëlzen Macukulli for believing in our work. We would like to thank the authors of all the individual chapters – without their expertise, patience, and dedication, this book would not have been completed.

We extend our gratitude to Katarzyna Tarasewicz, Richard Koss, Marcin Hapat, Małgorzata Zeniuk, Debbie de Wit, and Judy Pereira, who supported forming the final shape of the book.

We are grateful to our Families, Friends, and all our Colleagues in the Balkan states. Without their support this endeavor would not have been possible.

A special word of thanks goes to the Editor of the Studies in Critical Social Sciences Series, Professor David Fasenfest, who offered constructive remarks and coordinated the study.

Figures and Tables

Figures

2.1 Life expectancy in North Macedonia 2005–2015   50
5.1 Pension fund's income from contributions and government transfer (million euro), 2016–2018   119
5.2 Demographic transition in Montenegro   131
5.3 Population by age groups: 1991–2091   132
5.4 Ratio of expenditures and revenues of the pension fund (scenario 1)   136
5.5 Number of employees per number of pensioners (scenario 1)   137
5.6 Ratio of expenditures and revenues of the pension fund (scenario 2)   138
5.7 Number of employees per number of pensioners (scenario 2)   139
8.1 Tourist arrivals in collective accommodation in Montenegro, 2010–2018   202
8.2 Unemployment in Montenegro's regions (%)   209
8.3 Unemployment rate in the Western Balkan states (2006–2019)   210

Tables

2.1 The number of pensioners and birth rate in Macedonia   48
2.2 Status of pension beneficiaries by paid pension type, and the percentage of employment/unemployment rate in 2017 in North Macedonia   52
2.3 Average amount of pension and pensioners structure by pension type in 2017 in North Macedonia   53
2.4 Terms and conditions for pension and disability insurance   54
3.1 Poverty rate in the Republic of North Macedonia   66
3.2 Risk of poverty, depending on the number of household members and social transfers   68
3.3 Percentage of unemployed out of people that are living in poverty   72
3.4 Percentage of poverty of persons living in households with five or more members   73
3.5 Percentage of household where the head of the household has no education or primary education   73
3.6 Relative poverty according to the number of household members (1997–2007)   74
3.7 Relative poverty according to the economic status of members of the household (1997–2007)   74

FIGURES AND TABLES

3.8 Relative poverty according to the level of education of the head of the household (1997–2007) 75
4.1 Overview of the number of unemployed persons from 1976 to 1990 89
4.2 Gender structure of the unemployed in the Republic of North Macedonia 92
4.3 Age structure of the unemployed in the Republic of North Macedonia 93
4.4 Unemployment rate among young people aged 15 to 24 years 94
4.5 Number of job seekers for more than a year 95
4.6 Economic growth rate with employment and unemployment rate 96
4.7 Overview of active labor market policy measures by category for 2007–2015 101
4.8 Benefits for employers foreseen by the project "Macedonia employs 2" 101
5.1 Comparison of the basic features from the pension law from 2004 and 2010 118
5.2 The pension system in Montenegro (changes in indicators from 2006 to 2018) 120
5.3 The pension system in Montenegro, 2006–2018 (descriptive statistics of indicators) 123
5.4 Fiscal indicators in Montenegro, 2006–2018 (%) 125
5.5 Population in Montenegro 1991–2091 (cohort model projections) 129
5.6 Dependency ratio in Montenegro 1991–2091 (cohort model projections) 133
5.7 Forecasting revenues and expenditures of the pension system in Montenegro, 2019–2056 (scenario 1) 136
5.8 Forecasting revenues and expenditures of the pension system in Montenegro, 2019–2056 (scenario 2) 138
5.9 Forecasting revenues and expenditures of the pension system in Montenegro, 2019–2056 (scenario 1) 142
5.10 Forecasting revenues and expenditures of the pension system in Montenegro, 2019–2056 (scenario 2) 146
7.1 Overview of social assistance benefits 179
7.2 Social welfare beneficiaries 184
8.1 Montenegro: Macroeconomic projections (2018–2021), low-growth scenario 203
8.2 Growth rate in the Western Balkans (%) 205
8.3 General government finances (% of GDP) 206
8.4 Number of unemployed persons and unemployment rates by sex in Montenegro 208
8.5 Net migration rate in the Western Balkan states 212
8.6 Net migration in Montenegrin municipalities, 2018 215
8.7 Elements of migration with regard to the whole society in 1991–2011 216

Abbreviations

ALMP	Active Labor Market Policies
AP	Action Plan
AROPE	At risk of poverty or social exclusion indicator
CeMI	Center for Monitoring and Research
CPI	Consumer Price Index
CSW	Centers for Social Work
DPS	Democratic Party of Socialists of Montenegro
DRG	Diagnosis Related Groups
EAM	Employment Agency of Montenegro
EC	European Commission
FRY	Federal Republic of Yugoslavia
HIF	Health Insurance Fund
HIFM	Health Insurance Fund of Macedonia
ILO	International Labor Organization
IMF	International Monetary Fund
IPA	Instrument for Pre-Accession Assistance
ISA	Institute for Social Activities
LSG	Local Self-Government
LSGU	Local Self-Government Units
MLSW	Ministry of Labor and Social Welfare
MONSTAT	Statistical Office of Montenegro
MOP	Family material support
NPAA	National Program for Adoption of European Union Law
OSCE	Organization for Security and Co-operation in Europe
PAYG	pay-as-you-go system
PIO Fund	Pension and Disability Insurance Fund
RNM	Republic of North Macedonia
SFA	social financial assistance
SFRY	Socialist Federal Republic of Yugoslavia
SILC	Survey on Income and Living Conditions
SPF	social protection fund
SSW	Services for Social Work
SWC	Social Welfare Centers
UNDP	United Nations Development Program

Notes on Contributors

Maja Baćović
is an associate professor at the Faculty of Economics of the University of Montenegro. She is a former member of the Committee for Economic Research and former member of the Centre of Young Scientists of the Montenegrin Academy of Arts and Sciences. She acted as the vice rector for International Cooperation (University of Montenegro) (2015–2017). She is the author of four books and several papers in WoS indexed journals. Her two most recent papers are "Total factor productivity growth in upper middle-income Balkan countries from 2000–2017, total economy and sectoral approach: growth accounting method" (Argumenta Oeconomica, 2021); and "STEM Education and Growth in Europe" (co-author with Zivko Andrijasevic and Bojan Pejovic, Journal of the Knowledge Economy, 2021). Her ORCID is: https://orcid.org/0000-0002-8865-3924.

Katerina Veljanovska Blazhevska
is an associate professor in political systems and Vice-Rector for International Cooperation at MIT University – Skopje, Faculty of Security Sciences, the Republic of North Macedonia. In June 2012 she was granted a full scholarship for the International Summer School (Master Course) at the University of Oslo, Kingdom of Norway, Department of Politics and Media Communications. In October 2014, she was granted full scholarship of the International Visegrad Fund to implement an international scientific-research project at the National Defence University of Warsaw, Poland. During her scientific stay, she was hired as a visiting professor at the Department of National Security. In April 2016, she gained a scholarship from the Austrian Government and Austrian Study Centre for Peace and Conflict Resolution – ASPR, for the International Civilian Peacekeeping and Peacebuilding Training Program (IPT). In November 2018 and June 2019, she was awarded a Jean Monnet scholarship for conference presentation of scientific research in the framework of new security challenges. In 2019, she received official recognition by the 4th Macedonian President Prof. Gjorge Ivanov, who served two consecutive terms as the President of his country (2009–2019), for "10 years of International training for young leaders", for continuous support and common vision. Katerina Veljanovska Blazhevska has gained extensive experience in the field of political and security relations. She is also a licensed consultant in communication skills and public relations, career development mentor and public policy expert. She is the author of four books, two manuals and a large number of scientific-research papers in her

scientific field of interest (political systems – security – public policy). Her latest book is European and Security Policy – Through the Prism of Theory and Practice (2019, IPP). Her ORCID is https://orcid.org/0000-0001-9993-7618 and e-mail address: veljanovska_katerina@yahoo.com.

Agata Domachowska

is an associate professor (dr. hab., prof. UMK) at the Faculty of Humanities (Nicolaus Copernicus University, NCU) and a senior analyst at the Institute of Central Europe. She has conducted research at the University of Pittsburgh, George Washington University and the Humboldt University of Berlin as well as in archives and libraries in Serbia, Montenegro, Albania, North Macedonia and Croatia. She also did an internship at the European Parliament and a training stay at the Polish Embassy in Tirana (Albania). She is a member of The Laboratory for the Study of Collective Memory in Post-communist Europe and the Balkans. She is the recipient of numerous scholarships and grants including a Kosciuszko Foundation in New York, the 2015 ASEEES Davis Travel Grant, the Polish Ministry of Education. Her research focuses on identity and historical narratives, nation-building and the politics of memory in the Western Balkans, Balkan diasporas, politics and culture of western Balkan states. Selected publications: "'The Yellow Duck' Attacks – An Analysis of the Activities of the Ne da (vi)mo Beograd Initiative in the Serbian Public Space" (Slavia Meridionalis, 19, 2019); "The attitude of Poland and Polish Society toward the 1999 Kosovo refugees. Slovanský přehled: historická revue pro dějiny střední, východní a jihovýchodní Evropy", (Slavonic Review: Review for Central, Eastern and Southeastern European History), 105(1), 2019); "From Saint Sava to Milosevic – The Pantheon of (Anti) heroes in Serbian Presidential Election (2017)" (Journal of Nationalism, Memory & Language Politics 13(1), 2019). Her ORCID is https://orcid.org/0000-0002-8521-9399 and e-mail address: a.domachowska@umk.pl.

Dorota Domalewska

is an assistant professor at the National Security Faculty, War Studies University, Warsaw, Poland. She is the Head of the Department of Security Education. During the years 2012–2015, she was a lecturer at Stamford International University and Rangsit University in Thailand and, in 2019, a research fellow at Rangsit University, Thailand. She carries out interdisciplinary research blending the field of security, communication and education. She is the author of "Multidimensional communication from a security perspective. Communication in crisis situations and strategic communication" (Warsaw: War Studies University, 2020, in Polish), and "Determinants of the modern security environment" (co-editor with Radosław Bielawski,

Warsaw: War Studies University, 2020, in Polish). She has published numerous articles on security education, immigrant integration processes, strategic communication in social media, and societal security. Since 2016, she has been an Associate Editor and, since 2020, Editor-in-Chief of Security and Defence Quarterly, ISSN 2300-8741. Her ORCID is https://orcid.org/0000-0002-1788-1591 and e-mail address: d.domalewska@akademia.mil.pl.

Tomasz Ferfecki
works at the Ministry of National Defence in Warsaw, Poland. His main research interest includes Western Balkan region, particularly issues focused on the relations between the European Union, NATO, Russia, Montenegro and Serbia on the political, social, economic and military level. He is an author of articles concerning the security situation in the Western Balkans e.g., "Serbia's cooperation with the Russian Federation in the military area as a challenge for the development of Serbia-NATO cooperation" (Wiedza Obronna, 2017) and "Strategic communication of the Russian Federation in the military area of the Republic of Serbia" (Chorzow Studies in Politics, 2019).

Afet Mamuti
is an associate professor at the University of Tetova, the Republic of North Macedonia. He is a member of the Board of Directors at the Clinical Hospital in Tetovo and a member of the Editorial Council of International Journal of Legal Sciences "Justicia", Faculty of Law, University of Tetova. He carries out research in the field of health insurance and disability pension insurance. His recent publications include "The New Reproductive Technology and Parent-Child Relationship" (Revista de Științe Politice, Revue des Sciences Politiques, 51, 2016); "Protection of Ownership Rights under The Legislation of Macedonia" (Vizione, 29, 2018); "The role of the state and family in implementing the principle of special protection of children" (Vizione, 28, 2017). His e-mail address is afet.mamuti@unite.edu.mk.

Katerina Mitevska Petrusheva
is an assistant professor at the Faculty of Education, International Balkan University in Skopje, the Republic of North Macedonia. Her recent works include "Analysis of Theoretical Approaches to Education" (co-author with Kire Sharlamanov, Katica Stoimenovska, International Journal of Scientific & Engineering Research, 10(2) 2019); "Requirements for teacher education in vocational education and training" (co-author with Biljana Popeska and Snezana Jovanova-Mitkova, Proceedings of University of Ruse-2018, 57(6.2), 2018); "Perspectives of students – future natural sciences teachers regarded

teacher's role as educator" (co-author with Biljana Popeska and Orce Mitevski, Contemporary Educational Researches Journal, 7(3), 2017); "Establishing the relation between teacher and the student in a context of teacher's educational role – perspective of the future physical education teachers" (co-author with Biljana Popeska, Research in Kinesiology 44(2), 2016).

Natalija Perišić

is an associate professor of social policy at the Faculty of Political Science, Department of Social Policy and Social Work, the University of Belgrade, where she lectures on national and European social policy, ageing and migration at the undergraduate, masters and PhD levels. She is also a lecturer at the Master in Migration Studies program at the University of Belgrade. She is a Visiting Professor at the University of Tuzla – Faculty of Philosophy, Bosnia and Herzegovina, the University of Eastern Sarajevo – Faculty of Philosophy, Bosnia and Herzegovina and the University of Niš – Faculty of Philosophy, Serbia. She is Head of the Department of Social Policy and Social Work and a coordinator of MIGREC, a project currently funded under the European Union's Horizon 2020 scheme. Her scientific and research interests include the nexus between ageing, migration and welfare state, national and European social policies and gender perspectives. She has published about 50 papers in national and international journals and contributed to several edited books. Some of her contributions include "Responses of the Serbian Welfare State to the Global Economic Crisis" (co-author with Jelena Vidojević, Revija za socijalnu politiku, 22(2), 2015); "The Serbian Welfare State – A Transition Loser" (in Challenges to European Welfare Systems, edited by Klaus Schubert, Paloma de Villota, and Johanna Kuhlmann, Heidelberg, New York, Dordrecht, London: Springer, 2016); "Readmission in Serbia – Huge Challenges, Weak Opportunities" (in Diversity of Migration in South-East Europe edited by Mirjam Zbinden, Janine Dahinden, Andnan Efendić, Bern: Peter Lang, 2016); "Domestic Violence Against Immigrant Women in Transit – The Case of Serbia" (Temida, 22(1), 2019); "Montenegro" (in Health Politics in Europe: A Handbook, edited by Ellen M. Immergut, Karen M. Anderson, Camilla Devitt, and Tamara Popić, Oxford: Oxford University Press, forthcoming). Her ORCID is https://orcid.org/0000-0001-7678-7231 and e-mail address: natalija.perisic@fpn.bg.ac.rs.

Kire Sharlamanov

is an associate professor at the Faculty of Humanities and Social Sciences, International Balkan University in Skopje, the Republic of North Macedonia. He is a member of the steering committee at the Association of Sociologists of North Macedonia for 2019, a member of the management committee at

"Professionalization and Social Impact of European Political Science", COST CA 15207 (2016–2020), Coordinator, Gilberto Capano, and a member of the management committee at the European Network for conflict research (ENCoRe), COST (2012–2016). He is author of numerous articles, including "Concept of Power in Castells Communication Theory" (co-author with Demiri Bejtulla, International Journal of Scientific and Engineering Research, 9(9), 2018); "Sociological Analysis of Spin and Spin Doctors" (co-author with Aleksandar Jovanovski, International Journal of Scientific and Engineering Research, 7(12), 2016); "The Social Protection System in Republic of Macedonia" (co-author with Aleksandar Jovanovski, International Journal of Scientific and Engineering Research 7(10), 2016); "Transition of the Pension System in Republic of Macedonia" (co-author with Aleksandar Jovanovski, International Journal of Scientific and Engineering Research, 7(9), 2016); "Usage of Political Marketing in Organization of Political Campaigns" (co-author with Aleksandar Jovanovski, International Journal of Scientific and Engineering Research, 6(11), 2015).

Marzena Żakowska
is an assistant professor at the National Security Faculty, War Studies University, Warsaw, Poland. She is Director of the Global Affairs and Diplomacy Studies and Chair of War Studies Working Group at International Society of Military Science. Her main field of expertise includes war and armed conflicts, Balkan states' security, migrations and social security. She is the author of such publications as "The roots of armed conflicts – multilevel security perspective" (Security and Defence Quarterly 3 (30), 2020), "Strategic challenges for Serbia's integration with the European Union" (Security and Defence Quarterly 2(11), 2016); "Mediation in Armed Conflict" (Security and Defence Quarterly, 4(17), 2017); "Determining Polish parliamentarians' tweets on migration: A case study of Poland" (co-author with Dorota Domalewska, Czech Journal of Political Science 3, 2019); "Migration from war-torn countries -an analysis of parliamentarians' tweets" (co-author with Dorota Domalewska, Przegląd Europejski, no. 2 (2019), in Polish). Her ORCID is https://orcid.org/0000-0002-32457684 and e-mail address: m.zakowska@akademia.mil.pl.

Abstracts

Chapter 1

Social policy in the Republic of North Macedonia has been characterized by constant changes that occurred as a result of shifting social and demographic structure, low economic growth and capacity, a permanently high unemployment rate, and increased demand for social protection services. In order to tackle these challenges, numerous legislation revisions have been undertaken, especially in the financing and administering of social services. The aim of this chapter is to give an overview and assessment of the social protection system in the Republic of North Macedonia (in particular its stakeholders) and to offer recommendations for improvement. The study is based on an analysis of secondary data such as research reports, policy documents, public perceptions on social issues, the experiences and perceptions of the beneficiaries of social assistance, and studies conducted by civil associations that work in the field of social work. The study also reviews strategic documents related to social policy such as the National Strategy for the Reduction of Poverty and Social Exclusion in the Republic of Macedonia 2010–2020, the Program for Employment and Social Policy 2020, and the Operational Plan for active employment programs and services. The analysis reveals that social policy in North Macedonia is oriented towards favoring services instead of cash transfers, increased consumer targeting rather than universal access, reduced state service provision at the expense of increased private initiatives, strengthening local government involvement in social protection, conditional cash transfers and reducing the institutional capacity of the state.

Chapter 2

Before gaining independence, the social security system of the Republic of North Macedonia was based on centralized Yugoslav Federation policies. Only after 1991 were concrete measures taken to establish a functional social security system in order to best meet the needs of its citizens. The Stabilization and Association Agreement between Macedonia and the EU requires that social security be adapted to the new social and economic requirements of society and the level of protection of the health and safety of workers be improved. The main rights of citizens regarding the social security system are ensured by the Constitution. The pension and disability system functions on the basis of the Principles of Solidarity (otherwise referred as the Pay-as-you-go (PAYG) principle) and the healthcare insurance system is based on compulsory and voluntary insurance. The aim of this chapter is to present theoretical and empirical views of the social security system of the Republic of North Macedonia through the doctrinal approach, with emphasis placed on health, pension and disability insurance, as well as the challenges present in this state. The development of the social security system will depend on demographic change and may only be achieved through reform and adapting to new social circumstances.

Chapter 3

Poverty remains one of the most serious social issues, especially when it afflicts a significant portion of the population over an extended period of time. It has serious consequences both for people living in poverty and for the community where those individuals live. Hence, every society seeks to reduce the number of people that live in poverty through its social policy and the established system of social security. This chapter aims to show the poverty rate in the Republic of North Macedonia, its structure and amplitudes over time, the reasons that cause it, and the measures taken to reduce it. To achieve this objective, secondary analysis of data was carried out, in particular analysis of data obtained from the government agencies that coordinate poverty reduction programs and social policy institutions in the Republic of North Macedonia. The research results indicate that the poverty rate in the Republic of North Macedonia over a long period of time has increased compared to most countries in the region. Although poverty has been reduced over the last few years, it remains at a high level compared to other countries.

Chapter 4

Unemployment is one of the most serious social issues, especially when it has structural characteristics. This chapter presents the evolution of unemployment in the Republic of North Macedonia, the reasons for the manifested amplitudes over time, and the attempts to reduce it and bring it under control through measures taken on the labor market. The research is conducted based on secondary sources of information: analysis of data obtained from the official state institutions in charge of recording unemployment and addressing this significant social challenge, as well as analysis of the most significant publications of academic scholars. The results of the research show that unemployment has been the most serious social problem in the Republic of North Macedonia for a long time. Since the country gained independence there have been constant but insufficient attempts to overcome this problem and the state institutions are far from resolving this problem satisfactorily. However, there has been a significant reduction of the unemployment rate in modern Macedonian society compared to the early 1990s.

Chapter 5

The pension system in Montenegro, although multi-pillar by law, is largely based on a mandatory public pay-as-you-go system that is operated by Montenegro's public pension fund and is subsidized by the Government. Since the two reforms in 2003 and 2010, the financial sustainability of the pension fund has been improved, but it still has not achieved its full capacity. Despite growing employment and efforts to reduce the informal economy, the ratio of workers to retirees has only moderately decreased since 2006 due to the aging population. This chapter aims to present recent developments in the Montenegrin pension system and to analyze the sustainability of the system in the future, bearing in mind the continued aging of the population, the mounting public debt and the high fiscal burdens that discourage investment. The framework of the study is based on two key characteristics of the Montenegrin pension system: the unsatisfactory ratio of workers to retirees and the insufficient pension funds and disability insurance. The study employs quantitative methods, and population projections were created by applying the cohort component method. The pension fund's forecasted expenditures and revenues were estimated by applying the arithmetic approach. Two forecasting scenarios, the aging population and wage growth are presented. The results show that the financial sustainability of the pension system in its current form may be improved by 2056, but it cannot be achieved in full. Although two comprehensive reform packages were implemented to increase the retirement age, introduce a points system in pension calculation, and change the pension adjustment formula, further reforms are recommended. To provide a pension system that is more sustainable from both a fiscal and a social perspective, further reforms may be directed at prolonging labour market participation by strengthening the early retirement policy and revising the early retirement scheme.

Chapter 6

The period of transition after 1989 did not introduce radical transformations to the Montenegrin health care system. Gradual reforms started as late as in 2004 and have resulted in the sustained dominance of the public health care system over the private sector. The purpose of this chapter is to explore the effects of the public health care sector reforms after 1989 in Montenegro regarding access to and the quality and sustainability of health care services. The study is based on qualitative analysis and assessment of the provision of health care by various sectors, with an emphasis on the public sector. The chapter starts with alternative roles of the state concerning health care – as a regulator, funder/purchaser and provider/planner, and takes them into consideration further within the Montenegrin context. The research shows the mixed results of health care reform. While coverage of the population by health care services is high, there are certain gaps. There is a failure to maintain high quality, and the funding mechanisms are not sufficient for a sustainable health care system. The progress of the Montenegrin health care reforms, therefore, seems moderate.

Chapter 7

After a decade of isolation from international processes following Yugoslavia's disintegration, the Republic of Montenegro currently aspires to become a part of the European Union. This comes with many challenges to adopt EU social policy principles and its social protection system including EU standards, requirements and best practices. The aim of this chapter is to scrutinize the social protection system in Montenegro by analysis of the legal framework, organization of institutions, financing mechanism as well as benefits and allowances schema. The study was based on secondary research using data from legal documents, the Statisitcal Office of Montenegro, the Ministry of Labor and Social Welfare of Montenegro and the European Commission. The chapter examines the following topics: legal framework, structure of social protection, financial benefits and allowances, financing system of social protection and strategic reforms. The study indicates the need for a strong continuing reforms process of the social protection system to improve structure and quality of service provision, achieve broader social justice, increase protection of vulnerable groups such as elderly people and create better child protection system.

Chapter 8

Montenegro, a small Balkan state, has to grapple with many economic issues. The labor market situation has not improved in recent years. The unemployment rate has remained stubbornly high, especially among young people. What is more, around 20% of the employed in fact work in the informal economy. Large numbers of the unemployed pose a serious challenge not only to the Montenegrin economy, but also to the capacities of social security system. The economic situation and the level of unemployment also have an impact on the scale of emigration. The aim of this chapter is to present two key challenges to the social security of Montenegro – unemployment and emigration. The analytical basis of this research is a review of economic, sociological and security-related literature, including a secondary data analysis of public policy documents, statistics and media reports. Considering the subject of this study, qualitative research seemed necessary while the research topic justifies the application of content analysis and desk research in order to analyze secondary data sources. The chapter begins by presenting briefly the economic situation in Montenegro – what changes have taken place in the economy over the last 30 years. Next, the unemployment level in Montenegro is described. The last part of the analysis presents the problem of emigration resulting from the economic situation in Montenegro and the level of unemployment. Despite efforts to accelerate economic growth and reduce the level of unemployment, economic slowdown is expected, which will in turn further increase migration flows.

Social Policy in the Republic of North Macedonia and the Republic of Montenegro: Developments and Challenges

Marzena Żakowska and Dorota Domalewska

The Republic of North Macedonia and the Republic of Montenegro share a history of difficult political transformation and genesis of statehood after the breakup of Yugoslavia. The socialist heritage has influenced their economic and social policies, and also shaped the path of the EU accession process of both countries. North Macedonia and Montenegro applied for EU membership in 2004 and 2008 respectively and now the two are candidates to join the European Union.[1] The EU runs wide-ranging programs supporting the states' social protection mechanisms and instruments in order to coordinate them and develop efficient and equitable social assistance measures. EU Membership will stimulate economic development and private investment which will in turn have a positive impact on the resolution of social security issues.

This second of a three-volume publication presents a multifaceted analysis of the social security systems of North Macedonia and Montenegro from the

---

1 The Republic of North Macedonia gained candidate status in December 2005 and opened accession negotiations on March 2020 whereas the Republic of Montenegro was granted candidate status in December 2010 and opened accession negotiations in June 2012. The European Council point out that for North Macedonia the tempo of accession negotiations depends on reforms to address remaining structural weaknesses in the rule of law, fundamental rights, the functioning of democratic institutions, public administration reform, economic development and competitiveness including improving macroeconomic, budgetary and structural policies. For Montenegro, on the other hand, the European Commission identifies the need to maintain macroeconomic stability and emphasizes the need to reduce the deficit, public debt and high unemployment. Montenegro has managed to temporarily close two of the 35 negotiating chapters, but 22 remain open, confirming that the country is a likely candidate for accession to the EU by 2025 as suggested by the European Commission's new 2018 enlargement strategy, see: Council of the European Union, Council Conclusions on Enlargement and Stabilization and Association Process, https://www.consilium.europa.eu/en/press/press-releases/2019/06/18/council-conclusions-on-enlargement-and-stabilisation-and-association-process/ (accessed November 7, 2020); European Commission, Montenegro 2018 Report, https://www.europarl.europa.eu/doceo/document/TA-8-2018-0482_EN.html (accessed November 7, 2020); Velina Lilyanova, Montenegro – a Lead Candidate for EU Accession, https://www.europarl.europa.eu/EPRS/EPRS-AaG-628238-Montenegro-lead-candidate-for-EU-accession-FINAL.pdf (accessed November 7, 2020).

perspective of social security policy and provides recommendations for competitive and sustainable development. It is the outcome of a four-year project realized in the period 2016–2020 and coordinated by Marzena Żakowska, funded by the Faculty of National Security at the War Studies University, Warsaw, Poland and carried out by an appointed international team of scientists and experts. The outline includes a vast spectrum of topics focusing on the pension system, healthcare, and disability insurance. Moreover, it also covers problems of labor market structure, unemployment, poverty, and migration.

At the beginning it should be emphasized, that the pension system in both countries is based on the pay-as-you-go (PAYG) principle and has undergone a reform process. Montenegro started reforms in 2004 by introducing the following changes to the system: raising the retirement age, extending the calculation period, launching changes in the method of calculating the pension, abolishing the general possibility of early retirement, and tightening the rights and controls of people with disabilities. The reform of the pension system in North Macedonia began in 2006 with the division of the pension security system into three pillars, two obligatory and the third – voluntary. The first pillar is based on the principle of intergenerational solidarity and includes contributions for old-age, disability, survivors' pensions, and the minimum pension, while the second and third are based on the principle of full funding. The second pillar provides an additional part of the pension for those retirees who pay contributions to this pillar and the third pillar imparts additional material security.[2] In these states, pension and disability insurance systems are based on generational solidarity.

Furthermore, North Macedonia and Montenegro embarked on major reforms in the organization, governance, financing, and provision of healthcare. These reforms, which were based on macro-level policy changes, aimed to increase financial sustainability, improve access to healthcare services for the entire population, improve the quality and efficiency in service delivery, and optimize health outcomes. With the reforms implemented since the country's independence in 1991, North Macedonia moved from a state-based healthcare system to private-public mixed one, which helped to improve long-term sustainability and efficiency. The North Macedonia Health Insurance Fund (HIF) was set up as the public purchaser of health services and total healthcare

---

[2] Blagica Petreski and Pavle Gacov, Sustainability of the Pension System in Macedonia. Comprehensive Analysis and Reform Proposal with MK-PENS – Dynamic Microsimulation Model, https://www.financethink.mk/wp-content/uploads/2020/11/Pension-analysis-EN.pdf (accessed November 10, 2020).

expenditure has increased.[3] The healthcare system has been decentralized and local authorities are responsible for managing primary healthcare, supporting patients with special needs, and other services. Special emphasis has been placed on reducing inequalities in access to healthcare services and maintaining high quality of services across the country and population. As a result of reforms efficiency gains were achieved and health benefits to the entire population were maximized. In contrast, the Montenegrin healthcare system is organized as a predominantly centralized system based on the public sector even though the healthcare market was liberalized allowing private providers to enter the market, in particular dental clinics, medical centers and pharmacies. The Montenegro Health Insurance Fund (HIF) manages the funds for services and healthcare providers on the basis of a contract.[4] The Government of Montenegro prioritizes healthcare with the objective of improving its efficiency and quality.

Among the main challenges for North Macedonia and Montenegro are the reduction of unemployment rates, and the maintenance of macroeconomic stability.[5] Both countries are struggling with the negative impact of the shadow economy on the labor market and social integration processes.[6] These unfavorable phenomena on the labor market are a heavy burden on the pension system. Additionally, the constantly deteriorating demographic trends are a huge challenge. Although in the last decade the unemployment rate in both countries has been reported significantly reduced, it is still among the highest in Europe (20.8% in Macedonia and 15.2% in Montenegro in 2018).[7] The biggest problems are on the one hand the low participation of women in the labor market and the small number of new jobs, and on the other hand low wages, job instability, employment discrimination and unequal treatment of employees. To remedy this situation the following actions are required:

---

3   Law on Health Insurance, Official Gazette, no. 07–12961, 2010, https://www.refworld.org/pdfid/5aa125974.pdf (accessed November 10, 2020).
4   Law on Health Care of 2016, Article 77.
5   European Commission, Montenegro 2018 Report, https://www.europarl.europa.eu/doceo/document/TA-8-2018-0482_EN.html (accessed November 7, 2020); European Commission, North Macedonia 2020 Report, https://www.europarl.europa.eu/doceo/document/A-9-2021-0040_EN.html (accessed November 12, 2020).
6   Peter Sanfey and Jakov Milatović, "The Western Balkans Regional Economic Area: From Economic Cooperation to Economic Integration", in Western Balkan Economies in Transition. Recent Economic and Socila Developments, ed. Reiner Osbild and Will Barlett (Cham: Springer, 2019), 26.
7   Eurostat, Unemployment in the EU Regions in 2018, https://ec.europa.eu/eurostat/documents/2995521/9/4686z/1-29042019-BP-EN.pdf/329a9132-20c0-485b-aa22-b34864c22fde (accessed November 12, 2020).

- a more effective education system responding to the needs of the labor market;
- an active labor market policy, increasing the participation of women and social groups at risk of exclusion in the labor market;
- increased private sector investment and job creation in high-potential sectors;
- policy influencing the supply of and demand for labor in order to maintain a balance;
- the creation of new jobs in the private sector by increasing productivity and competitiveness.[8]

The implementation of these measures will also create an opportunity to improve the performance of the public finance sector in the provision of more inclusive social services and a labor market re-entry plan for the unemployed. Currently, fiscal deficits and high public debt impede the pace of long-term private sector development required to enable sustainable prosperity and rapid EU accession.[9] The long-term strategy to decrease unemployment entails linking the employment policy to the education system. North Macedonia and Montenegro face complex problems with the quality of education, which is manifested in the relatively low academic achievement of students.[10] The education system needs to be geared to the needs of the labor market so that graduates immediately find employment using their qualifications and do not end up swelling the ranks of the unemployed. Additionally, vocational training at the level of higher

---

[8] International Bank for Reconstruction and Development, International Finance Corporation, Multilateral Investment Guarantee Agency, Country Partnership Framework, Montenegro. Report No. 105039-ME, https://documents1.worldbank.org/curated/en/715681467996758549/pdf/105039-CPS-P152920-PUBLIC-R2016-0095-2.pdf (accessed November 14, 2020).

[9] The World Bank, Montenegro, https://www.worldbank.org/en/country/montenegro/overview#2 (accessed November 14, 2020).

[10] In the annual Program for International Student Assessment (PISA) test, students from secondary schools in the Republic of North Macedonia and Montenegro scored below the OECD average. In the reading test, students from the Republic of North Macedonia and Montenegro scored 393 and 421 points, compared with the OECD average of 487 points. Moreover, in the math test, young people from North Macedonia scored 394 points, from Montenegro – 430 points, while the average in OECD countries was 489. See: OECD, North Macedonia Student Performance (PISA 2018), https://gpseducation.oecd.org/CountryProfile?primaryCountry=MKD&treshold=5&topic=PI (accessed November 14, 2020); OECD, Montenegro Student Performance (PISA 2018), https://gpseducation.oecd.org/CountryProfile?primaryCountry=MNE&treshold=10&topic=PI). (accessed November 14, 2020).

and vocational schools should increase the chances of young people finding employment. Apprenticeships are not only intended for young people and can improve employability for adults too. Thus, apprenticeships perform a vital role in providing employability skills for the young and old as well, enabling the young to enter the employment market and the old to update and upgrade their work-related skills to extend their working life. Continuity of employment will also be supported for individuals.

Another issue is the persistence of income inequalities despite the reduction in the levels of poverty in recent years in North Macedonia and Montenegro. This shift can be partly explained by the overall increase in income in society. The at-risk-of-poverty rate is 21.9% in North Macedonia and 23.6% in Montenegro.[11] However, this situation does not resolve the growing problem of the persistence of high-income inequalities and these countries have similarly high rates of inequality in income distribution.[12] It should be noted that the gradual decline in poverty and the improvement in welfare recorded in recent years has been interrupted by the recession started in 2020 caused by the COVID-19 pandemic. It is estimated that the pandemic may increase the poverty rate in Montenegro by around 1.5-3%, while in North Macedonia by around 3-6% depending on the duration of the crisis.[13] Such high forecasts are associated with a decrease in income and remittances. Since a substantial number of the new poor are at risk of not being included in social welfare programs, outreach activities at the local level are undertaken to increase access to social assistance programs.[14] The implementation of social assistance tasks is inextricably linked with distribution of funds for their application and service. From 2005 to 2018, total spending on social protection in North Macedonia increased by 2.1%, and in 2018 accounted for 15.3% of GDP. Social protection spending in Montenegro was 16.6% of GDP in 2017; and since 2005, it has

---

[11] Eurostat, Income Poverty Statistics, https://ec.europa.eu/eurostat/statistics-explained/index.php?title=Income_poverty_statistics&oldid=440992 (accessed November 15, 2020).

[12] Ibid.

[13] World Bank Group, The Economic and Social Impact of COVID-19, Western Balkans Regular Economic Report, no. 17 (2020): 4, http://documents1.worldbank.org/curated/en/236311590680555002/pdf/The-Economic-and-Social-Impact-of-COVID-19-Poverty-and-Household-Welfare.pdf (accessed November 15, 2020).

[14] International Bank for Reconstruction and Development, International Finance Corporation, Multilateral Investment Guarantee Agency, Country Partnership Framework, The Republic of North Macedonia for the period of January 2019-June 2023. Report No. 135030-MK, http://pubdocs.worldbank.org/en/705311555590000225/North-Macedonia-CPF-2019.pdf (accessed November 15, 2020).

remained at an average level of 17.9%.[15] The issue of financing social protection in both countries is associated with many difficulties, such as susceptibility to structural changes in the labor market, dependence on the budget of the central and local government sector and lack of contributions from the gray zone. An aging society and high migration also have a significant impact on the financing of social assistance.

The issues mentioned above have been discussed in detail in the chapters of the book. In the first chapter, "The social security policy of the Republic of North Macedonia: Reform process, opportunities and perspectives", Katerina Veljanovska Blazhevska examines national policies and approaches related to social security. The author points out several serious impediments to stable and efficient social security: its fragmentation, poverty, and social exclusion. Finally, wide-ranging recommendations are offered for more efficient social protection, such as supporting employment policies and training programs for the young and unemployed, implementing comprehensive social policies, and following good practices from the European Union. Afet Mamuti in the chapter "Health, pensions and disability insurance in the Republic of North Macedonia: Recent developments" provides a detailed analysis of social protection policies in the field of healthcare, the pension system and disability insurance. The author shows the transformation of policies in specific issue areas aligning them with European Union legislation. The following two chapters describe two case studies that focus on specific areas vital to ensure social security stability and efficiency. In chapter three, entitled "Poverty as a social phenomenon in the Republic of North Macedonia", Kire Sharlamanov and Katerina Mitevska Petrusheva examine poverty dynamics in the country and review policies that have been implemented to alleviate poverty and reduce inequality. In chapter four, entitled "Unemployment in the Republic of North Macedonia: Characteristics and perspectives" Kire Sharlamanov and Katerina Mitevska Petrusheva discuss correlation between unemployment, social security, and economic growth. Moreover, the authors give recommendations for policy change and new initiatives to reduce unemployment in the country.

Part Two covers a variety of social security sectors in Montenegro. In the chapter "Pension system and reforms in Montenegro" Maja Baćović investigates fiscal and demographic indicators as well as patterns of pension provision to give a well-informed picture of the Montenegrin pension system. Long-term fiscal projections related to revenue and pension expenditure allow

---

15 Maja Gerovska Mitev, Financing Social Protection. North Macedonia (Brussels: European Social Policy Network, 2019), 4; Mirna Jusić and Nikolina Obradović, Enlargement Policy and Social Change in the Western Balkans (Sarajevo: Dialog Sudosteuropa, 2019).

important recommendations for further reforms to be made for social policy. Natalija Perišić in the chapter "The public health care sector in post-transition Montenegro" provides an overview of the healthcare system reforms implemented in Montenegro which aimed at increasing efficiency in the delivery of health services. The author also describes serious problems encountered in implementing reform particularly the failure to maintain ambitious standards and the difficulty in sustaining the health care system. Therefore, the healthcare reform in Montenegro has an unfinished agenda. Marzena Żakowska and Tomasz Ferfecki in the chapter "Social protection system in Montenegro" address the issue of social security transformation and explore policies, legislation and regulations related to social protection in Montenegro. The authors examine the principles governing benefits and allowances as well as healthcare as the primary focus of social policy. Finally, funding mechanisms for the welfare programs are explained. Agata Domachowska in the chapter "Unemployment and emigration as the (main) challenge for the social security system and stability of a multiethnic state: The case of Montenegro" examines the key factors behind mixed labor market outcomes in Montenegro. On the one hand, tourism growth and an extended period of political stability have brought positive economic outcomes but on the other hand, the labor market is characterized by informal economy, corruption, high emigration and projected economic downturn, typical features characterizing periods of transition to a market economy.

We hope that the volumes stimulate public discussion of social security policy in the Republic of North Macedonia and Montenegro and offer valuable guidance to policy makers and other experts in the fields of social security.

Bibliography

Council of the European Union. Council Conclusions on Enlargement and Stabilization and Association Process. Accessed November 7, 2020. https://www.consilium.europa.eu/en/press/press-releases/2019/06/18/council-conclusions-on-enlargement-and-stabilisation-and-association-process/.

European Commission. Montenegro 2018 Report. Accessed November 7, 2020. https://www.europarl.europa.eu/doceo/document/TA-8-2018-0482_EN.html.

European Commission. North Macedonia 2020 Report. Accessed November 12, 2020. https://www.europarl.europa.eu/doceo/document/A-9-2021-0040_EN.html.

Eurostat. Unemployment in the EU Regions in 2018. Accessed November 12, 2020. https://ec.europa.eu/eurostat/documents/2995521/9746862/1_29042019_BP_EN.pdf/329a9132-20c0-485b-aa22-b34864c22fde.

Eurostat. Income Poverty Statistics. Accessed November 15, 2020. https://ec.europa
.eu/eurostat/statistics-explained/index.php?title=Income_poverty_statistics
&oldid=440992.
Gerovska Mitev, Maja. Financing Social Protection. North Macedonia. Brussels:
European Social Policy Network, 2019.
International Bank for Reconstruction and Development, International Finance
Corporation, Multilateral Investment Guarantee Agency, Country Partnership
Framework. Montenegro. Report No. 105039-ME. Accessed November 14, 2020.
https://documents1.worldbank.org/curated/en/715681467996758549/pdf/105039
-CPS-P152920-PUBLIC-R2016-0095-2.pdf.
International Bank for Reconstruction and Development, International Finance
Corporation, Multilateral Investment Guarantee Agency, Country Partnership
Framework. The Republic of North Macedonia for the period of January 2019-June
2023. Report No. 135030-MK. Accessed November 15, 2020. https://thedocs.worldbank
.org/en/doc/705311555590000225-0080022019/original/NorthMacedoniaCPF2019
.pdf.
Jusić, Mirna, and Nikolina Obradović. Enlargement Policy and Social Change in the
Western Balkans. Sarajevo: Dialog Sudosteuropa, 2019.
Law on Health Care of 2016. Text no. 47.
Law on Health Insurance. Official Gazette, no. 07–12961, 2010. Accessed November 10,
2020. https://www.refworld.org/pdfid/5aa125974.pdf.
Lilyanova, Velina. Montenegro – a Lead Candidate for EU accession. Accessed
November 7, 2020. https://www.europarl.europa.eu/EPRS/EPRS-AaG-628238
-Montenegro-lead-candidate-for-EU-accession-FINAL.pdf.
OECD. Montenegro Student Performance (PISA 2018). Accessed November 14, 2020.
https://gpseducation.oecd.org/CountryProfile?primaryCountry=MNE&treshold
=10&topic=PI.
OECD. North Macedonia Student Performance (PISA 2018). Accessed November
14, 2020. https://gpseducation.oecd.org/CountryProfile?primaryCountry=MKD
&treshold=5&topic=PI.
Petreski, Blagica, and Pavle Gacov. Sustainability of the Pension System in Macedonia.
Comprehensive Analysis and Reform Proposal with MK-PENS – Dynamic
Microsimulation Model. Accessed November 10, 2020. https://www.financethink
.mk/wp-content/uploads/2020/11/Pension-analysis-EN.pdf.
Sanfey, Peter, and Jakov Milatović. "The Western Balkans Regional Economic Area:
From Economic Cooperation to Economic Integration". In Western Balkan
Economies in Transition. Recent Economic and Social Developments, edited by
Reiner Osbild and Will Barlett, 15–28. Cham: Springer.
The World Bank. Montenegro. Accessed November 14, 2020. https://www.worldbank
.org/en/country/montenegro/overview#2.

World Bank Group. The Economic and Social Impact of COVID-19. Western Balkans Regular Economic Report, no. 17 (2020). Accessed November 15, 2020. https://documents1.worldbank.org/curated/en/236311590680555002/pdf/The-Economic-and-Social-Impact-of-COVID-19-Poverty-and-Household-Welfare.pdf.

PART 1

Social Security in the Republic of North Macedonia

CHAPTER 1

The Social Security Policy of the Republic of North Macedonia: Reform Process, Opportunities and Perspectives

Katerina Veljanovska Blazhevska

1   Introduction

Over the past decade, a constant series of changes resulting from shifting social and demographic structure, a persistently high rate of unemployment, low economic growth and capacity and growing demand for social protection services have shaped social policy in the Republic of North Macedonia. The most visible changes were those in policies related to employment, social protection, and social security. The changes in these policies in North Macedonia, then, are particularly worthy of analysis, in particular those processes of pluralization, social inclusion, activation, deinstitutionalization and decentralization. These social policy processes have been the subject of debate, and have been implemented in other European social states, and are not peculiar to North Macedonia. Indeed, as Palier points out, one could have the impression that privatization, 'neo-liberalization', cuts to social transfers, and parting with social-democratic ideals generally reflect the current changes in Europe. Do these common trends, Palier asks, dictate uniformity in the approach to changing social policies in the face of different social and macroeconomic conditions?[1]

Similarly, to most European countries, North Macedonia has a comprehensive system for social security which comprises:
- contributory benefits, such as pension and disability insurance;
- passive and active labor-market program;
- social assistance programs for protecting income and consumption of the poor. Unemployment benefit, based on contributions and conditional on prior employment history, is representative of passive policies.[2]

---

[1]   Bruno Palier, Is There a Social Route to Welfare Reforms in Europe? Paper presented at the annual meeting of the American Political Science Association, Marriott, Loews Philadelphia, and the Pennsylvania (Convention Center, Philadelphia: PA 2006).

[2]   World Bank Review of the Social Protection System in the Republic of Macedonia, 2008.

The system of social protection of the Republic of North Macedonia includes benefits and services based on contributions, as well as those financed on the basis of taxation. The Law on Social Protection (2009) points out that working people and households, who are not financially secured and who are not able to acquire financial means for living through other legal acts, have the right to use social financial assistance.[3]

According to official data for households receiving social financial assistance, it can be seen that since 2005 there has been a decrease in the number of households receiving this social financial assistance. This cannot be seen as meaning that the need for social assistance has fallen, but rather that the rules have grown more rigid and the procedures for the verification of eligibility for assistance have grown more intensive.[4]

Official data on poverty in North Macedonia shows that almost a quarter of the population in the country lives below the poverty threshold, that youth unemployment population exceeds 50% and that the average net-salary is only two thirds of the consumer basket published by the trade unions. In 2011, almost half of the population, or 44.5% of households in the country, were affected by one of the three following risks: risk of poverty (22.9%), risk of material deprivation (30.8%) and/or the risk of unemployment (17%). According to the latest data, the percentage of persons in the Republic of North Macedonia who are poor account for 22.1% and this is dominated by persons who are seriously materially deprived, and whose income does not allow them to lead a normal life.[5] North Macedonia has developed a non-functional normative framework of social protection. The Ministry of Labor and Social Policy has the key role in defining the policies, management, and enforcement oversight of the legal framework in the area of social protection. The Living in Poverty identifies the Centers for Social Work as the weakest part in the functionality of the system of social protection because they face too much bureaucracy, but do not receive the expected level of support. Social protection in Macedonia provides inadequate social financial assistance, in terms of availability and coverage.

---

3 Susanna Bornarova, Maja Gerovska-Mitev, Social Exclusion, Ethnicity and Seniors in Macedonia (Skopje: Faculty of Philosophy, 2009).
4 Maria Donevska, Maja Gerovska, Dragan Gjorgjev, and Tanja Kalovska, Social Protection and Social Inclusion in the Former Yugoslav Republic of Macedonia (Macedonia: European Commission, 2007), http://www.iut.nu/wp-content/uploads/2017/03/Social-Protection-and-Social-Inclusion-in-the-Former-Yugoslav-Republic-of-Macedonia.pdf (accessed March 12, 2018).
5 Ministry of Labor and Social Policy Republic of North Macedonia, National Program for Development of Social Protection 2011–2021.

The aim of this chapter is to give a clear overview of the situation regarding social security in the Republic of North Macedonia. In this regard, the mandatory actors who contribute to the implementation of the social security system in the country, as well as the positive and negative aspects of the functioning of social security within the system, are especially highlighted. The chapter presents analysis as an overview of the existing system of social protection in the Republic of North Macedonia with recommendations for its improvement.

2   The System of Social Protection in the Republic of North Macedonia

Social protection may be defined as a system of measures, activities and policies aimed at the prevention of and overcoming fundamental social risks which an individual faces over their lifetime. These are designed to counter poverty and social exclusion and to bolster people's own ability to protect themselves. In the Republic of North Macedonia, constant updates are made to the social protection system to try and ensure that the most vulnerable groups will be able to access those rights and services. In this regard, social protection is achieved through the implementation of measures for prevention of the occurrence and reduction of the consequences of social risks for citizens, the provision of cash benefits and the establishment and development of services in the area of social protection (professional services by professional persons and expert teams, accommodation in institutions for institutional or non-institutional protection). For the development of the area of social protection and social inclusion, appropriate national strategic documents have been prepared and implemented, such as the Social Protection Development Program 2011–2021, the National Strategy for the Reduction of Poverty and Social Exclusion 2010–2020, the National Strategy for Equalization of Rights the persons with Disabilities 2010–2018, the National Strategy for the Elderly 2010–2020, the National Strategy for Deinstitutionalization. To monitor and evaluate the implementation of these, special multi-sectoral national coordinating bodies have been established. In addition, measures have been implemented for subsidizing energy consumption, and conditional cash benefits for regular secondary education for children from households that are beneficiaries of social financial assistance. Other measures provide for the employment of persons who had the status of a child without parents and without parental care until the age of 18, and for subsidizing the employment of beneficiaries of social financial assistance, and detail the beneficiaries, the measures, the holders and the sources of funds. In order to provide greater social security for the most materially vulnerable families, the amount of social assistance and permanent financial assistance is continuously increasing, by 5% annually in 2013 and 2014, and in 2015 the amount of these benefits was increased by 10%.[6]

In Northern Macedonia, the social assistance system provides particular groups of the population, e.g., the unemployed or the disabled, with guarantees of minimum resources or income. It can thus be described as a categorical, rather than a universal system. Moreover, the system does not have one comprehensive program, but instead is fragmented into many types of programs. In total, there are 16 separate benefit schemes that are defined by laws as 'entitlements' or 'rights' and two social programs. Of those, eleven are social and five are child protection benefits. The main program is social financial assistance (SFA). The other programs include permanent social assistance (for those who are permanently unable to work, such as the disabled or elderly); cash assistance for orphans; child allowances; benefits for care givers; one-time cash benefits; salary supplements for family members who face reduced work opportunities because of having to care for children with disabilities; housing and health insurance benefits, etc. Further measures have been introduced by the government in the past few years, which are intended to further reduce poverty, although some of these (e.g., to support fertility) are essentially part of demographic policy.[7]

The Ministry of Labor and Social Policy also introduced additional measures for improving the protection of persons at risk of social exclusion by introducing new monetary rights from social protection and development of social services. Thus, in order to improve the conditions for the daily functioning of persons with disabilities in 2012, the rights to mobility and of the blind were introduced, and in 2014, the exercise of the rights of the deaf was introduced. In 2015, the Ministry of Labor and Social Policy also increased the special allowance for the materially insecure parents of children with developmental disabilities by 25%, and a cash compensation of 8,000 denars was introduced for parents who have children with developmental disabilities and who will take care of these children for the next 15 years without placing them in an institution, if they cannot exercise the right to old age or other kind of pension. As of June 2015, the cost of accommodation for persons in foster care families and the foster care allowance has increased by 25%. Lately, the social protection

---

6 Ministry of Labor and Social Policy the Republic of North Macedonia, Projects in the Field of Social Protection, https://www.mtsp.gov.mk/proekti-od-oblasta-na-socijalnata-zashtita.nspx (accessed May 12, 2018).
7 Marjan Petreski and Nikica Mojsoska-Blazevski, Overhaul of the Social Assistance System in Macedonia: Simulating the Effects of Introducing Guaranteed Minimum Income (GMI) Scheme, Finance Think Policy Studies 11 (11) 2017.

system is directed primarily towards the development and strengthening of non-institutional forms of care for the vulnerable categories of citizens, by establishing the services of daily and temporary care and improving the care of children in foster care families.[8]

A substantial role in the reduction of poverty is played by pensions. In 2015, before social transfers, the poverty rate was 40.5%, but the AROPE was reduced by pensions to 24.8. Social transfers, however, had only a small effect on poverty, reducing the AROPE (after pensions) by only an additional 3.3 percentage points, 21.5%. This is similar to the situation across EU countries, where also social transfers only contribute little to poverty reduction. The most significant protection against poverty is a person's status in the labor market. Even in the face of an overall high poverty rate in North Macedonia (21.5% in 2015), those who are employed are at a relatively low risk of poverty, as only 8.9% of employed persons live in poverty (i.e., are at-risk of poverty and social exclusion – the AROPE). Poverty is highest among the unemployed (39.7%) and other inactive persons (other than pensioners), at 26.7%. There are generally three main arguments for more profound reform of the social assistance system in the country:

- the low effectiveness of the social transfers in reducing poverty;
- the low spending on social assistance programs;
- the labor market disincentives arising from the social assistance given the low general level of wages and the large grey economy.[9]

The state realizes its social function through the network of public institutions for social protection. The social protection system is composed of centers for social work (30), which have public authorization for the activities in the field of social protection. Centers for social work have public authority, administer social security benefits, and provide social services. Administration of monetary rights from social protection is wholly facilitated through an established system of exchange of information ex officio with the institutions that maintain databases needed in the procedures for exercising the social security monetary rights. By opening new dispersed departments in the centers for social work, even greater availability of social protection has been provided to all citizens, especially to those living in rural areas, the elderly and the disabled.

---

8 Clarire Annesley, "Lisbon and Social Europe: Towards a European 'Adult Worker Model' Welfare System", Journal of European Social Policy 17, no.3 (2007), 2007: 195–205, https://doi.org/10.1177/0958928707078363.

9 Nikica, Mojsoska-Blazevski, Marjan Petreski, and Desperina Petreska, Increasing Labor Market Activity of Poor, Females and Informal Workers: Let's Make Work Pay in Macedonia. Eastern European Economics 53, no. 6 (2015).

3   The Process of Social Policy Involvement

The application of the principle or policy of activation in European social states became dominant in the late 1990s. Such a principal can be detected, above all, in employment policies, but also in others, such as social protection and social security. However, activation in social policy within a European framework differs greatly from the same approach characteristic for the United States of America. As Annesley points out,[10] the European approach, which draws on the experiences of Scandinavian countries, relies on offering support through welfare state, as opposed to those wishing to leave the social protective system having to face punitive measures for entering the labor market. European activation in social policy focuses more on training, education, and the targeting of social services to specific vulnerable groups. In contrast, the neo-liberal approach to activation includes techniques such as limiting social benefits, conditioning social benefits by engagement in work, reducing the number of social benefits as a condition for a more active job search, etc. Analyzing the situation in North Macedonia, especially the conditions, the amount and the length of the monetary compensation received as part of unemployment insurance, as well as the conditions with the social financial assistance that can be used by the working people, it is quite obvious that the conclusion is that activation in North Macedonia follows the neoliberal approach.

Namely, the right to monetary compensation in case of unemployment has been subject to a consistent reduction from 1997 onwards. Simultaneously with taking rigid measures for beneficiaries of cash benefits in case of unemployment, active measures for training, additional qualification and prequalification were implemented. These measures are not characterized by the rigidity of their availability, although in some cases they can be re-examined because the most vulnerable social groups – the unemployed without any qualifications or education cannot use the training services offered. Social (monetary) assistance is an additional example of the rigid use of the principle of activation in social policy. Namely, the beneficiaries of social assistance (with certain exceptions, such as pensioners, persons who prove that they are incapable of work due to old age, disability or sickness, persons in employment, schoolchildren, and students), if they refuse to be employed for up to five days a month (for public works), the household will lose the right to use social assistance for the next 24 months. Another measure that is expected to motivate more

---

10   European Commission, Joint Report on Social Inclusion, Office for Official Publications of the European Communities, Luxembourg, 2004.

social assistance beneficiaries to register with the Employment Agency for work within the mandated timeframe is the higher frequency of visits by social workers to beneficiaries' homes. If this is not complied with in time, exclusion from the social assistance system follows, as well as the increased number of criteria on which the right to social assistance depends (e.g., the owner of a car cannot be a beneficiary of social help). As far as justifying targeting as a mechanism for improving the effectiveness of social protection, it must be brought about by the real opportunities and needs of the labor market in North Macedonia. Currently, targeting in social protection in the case of North Macedonia does not improve the situation with the exit of users from the social protection system and their inclusion in the labor market. This raises the question of how many of these activation measures are justified by the economic and social reality of North Macedonia and how much they are based on previous thorough analyses of the needs and conditions of socially vulnerable groups in North Macedonia.

4 Pluralization of the Essential Services of the Social System

The trend of pluralization in social protection can be interpreted as an effect of the crisis of the welfare state in Europe, which was felt more intensively during the 1980s. In the countries of Central and Eastern Europe, these practices experienced a transition in the mid-1990s. Due to reduced economic resources, the public sector, then the main social provider, began to limit the range of its services, while also providing legislative opportunities and initiatives for greater entry of civil and private actors into social protection. The pluralization of social protection in Europe occurs in many forms: public-private partnerships, contracting, quasi-bazaars, etc.[11]

The pluralization of the provision of social protection services in North Macedonia was institutionalized for the first time with the amendments to the Law on Social Protection in 2004, but they are much more profoundly treated with the latest changes that are part of the Law on Social Protection in 2009. Although, in reality, the emergence of the private and civil sector in social protection in North Macedonia began in the mid-1990s, this trend is distinct from that in Western European countries, however. The reason for this difference is that in North Macedonia, there was no previous tradition

---

11 Ministry of Labor and Social Policy, the Republic of North Macedonia, Program for Dealing with the Problems of Socially Excluded Persons, 2004, www.mtsp.gov.mk (accessed March 18, 2018).

of these actors functioning as providers of social protection. This particularly refers to the absence of any prior experience of the private sector in social protection in North Macedonia's past. In the past, the civil sector in North Macedonia has also not been formally institutionalized and can only be recognized in informal family and neighborhood assistance, as well as in the social activity of church communities. The lack of prior experience of these actors in social protection contributed to the feeling of mistrust among social service users towards these actors as social protection providers. Currently, there are about 6,000 registered citizens associations in North Macedonia. Sources of funding for non-governmental organizations (NGOs) come from the central budget, the budget of individual ministries, funds received through the lottery and other games of chance, as well as through the Secretariat for European Affairs (in the context of activities related to European integration).

However, the bulk of the funds of non-governmental organizations derive from international donors and foundations. In the context of non-governmental organizations in the area of social protection, very few work in the field of labor and social policy. This register is composed of organizations that have met the criteria for professionalism, competence and quality, and only they can apply in the tender calls published by the Ministry of Labor and Social Policy of the Republic of North Macedonia. The areas in which NGOs are active in the social sector in Macedonia are in fact those in which the state has less developed capacities and forms of assistance, such as day care centers for socially vulnerable categories, SOS lines, assistance to specific categories such as women, members of various ethnic communities, programs for support of non-formal education, etc. While the practice of contracting between the non-governmental and public sectors is increasing, the quality of such cooperation is still not satisfactory. This is especially evident in the creation of national strategies and action plans, when the participation and experience of non-governmental organizations is treated solely from a formal character, but not through the institutionalization of their proposals, suggestions, and comments in specific policies. Nevertheless, the non-governmental sector remains a significant player in complementing gaps in government activities directed towards socially vulnerable categories, at the same time being characterized by greater efficiency and flexibility of offered services.

Currently, only two pension companies operate in North Macedonia, which operate on the market under the same conditions, so that there is no competitive basis for the selection of one or the other fund. The emergence of the private sector into pension insurance should in principle be an improvement in the opportunities for a higher and more secure pension future. However, the

mandatory private pension pillar is equally risky for both the individual and the society, primarily because of:
- high administrative costs charged by pension companies in the amount of 7.9% of the payment of user contributions;
- the greater (inappropriately predicted) outflow of the first (mandatory state) passers-by to the second (compulsory private) pension pillar, which greatly increased the transitional costs of this pension reform, which will again be the burden of all taxpayers in the state;
- insufficiently developed financial instruments on the domestic market in which the pension funds can invest, which leads to the question of the possibility of higher earnings or the increase of the pension yield.

5 Need for Social Inclusion

In the Republic of Macedonia there are many target groups that need different kinds of help and support for normal functioning, including the elderly, the disabled, the homeless, single parents, victims of domestic violence, HIV positive people, those addicted to alcohol, drugs, or other substances and recovering addicts now in treatment. In Macedonia 16.6% of the population is old, whereas 6.5% people are with disabilities, 30% people live in poverty and social exclusion, 258 people are living with HIV/AIDS, there are 236 street children, 45 homeless people and other categories of citizens who need some kind of social service, and 34,504 family are welfare beneficiaries.[12]

There is no universally accepted definition of social exclusion in the Republic of North Macedonia which could be used to analyze this issue. Exclusion can be analyzed from several perspectives, but the most important are the economic, health, educational, ethnic, geographical and cultural perspective.[13] Despite the lack of a formally accepted definition of social exclusion, in its (2004) program the Ministry of Labor and Social Policy specifically addresses the problem of four socially excluded groups:
- drug users and their family members;
- street children / street children and their families;

---

12 Improving the Provision of Social Service Delivery in South Eastern Europe through the Empowerment of National and Regional CSO Networks, From Idea to Initiatives to Reform the Public Social Services in Macedonia (Macedonia: Iris Network, 2015).
13 Ludwig Boltzmann Institute of Human Rights. Decentralization of the Social Protection in the Republic of North Macedonia Factual Situation, Challenges and Opportunities at Local Level (Skopje: Ludwig Boltzmann Institute of Human Rights, 2012).

- victims of domestic violence;
- the homeless.

This separation of these target groups according to the Ministry of Labor and Social Policy aims to improve the effective access of people who previously did not have systematically organized social protection services provided (2004). One of the newly proposed changes in the social protection system in North Macedonia, which according to the creators of social policy aim to improve the effectiveness of the system, but also contribute to better social inclusion of certain groups in the society, is the introduction of conditional cash transfers. The idea behind such a program generally consists in conditioning the financial assistance by investing in human capital in the younger generation, that is, sending children to school or carrying out regular health checks and examinations.

6   The Pillar of Decentralization and Deinstitutionalization

The financing of social financial assistance at the local level (e.g., social assistance) is not yet subject to decentralization. For this, there are currently no appropriate legal solutions, nor the necessary institutional and economic prerequisites.[14] Social work centers, although these operate at the municipal level, are also not properly decentralized, but are still decentralized central government units. Specific problems that arise in the process of greater decentralization in social protection are:

- the lack of legal provisions in the Law on Local Self-Government[15] (Article 22, paragraph 7), where no decentralization of the financial transfers is envisaged;
- the lack of a body for implementing a second instance procedure at the local level, as well as a lack of human resources in most centers for social work in dealing with and administration of social transfers and provision of social services.

Unlike all the previously noted reform processes, deinstitutionalization in North Macedonia may be accepted with the greatest consensus, and the number of challenges it faces is the least compared to other reform efforts. The

---

14   Law on Local Self-Government, Official Gazette of the Republic of North Macedonia, no. 5 dated 29.01.2002, reviewed on 10/05/2018.
15   Strategy for De-institutionalization of Social Services in the Republic of North Macedonia (2007–2014).

institutional form of protection in North Macedonia was until recently the dominant way of providing services.

However, thanks to the trend of deinstitutionalization, a large number of new non-residential services were opened as a way to reduce the number of institutional residents, but also as an aspiration to improve the quality of their lives. They are targeted at several categories of users:
- children with special needs;
- drug users;
- victims of domestic violence;
- street children;
- the homeless.

According to the Strategy for deinstitutionalization (2007–2014), the process of transformation of institutions was foreseen to last for seven years and to include three phases in which different institutions were to be transformed. According to the Strategy, the reform proceeds in two directions:
- assessment of the current network of all types of accommodation and giving priority to the development of accommodation network consisting of foster families and small homes;
- assessment of the type and quality of accommodation services provided in the system of social protection.[16]

During this reform, the Ministry of Labor and Social Policy was set up to fund, train and support the establishment and effective functioning of preventive services, temporary accommodation services, reintegration services, and small family homes. The main goal of the deinstitutionalization process is the need for improved capacity building and human resources for non-institutional protection, with which the professions involved in this process will contribute not only to improving the quality of non-residential services, but also to better integrating their users into society in general.[17]

7 Analysis of the Current Situation within the System of Social Security in the Republic of North Macedonia

This analysis is an overview of the existing system of social protection in the Republic of North Macedonia with recommendations for its improvement.

---

16 Ministry of Labor and Social Policy the Republic of North Macedonia, Draft Version of the Strategy for De-institutionalization (Skopje, 2007).
17 Igor Nikolovski, Promotion of Social Inclusion through Effective Utilization of the EU Funds (Skopje: IDSCS, 2017).

The basis for the analysis is the data from the reports from conducted research on the work of the centers for social work in the Republic of North Macedonia, public perceptions of social issues, experiences and perceptions of the beneficiaries of social assistance, and a survey of civil associations that carry out activities in the field of social work conducted within the project "Improving social inclusion through effective utilization of EU funds" implemented by the Institute for Democracy 'SocEmaxCivilis' and project partners.[18] The analysis also uses data from strategic documents related to social policy such as the National Strategy for Reduction of Poverty and Social Exclusion in the Republic of North Macedonia 2010–2020, the Program for Employment and Social Policy 2020, Operational Plan for active employment programs and services.

In the Republic of North Macedonia, the unemployment rate is still high (in 2015, it was 26.1% or expressed in an absolute number of 248,933 people, in March 2018 it was 22.4%) and is much higher than the European average unemployment rate (9% in 2015).[19] Unemployment, which, in itself, is a problem, causes negative reactions in almost all segments of society: the social sphere, fiscal policy, demographic policy, regional policy and, of course, the economic growth and development of the state. Taking into account the fact that the high unemployment rate is a long-term phenomenon in North Macedonia, the losses for the state from this negative trend are multiple. Persons covered by the social protection system are mostly long-term unemployed persons, most of them inactive people, living on the verge of poverty, considering the relatively low amount of social welfare funds. There is discouragement among long-term unemployed persons that they are losing over time the knowledge and skills they had acquired during the educational process. Thus the process of their reintegration into the labor market is much more difficult and more expensive and these people are prone to informal work. The need for a set of related activities with the joint action of the Centers for Social Work and the Employment Centers for beneficiaries of social assistance is important to support their transition from unemployed to persons who will seek their employment.

The relatively high amount of funds allocated for social assistance, which as a total amount, on average, viewed from the state budget in the past few years, amounts to 6,166,500,000.00 (billion) denars in 2014, 7,178,000.00 (billion)

---

18 Foundation Friedrich Ebert, Framing Social Policy: Actors, Dimensions and Reforms (Skopje: UKIM, 2016).
19 Foundation for Democracy, Social Protection in the Republic of Macedonia: How to Measure a System for Every Citizen (Skopje: Foundation for Democracy, Westminster, 2016).

denars in 2015 annually without a real impact on the social categories of persons. This impedes the quality of the labor market in terms of investing greater resources and human potential for creating quality active labor market policies. These would make the beneficiaries of social assistance able to be involved in some of the training programs and become competitive and sought after in the labor market or have the possibility of opening their own business. All this would relax the national budget. On the other hand, recipients of social assistance easily cross into the group of long-term unemployed (over one year). For example, almost half (47.9%) of surveyed welfare recipients reported receiving some form of social assistance for a period of two to five years, while over one third (36.9%) of respondents – recipients of social assistance – reported receiving social assistance for more than six years. This implies that they lose their work skills and qualifications over time and are further distancing themselves from the labor market. On the other hand, only 3.6% of the surveyed social assistance beneficiaries have been involved in some kind of training for acquiring working skills that would improve their employability and help them find work in the labor market. The majority of them look at the future with pessimism and find it very difficult to find work in the Republic of North Macedonia. The need to encourage and activate the recipients of social assistance and their inclusion in active employment programs and services is more important, given that a large proportion (more than 50%) are not familiar with active employment measures, and more than 40% of those who are familiar, fear losing the right to use social assistance if they engage in some of the active employment programs.[20]

Young people (aged 15–29) in the Republic of North Macedonia are among the most vulnerable categories and are easily susceptible to social exclusion, taking into account the period of first employment. For example, in 2014 young persons took, on average, 31.2 months (2.5 years) from the time of completion of their education to finding their first employment considered to be stable or satisfactory. The duration of the transition is considerably longer for young men than for young women, with an average difference of 14 months. The average duration of the transition from school to the first stable/satisfactory employment was 37 months for young men and 23 months for young women. Young people who have completed only elementary education need up to 62 months to complete the transition. The economic and social costs of financial support for so many young people during these long periods of transition are an obstacle to the country's development potential. Taking into account the above,

---

20 Ibid.

the desire for greater social inclusion of unemployed young people is important. The opinion of the majority of social assistance beneficiaries regarding the amount of social assistance payments is compatible with public opinion, which is that they are not at all sufficient to meet their basic needs (79.8% of public opinion considers that the amount that socially disadvantaged people receive as social assistance is insufficient to provide for a dignified life). Also, the monthly reporting obligations to the Center for Social Work and transport to the Center represent an additional burden. Public opinion, which mostly considers that the state is not sufficiently committed to the socially disadvantaged, and a high percentage of citizens (over 70%) believe that the state does not sufficiently plan in the national budget for the needs of the socially endangered and that in the future more funds should be allocated for the socially disadvantaged.[21]

The insufficient involvement of the Units of Local Self-Government (the municipalities) makes it difficult to decentralize the services of social protection and address poverty and social exclusion at the local level. In the municipalities, there are different categories of vulnerable groups of citizens who are on the margins of the society or are in different situations of social risk. With the process of decentralization, it is necessary that local self-government is increasingly taking over the competence in several spheres, in the area of the development of social services, adapted to the specific needs of the population in the local community. As a consequence of the absence of sufficient financial resources and institutional capacities, a number of local self-government units have not yet developed effective systems of support and care for the social needs of vulnerable people, nor do they have adequate information and databases on the number of vulnerable groups, for the types of vulnerability, their specific needs and constraints, which would be further used for the preparation of appropriate local programs and solutions based on local needs of the population. In the past period in this part, the practice of establishing centers for social services (in four pilot municipalities) and local co-ordination bodies for social protection (in three pilot municipalities) has been recognized as good practice and as mechanisms for the development of preventive work, planning and undertaking activities in the area of social protection. A good practice is also the Municipal Work Program, i.e., a program for delivery of social services in the local community, which promotes the system for providing social services at the local level by replenishing the existing

---

21 Returning New Social Policy: Actors, Dimensions and Reforms (Skopje: University St. Kiril and Methodius, Faculty of Philosophy, Friedrich Ebert Foundation, 2008).

and/or introducing new services. This program seeks to assist in the social inclusion of persons who have greater difficulty participating in the labor market through their part-time engagement in order to acquire certain skills, but at the same time to increase the supply of social services, in accordance with the needs of the population in given local government. In the course of 2015, 42 municipalities were involved in this program, with 318 unemployed (social category) persons engaged. In any case, there is a need for further coordination and involvement of all stakeholders in the community in the process of providing quality and innovative social services. This is especially important in the part of the preparation of social protection programs at the local level, but which have not been appropriately budgeted by municipalities' own resources.

The insufficient staffing of the Centers for Social Work with appropriate professional staff directly involved in the implementation of activities in the field of social protection (social workers, pedagogues, psychologists, defectologists, sociologists), as opposed to 46% of the total number of employees in the Centers for Social Protection belonging to the administrative and technical services, reduces efficiency in working with end-users – recipients of social assistance and other socially endangered persons. This unfavorable situation is accompanied by the lack of means of transportation and obsolete equipment, which makes the significant part of the field work of the employees of the Centers for Social Work difficult. In accordance with the manual on norms and standards for space, equipment and professional staff and resources in public institutions – the Centers for Social Work, for qualitative change in the process of planning of employment, the introduction of planning is needed in accordance with the real needs of the SWC. These are determined by analyzing the scope of work in previous years, the identified priorities and the specifics of the region and the projected scope of work in the coming years. One of the basic criteria for determining the required number of employees is the number of cases with which one employee can be charged during the year, and this is determined through defined norms. The Institute for Social Activities (ISA) also receives an extended function of a human resources manager in the social protection system in the Republic of North Macedonia. This implies the establishment of a human resource management system in the ISA that will take care of staff planning, monitoring the work of employees, evaluating the results of their work, taking care of the career development of professional and other staff, and strengthening the capacities of organizations in the social protection system.

The Centers for Social Work have a limited capacity to apply and implement IPA projects. The problem according to the statements of employees from the

CSW stems from the lack of project management trainings, as well as the fact that a large part of the total number of social work centers stated that they do not have employees with English language skills, and communication with foreign donors is in English. Bearing in mind that a relatively large amount of funding from IPA funds for social inclusion is available, the rapid overcoming of human resources problems that the Centers for Social Work are facing pose a challenge for the further quality work of the Centers for Social Work. In accordance with the manual on norms and standards for space, equipment and professional staff and resources in public institutions – Social Welfare Centers, the ISA should analyze the training needs of the employees in the CSW and the social protection institutions, according to which they should develop a training plan, to develop training programs and to provide trainers for the implementation of the training. Training should be provided for all professional and administrative employees. The ISA should prepare a training plan for the professional and administrative staff at the CSW, which should include topics on the required trainings and a dynamic plan for the realization of the trainings. The daily work of the Centers for Social Work in the Republic of North Macedonia includes, *inter alia*, cooperation with the police, courts, units of local self-government, educational institutions and civil society organizations.

From the conducted survey of the Centers for Social Work, it was concluded that the communication and cooperation with the civic organizations is the weakest, and something better with the Units of Local Self-Government. Taking into account that most of the civil society organizations perform activities in the social sphere, and from the analysis conducted at the CSW, the lowest level of cooperation with the civil society organizations is determined. The need for further deepening of the cooperation is more than important in order to avoid duplication of similar efforts for achieving identical goals and achieving maximum effects when delivering services to end-users. The situation is similar regarding the cooperation of the Centers for Social Work with the Units of Local Self-Government. The survey found that most of the Centers for Social Work do not participate in the preparation of programs or action plans for social inclusion at the local level, and bearing in mind the legal regulation (Law on Local Self-Government) that states that the Units of Local Self-Government are one of the holders of the implementation of the social protection system, this imposes the need to deepen the cooperation of the Centers for Social Work with the Units for Local Self-Government in order to improve the efficiency and the expertise when creating programs or local action plans for social inclusion.

8 Conclusion

Introduction and implementation of a set of activities would start with regular monthly submission of data from the Centers for Social Work to the Employment Centers for the beneficiaries of social assistance. Then those persons, through the information mechanisms developed by the Employment Agency of the Republic of North Macedonia, would be called to register as active jobseekers, if they have not already done so. The next step would be to make profiling, to develop an individual plan for employment of hard-working people, and on this basis, the person should be properly involved in some of the training programs or opening their own business. If, after the completion of a specific training, the beneficiary of the social assistance is not employed, it would then be necessary to continuously repeat the process for inclusion in different types of training in order for the person to remain active in the process of seeking a job, i.e., preventing the process of re-training asocialization. Having in mind the fact that the average period for first employment of young people (aged 15–29) in the Republic of North Macedonia is a period in which young people are surely turning into the category of long-term unemployed persons. The probability that they will be included in the social protection system constitutes a great need for developing a system for rapid inclusion of young people after the completion of school in the process of training in real working conditions (internships), motivational training, advanced IT skills training, or offering favorable conditions for opening up their own business. In order to familiarize young people with the possibilities offered by the Employment Agency, in close cooperation with educational institutions, timely intervention in the final years of education (high school or university) is necessary. The Units of Local Self-Government (the municipalities) should also be activated and open local youth offices that would have in the first place the role of mediator in organizing meetings of young people who have completed their education and those who have already become long-term unemployed with representatives of the local business community to consider the possibilities of including young unemployed persons in some kind of flex-arrangement or to directly employ them, which would have a preventive effect on the relaxation of the social protection system.

Establishment of a mechanism for determining and adjusting the amount of social assistance in accordance with the established minimum monthly living expenses, which would be operated by the relevant state institutions (Ministry of Labor and Social Policy, State Statistical Office) and representatives of associations involved in the implementation of activities in the social sphere. For greater involvement of the Units for Local Self-Government (LSGs) in the implementation of the services of social protection and dealing with poverty and social and the exclusion at the local level, it is necessary to have a database of users of social assistance and that it be constantly updated. The LSGU database would be most easily developed in cooperation with the local Center for Social Work. Each of the LSGUs could apply for IPA projects, which would provide a greater amount of funds for the implementation of programs and services in the social sphere. The practice should be continued of establishing centers for social services and local coordination bodies for social protection in all municipalities in the Republic of North Macedonia as mechanisms for development of preventive work, planning and undertaking of activities in the area of social protection and the possibility of animation and inclusion in some from local activities in the area of social protection. According to the manual for norms and standards for space, equipment and professional staff and resources in the public institutions – Centers for Social Work (CSW), administrative staff, as well as professional staff, have continuous training according to the needs of the organization and the individual needs of the employees. Management staff should have compulsory training in management, finance and budgeting, and the rest of the staff will be provided vocational training in accordance with the needs of the workplace (finance and budgeting, analysis and reporting, etc.) and for the promotion of personal skills (communication skills, IT, teamwork etc.). Furthermore, if greater efficiency in the functioning of the CSW is to be achieved, a proportionally much larger share of professional staff is needed, directly involved in the implementation of activities in the field of social protection than other more technical administrative staff. This includes the need for renewal and introduction of appropriate equipment and vehicles. It is also necessary for a certain number of employees from each CSW to be provided with courses in English and project management training because of the great importance of securing additional resources for solving some of the above problems, but also for expanding the scope of activities or projects in the field of social protection. It is also necessary to separate the profile of a field social worker whose work will be aimed at improving the position of individuals and their families in urban and rural areas.

Good practices from the European Union for the decentralization of the social protection system can also be taken into account. One such example would be Lithuania where, from 2015, the development of the social protection system is carried out through a decentralization process, all municipalities are provided money for social assistance and is awarded in accordance with commonly equal conditions (they have lost the discretion to decide whether to increase the fee / benefit, except in cases not provided for in the Law on Social

Protection). Municipalities can also use municipal budget funds to provide additional social support, especially for vulnerable groups, where support by law is not regulated or insufficient.

From the analysis of the prominent reform processes in North Macedonia, it can be concluded that the once declared as universal social state is oriented towards favoring services instead of cash transfers; increasing targeting of consumers rather than universal access; conditioning of previously universal cash transfers; reduced state service provision at the expense of increased private initiative; a trend towards inclusion of local levels in the administration of social protection, but with the support of the centralization of the collection then the distribution of fiscal resources; and ultimately reduce the range of state institutional capacity and offering day care services primarily provided by civil and private service providers. Such a recalibration of the social state in North Macedonia confirms the "neoliberal trends" of the currently dominant ideological matrix, which seems attractive primarily because of the savings in social policy, which in conditions of low economic growth, high unemployment rate and great support on the system of social protection are seen as the only way out. At the moment, current views of social policy do not attach a productive dimension. However, what is most symptomatic and most problematic about the sustainability of previously prominent reform processes is their adoption without greater social consensus and without greater empirical evidence. All this makes these reforms feel remote to their users and unavailable to current facilities, opportunities and needs. Reforms in social policy should serve as a ladder up to greater opportunities, and not just a knit safety net that keeps users in their downturns. For this purpose, it is essential to impart greater orientation of the reforms to the local capacities and needs, to elicit the involvement of the beneficiaries in the creation of social programs, improve the access to social services based not only on rights, but also on needs and, finally, to affect the systematic creation of social protection measures not based on projects, shock-therapy and ad hoc solutions. Only in this way can you build your own model of social policy that will represent an individual response to uniform trend solutions, offering a different solution based on national opportunities and resources.

Bibliography

Annesley, Claire. "Lisbon and Social Europe: Towards a European 'Adult Worker Model' Welfare System". Journal of European Social Policy 17, no. 3 (2007): 195–205. https://doi.org/10.1177/0958928707078363.

Bornarova, Susanna, and Maja Gerovska-Mitev. Social Exclusion, Ethnicity and Seniors in Macedonia. Skopje: Faculty of Philosophy, 2009.

Donevska, Maria, Maja Gerovska, Dragan Gjorgjev, and Tanja Kalovska. Social Protection and Social Inclusion in the Former Yugoslav Republic of Macedonia. European Commission, 2007.

European Commission. Joint Report on Social Inclusion. Office for Official Publications of the European Communities. Luxemburg, 2004.

Foundation for Democracy. Social Protection in the Republic of Macedonia: How to Measure a System for Every Citizen. Skopje: Foundation for Democracy, Westminster, 2016.

Foundation Friedrich Ebert. Framing Social Policy: Actors, Dimensions and Reforms. Skopje: UKIM, 2016.

Foundation Friedrich Ebert. Returning New Social Policy: Actors, Dimensions and Reforms. Skopje: University St. Kiril and Methodius, Faculty of Philosophy, 2008.

Improving the Provision of Social Service Delivery in South Eastern Europe through the Empowerment of National and Regional CSO Networks. From Idea to Initiatives to Reform the Public Social Services in Macedonia. Macedonia: Iris Network, 2015.

Law on Local Self-Government, Official Gazette of the Republic of North Macedonia, no. 5, dated 29.01.2002, reviewed on 10/05/2018.

Ludwig Boltzmann Institute of Human Rights. Decentralization of the Social Protection in the Republic of North Macedonia – Factual Situation, Challenges and Opportunities at Local Level. Skopje, 2012.

Ministry of Labor and Social Policy Republic of North Macedonia. National Program for Development of Social Protection 2011–2021.

Ministry of Labor and Social Policy Republic of North Macedonia. Projects in the Field of Social Protection. Accessed May 15, 2018. https://www.mtsp.gov.mk/proekti-od-oblasta-na-socijalnata-zashtita.nspx.

Ministry of Labor and Social Policy The Republic of North Macedonia. Program for Dealing with the Problems of Socially Excluded Persons 2004. Accessed March 18, 2018. www.mtsp.gov.mk.

Ministry of Labor and Social Policy, the Republic of North Macedonia. Draft Version of the Strategy for De-institutionalization. Skopje, 2007.

Ministry of Labor and Social Policy, the Republic of North Macedonia. Strategy for De-institutionalization of Social Services in the Republic of North Macedonia (2007–2014).

Mojsoska-Blazevski, Nikica, Marjan Petreski, and Desperina Petreska. "Increasing Labor Market Activity of Poor, Females and Informal Workers: Let's Make Work Pay in Macedonia." Eastern European Economics vol. 53, no. 6 (2015): 466–490. https://doi.org/10.1080/00128775.2015.1103656.

Nikolovski, Igor. Promotion of Social Inclusion through Effective Utilization of the EU Funds. Skopje: IDSCS, 2017.

Palier, Bruno. "Is There a Social Route to Welfare Reforms in Europe?". Paper presented at the annual meeting of the American Political Science Association, Marriott, Loews Philadelphia, and the Pennsylvania Convention Center, Philadelphia: PA, 2006.

Petreski, Marjan, and Nikica Mojsoska-Blazevski. "Overhaul of the Social Assistance System in Macedonia: Simulating the Effects of Introducing Guaranteed Minimum Income (GMI) Scheme". Finance Think Policy Studies 11, no. 11 (2017).

World Bank. Review of the Social Protection System in the Republic of Macedonia, 2008.

CHAPTER 2

Health, Pensions and Disability Insurance in the Republic of North Macedonia

Afet Mamuti

1   Introduction

The general topic of this chapter is to establish the role and importance of social security for society in general and for the individual in particular in terms of quality of life. Social security is important to provide public support for people when they are facing a social risk. Social security includes the social protection of people vulnerable to poverty, unemployment, elderliness, homelessness, victims of domestic violence, and the category of marginalized people who, because of their circumstances, feel excluded from society. Social security serves to increase the efficiency of the system to ensure a better quality of life for all people and enable them to become involved in social, economic, and cultural life. Social security is primarily related to concrete services provided by the state in order to protect its citizens. In particular, answers will be given regarding the main types of social security: health insurance and pension and disability insurance. In this chapter, we have used concrete statistical data and empirical, comparative and descriptive methods in order to achieve clearer results. This study will serve to correctly understand the role of social security for society in general and its impact on the struggle with anomalies in society such as the risk of death, age, unemployment or disability. Theoretical and empirical data show that countries with sustainable economic development guarantee the more stable functioning of the system they implement. Even for countries like the Republic of North Macedonia[1] (so called North Macedonia), regardless of the pension system it implements, social security is always faced with sustainability dilemmas. This is also due to the permanent increase in the number of pensioners in relation to the number of employees. This further

---

1   Based on the Agreement between the Republic of Macedonia and the Republic of Greece (Prespa Agreement) of 17 June 2018, for the name issue, Macedonia was officially called the Republic of North Macedonia. Since most laws were passed prior to this date, in every place where reference is made to the Republic of Macedonia, it is the same subject as what today is called the Republic of North Macedonia.

increases the budget of the pension and disability fund and the state budget. The ratio between the number of employees and pensioners according to the World Bank and International Monetary Fund in Northern Macedonia is 2:1. This is not in line with European standards and in the long term, makes the fund budget unstable.

Investigating this topic is of a continuing concern due to the importance of the problem and the ongoing reforms being made in this sector in order to meet the challenges that lie ahead of the Fund for Health Insurance and Pension Disability Insurance. Improving the health system, modernizing it through the application of innovative medical technologies, and expanding accessibility to the patient is imperative. Through this chapter, it is intended that both scientists and experts in this field will identify and analyze the problems of the system applied by the country. Consequently, recommendations can be made in relation to economic and demographic factors for normative changes in order to avoid unnecessary expenditure by the Health Insurance Fund or the eventual collapse of the Pension and Disability Insurance Fund of the Republic of North Macedonia in the future.

2   Social Security in the Republic of North Macedonia

Social security problems are complex and efforts to solve them aim at the achievement of social welfare through constantly looking for the 'happiness' of the individual and the society. In the early stages of the development of human society, the issue of social problems was considered a problem that concerns only the individual and not the society. When social problems began to affect a larger number of people, then intervention was sought through social policy for the solution of these social problems and this intervention became a public issue. For our purposes, we can take this as meaning that to be a social problem an issue has to move from being private to public.[2] Social security is an organized way of governing how social assistance is provided to individuals. Social security is intended to provide material support to people when it is needed.

The term 'social security' was formally used for the first time in United States legislation – the Social Insurance Act of 1935 – although this act was intended to cover only the risks of age, death, disability and unemployment. In 1935, the Social Security Act was enacted, in part, to help ensure that older Americans

---

2   Stuart Isaacs, David Blundell, Anne Foley, Norman Ginsburg, Brian McDonough, Daniel Silverstone, and Tara Young, Social Problems in the UK (Oxon: Routledge, 2015), 12.

would have adequate retirement incomes and would not have to depend on welfare.[3] The ILO has adopted this term and used it due to its simplicity and inclusiveness. Social protection is the answer to the need for security in the wider sense of the word, through a process of social solidarity and not simply a system of instruments that guarantees this security.[4]

The right to social security and the ability to enjoy economic, cultural, and social rights allowing them to freely develop their personality belongs to each individual as a member of society. State and international cooperation, within the abilities of each state, are to serve this end. The quality of human health and life in this way is directly or indirectly affected by social security.

Social security as an object includes a whole set of social relationships that are addressed by social policy. Any condition or behavior that brings negative consequences for a greater number of people is considered as a social problem. Any such condition or cause needs to be addressed to find a solution.[5] By social insurance, we mean the basic actions of state institutions in terms of providing material and financial support for the basic needs of the population such as illness, poverty, unemployment, etc.

When talking about the issue of social problems, we mean the problems that people face in everyday life, such as unemployment, housing, poverty, social violence, domestic violence, healthcare, old age or sheltering the homeless, narcotics, social networking, homosexuality, gay marriage, abortion, racism, freedom of speech, terrorism, emigration, environmental issues, global warming, etc. Some theorists consider education policies to be outside the social sphere, while health and economic policies are often part of social policies because they have a direct impact on providing living conditions.

The Republic of North Macedonia, before its independence in 1991, carried out the question of designing and implementing social security policies within the Yugoslav Federation. Only after its independence in 1991 has it taken concrete measures to establish a functional and contemporary social security system in order to best fulfill the needs of its citizens. The independence period from the former Socialist Federal Republic of Yugoslavia (SFRY) in 1991 found North Macedonia unprepared in the face of new challenges. This was because the country had moved from a country with a planned economy to that of a market economy, which was also associated with declining GDP, rising

---

3 US Government Accountability Office, Social Security's Future, Washington DC 20548, October 2015.
4 Merita Xhumari, The Process and Institutions of Social Policy (Tirana: ABC, 2009), 13.
5 Ibid., 4.

unemployment, wage cuts due to inflation and a rising informal economy. This entire situation was also reflected in the emergence of difficulties in the creation and realization of the state budget from tax revenues and liabilities that had decreased.

North Macedonia recognizes the right to social security which is sanctioned by international acts such as the UN Universal Declaration of Human Rights, the UN International Covenant on Economic, Social and Cultural Rights (1966), the ILO Convention, the European Social Charter and so on. Even Article 9 of the International Covenant on Economic, Social and Cultural Rights clearly shows the commitment of member states to recognize everyone's right to social security.

The country's legislation has been amended several times in order to harmonize with EU legislation, also based on the National Program for the Adoption of the European Union Law (NPAA) to the earlier ones and from the Revision of 2017–2019, where a collective strategy is foreseen and priorities are set for improving the labor market situation, increasing employment and reducing unemployment, especially for young people and the disabled. This is intended to enhance inclusiveness in the labor market and increase the capacity of institutions to create policies for job creation by devoting themselves to the education system in creating the necessary staff for the labor market.

Even in the Republic of North Macedonia's constitution itself, the state's commitment is clearly visible to ensuring the fundamental values of the constitutional order through humanism, social justice and solidarity, and defining the country as a social state. The rights to social security expanded considerably after the Second World War. The present Constitution contains a special chapter referring to economic, social and cultural rights. The right to social security belongs to every member of society. Each member is entitled to this, with the support of national efforts and international cooperation within the abilities of each state, and is entitled to fulfil those economic, social and cultural rights to preserve his or her dignity and freely develop his or her personality, through national effort and international co-operation.[6] It is also important to mention the recent package of reforming laws that were voted by the Republic of North Macedonia's Assembly in May 2019 in the framework of social reforms such as the Law on Social Protection, the Law on Social Security for Elderly and the Law on Protection of the children. These laws will directly have effect on reducing child poverty, expanding the rights of people with special needs, and

---

[6] Universal Declaration of Human Rights of United Nations, 1948–1998 (New York: United Nations Department of Public Information), Article 22.

retirement care for elderly people who do not have an income from pensions or other sources of around 100 euro. Through these laws, 73,500 children would achieve their right to a child allowance instead of 3,200 children as it has been until now, then extending rights and increasing assistance for children with special needs and families who look after them. All these reforms have been made with a broad consensus among all affected parties and it is expected to have positive effects, considering it as a challenge for the country, as it should always find the balance between the needs and the opportunities based on the priorities of this department that aims to increase the social security.

The entire insurance system in Macedonia is currently based on the Law on Insurance Supervision, and on other special laws, by-laws and the implementation of EU legislation in the area of insurance. The insurance contract is an agreement in which the insurance contractor is obliged on the basis of the principle of reciprocity and solidarity to submit a certain amount of money to the insurance company (the insurer), whereas the company is obliged, if it comes to an affliction of the insured party, to pay the insured or any third person the compensation, respectively the sum insured.[7] According to these principles, the redistribution of the financial means from the rich to the poor, from the young to the old, from the healthy to the sick, and from the insurer to the other families in need, either old or young, are kept by the insurance contractor.

There are a number of types of social security, among which we can mention: pension insurance due to age, disability insurance in case of work injuries or illnesses, health insurance, unemployment insurance, family insurance, insurance for maternity and newborn coverage etc.

Based on the legislation of North Macedonia, all insurances are classified into 23 types, including:
- insurance against the consequences of accidents – disasters;
- health insurance;
- motor vehicle insurance (all-risk insurance);
- railway vehicle insurance (all-risk insurance);
- aviation insurance (all-risk insurance);
- floating vehicle insurance (all-risk insurance);
- freight insurance (cargo);
- fire and natural disaster insurance;
- other property insurance;

---

[7] Nikola Glavince, "Legal Solution Regarding Life Insurance", Economy and Business, no. 223 (2017): 60.

- motor vehicle liability insurance;
- aviation liability insurance;
- floating vehicle liability insurance;
- general liability insurance;
- credit insurance;
- border insurance;
- financial loss insurance;
- legal protection insurance;
- tourist assistance insurance;
- life insurance;
- marriage or birth insurance;
- life insurance in regard of parts in investment funds;
- tontine insurance;
- funds insurance.[8]

Among types of social security, the most important are pension insurance and health insurance, due to their inclusive effects on the country's economy and human life. This was also foreseen by government programs where, with the aim of creating social security policies and providing a more stable income for the Macedonian Pension and Disability Insurance Fund and the Health Insurance Fund. At the end of 2018, Parliament changed the payment rate by law, for compulsory disability pension insurance from 18% to 18.4% in 2019 and to 18.8% in 2020, while for health insurance this rate ranged from 7.3% to 7.4% in 2019 and to 7.5% by 2020.[9] Therefore in this paper we will focus only on these two types of social security.

3   Health Insurance in the Republic of North Macedonia

Health is a significant factor in the social condition of the population, which depends on the economic development of the country. Health cannot be considered as a commodity in the market which we can approach using the rules of the market economy. The state is committed to continuously improve the health of all its citizens based on their needs and through specific programs it

---

8   Law on Insurance Supervision, Article 5, Official Gazette no. 30, 2012, https://finance.gov.mk/wp-content/uploads/2009/05/LAW-ON-INSURANCE-SUPERVISION-2015.pdf (accessed March 10, 2019).
9   Amendments to the Law on Mandatory Social Security Insurance Contributions, no. 08-7421/1, 2018.

carries out campaigns to prevent certain diseases and increase the quality of health services at all levels. Because of the complex nature of health insurance for citizens themselves and for the state itself, it is of particular importance to find an adequate model that will fit the circumstances of a given country in order to achieve social security for all participants in the process and coverage for the largest number of citizens, offering services that are as cost-effective as possible. The resources of human beings, spatial capacities, and equipment or medical materials available to the state are always limited when compared to the needs and desires of people which are always limitless.

Over time, health insurance systems have been developed and changed in their efforts by:
- improving the health status of the population (ensuring access to health care);
- providing high quality and appropriate care;
- maintaining the sustainability and affordability of healthcare through cost control.[10]

Regardless of the system that the state may implement, each has its advantages and disadvantages. There is no healthcare system in the world that can meet all the demands and wishes of its citizens. Depending on the condition of a particular state, one system can guarantee better functioning than another. However, choosing an adequate health insurance system remains a challenge for any country. The most widespread system in Europe and the world of which Macedonia is part is the Bismarck Model, which was first set up by Otto von Bismarck in the 20th century, according to which health insurance is based on social security where part of a worker's wages is deducted as a part of the health insurance contribution and another part is made by the employer.

Based on practice to date, the Republic of North Macedonia as a social state, both in the past and the present, continues to support the financing of healthcare protection based on compulsory health insurance. Health insurance in Macedonia, as in most Western countries, is based on compulsory and voluntary insurance. Compulsory health insurance is imposed on all citizens of the Republic of North Macedonia for the provision of health services and money remittances based on the general, solid, equitable and effective use of funds under the conditions set forth in this Law.[11] In accordance with

---

10   Charles Normand and Axel Weber, Social Health Insurance: A Guidebook for Planning, 1994 (Geneva: WHO Library), 4.
11   Law on Health Insurance, Article 2 and 10, Official Gazette, no. 07–12961, 2010, https://www.refworld.org/pdfid/5aa125974.pdf (accessed March 12, 2019).

the Constitution, every citizen is guaranteed the right to healthcare protection and every citizen has the right and obligation to preserve and improve his health and the health of others.[12] From here it is clear that health insurance is based on the principle of solidarity, as citizens have a duty to preserve and improve both their own and the health of others. The level of health insurance is a challenge for all countries of the world and this also depends on other social, economic, political or social relations. No health insurance system can function separately from the influence of the country's governance system. Different countries use different methods of financing the healthcare. Funding of healthcare protection has evolved from individual payment when receiving the service, up to the payment through the health insurance of the employer or the employee, as well as financing by the Government through a social protection or taxation system, supplemented with private and non-governmental organizations.[13]

Funding as a function in the healthcare system refers to a system that is related to the mobilization, accumulation and distribution of money to cover the healthcare needs of people, the individual and the collectivity in the health system. The purpose of health financing is to make funding available, as well as to set the right financial incentives for providers, to ensure that all individuals have access to effective public health and personal health care.[14] Health insurance in Macedonia is based on the unity of measures for prevention, diagnosis, therapy and rehabilitation and based on the principle of access, efficiency, continuity, fairness, inclusiveness and the provision of quality health care.[15] Therefore, it can be said that in the framework of health care, a person is provided with health services regarding the condition of a patient's health; taking measures to improve their health status, such as preventing, combating and early diagnosis of diseases; health protection in relation to pregnancy and childbirth; prevention, recovery and remediation of oral and dental diseases; the coverage of therapeutic or rehabilitation procedures, autopsy of the

---

12 Constitution of the Republic of North Macedonia, Official Gazette, no. 52/91, 1991, Article 39, https://www.sobranie.mk/the-constitution-of-the-republic-of-macedonia-ns_article-constitution-of-the-republic-of-north-macedonia.nspx (accessed March 6, 2019).

13 Elizabeta Pacemska, Analysis and Control of the Financial Operations of Health Insurance Fund of Macedonia as a Prerequisite for Quality Health Care (Štip: Universitet Goce Delcev, 2013), 60.

14 World Health Organisation, The World Health Report 2000. Health Systems: Improving Performance (Geneva: World Health Organisation, 2000), https://www.who.int/whr/2000/en/whr00_en.pdf?ua=1 (accessed February 23, 2019).

15 Law on Health Protection, Article 5, Official Gazette, no. 07-1/04/1, 2012, https://www.refworld.org/pdfid/54edef434.pdf (accessed March 18, 2019).

deceased when required by the health institution and the coverage of health insurance for insured people (women) entitled to artificial insemination up to three times who meet certain conditions.[16]

Funding of health insurance for people who are insured with compulsory health insurance is also provided in cases when the insured are in temporary employment abroad or are abroad professionally, educationally, officially or privately. This right can be used by insured people in countries where the Republic of North Macedonia has concluded international social security agreements. This free-of-charge insurance usually covers any urgent medical assistance needed and not cases of insured people who have been diagnosed as having a history of acute illness or acute deterioration in a chronic illness. If the need for treatment persists, immediately after the emergency transfer, healthcare user needs to return to their home country for further treatment of the disease.[17]

Compulsory health insurance does not include health services such as aesthetic operations, the use of higher standards of health services than that offered by hospital health care, rehabilitation in spas without a doctor's recommendation; drugs that are not on the approved list, termination of pregnancy without doctor's recommendation, issuance of all medical certificates, recovery abroad without the consent of the Fund etc.[18] This insurance is provided through the "Health Insurance Fund" as a legal obligation, while the voluntary one is carried out through insurance companies. The Health Insurance Fund is presented as an independent financial institution that carries out public activities in the common interest. This insurance covers all people employed in the public and private sector whether in domestic or international institutions, who through the regular compulsory payment of contributions determined as a percentage of salary and use the health service they need. This insurance also includes a wide range of unemployed people, whether or not they are retired, social cash beneficiaries, unemployed jobseekers, inmates, foreigners who are studying or are obtaining professional training, etc. Furthermore, compulsory health insurance also covers, in addition to the insured person, the members of his or her family, if the same are not already insured, such as spouses, children born in marriage or out of marriage, stepchildren, adopted children and children entrusted for support. Children, in principle, have the right to be insured until adulthood and exceptionally up to the age of 26 if they continue their

---

16   Ibid, Article 16.
17   Rulebook on the Use of Health Services of Insured Persons Abroad, Article 34, Official Gazette, no. 105, 2011.
18   Law on Health Insurance, Official Gazette, no. 07–12961, 2010.

regular education.[19] Under the law, all insured parties pay contributions, while health services are actually used only by those who need it. People who are not insured on any of these bases should pay for health services by themselves and covers the entire cost from their own personal resources.

Beneficiaries of compulsory health insurance under the Law on Health Insurance, when using a certain service, participate privately in the service price. Insured people participate with their own resources when using health services or medicines, but at most pay 20% of the average health service costs, including medications.[20] The same goes for cases where the healthcare provider has the consent to be treated abroad, whereby we should participate with 20% of the total amount but no more than €200, while for the prostheses, orthopedic devices and other healthcare tools participation goes up to 50%. There is another category of people who are totally discharged from participating in the cost of healthcare insurance, such as children with special needs, social assistance beneficiaries, people who are residents in shelter centers and others. Current legislation does not foresee the release or change of participation in the service price depending on the type of illness, but all is of the same value, except for cases that are foreseen by the government program campaigns. Such campaigns have been held many times, such as AIDS, the immunization of the population, the prevention of tuberculosis, the early detection of cancer, the last campaign was for prevention of measles and many more.

The health insurance system in Macedonia covers all outpatient and hospital services, ranging across the prevention, diagnosis, recovery and rehabilitation of patients. Therefore, we can say that with compulsory health services, the insured are provided with healthcare services covering treatment of illnesses and injuries, the right to compensation in the form of salaries is provided in cases where the person is not capable of working because of an illness or injury, or compensation for absence from work due to childbirth and other cases.

The budget for compulsory health insurance is provided by health insurance contributions, the central budget participation, and additional contributions in cases of injury at work and occupational diseases and other sources. The data of the Ministry of Finance indicate that 95% of the healthcare budget is supplemented by health insurance contributions. According to the information from the Health Insurance Fund of Macedonia, the total healthcare budget for 2018 is 510 million euro, of which 459 million euro are dedicated to the

---

19   Ibid, Article 6 and 7.
20   Ibid, Article 32.

Health Insurance Fund of Macedonia, while the rest is devoted to the Ministry of Health through which programs for recovery and prevention are funded.[21]

Besides the problem of creating a healthcare budget, another important issue is the method of distribution of these funds, as the healthcare in Macedonia is organized into the primary, secondary and tertiary levels. Therefore, the use of these tools for the promotion, prevention, treatment and rehabilitation of various diseases as well as the salaries of employees and other means of work should be carefully planned.

Contributions for health insurance along with other contributions are deducted directly from the gross salary of the employee or from other sources of income. The rate of social contributions for compulsory health insurance is now 7.4% of gross salary.

As a rule, a criterion for creation of the budget for the upcoming year is taken from the budget of the previous years and the same is part of the State budget proposed by the Ministry of Finance and approved by the Parliament. The amount of the budget together with a detailed plan is proposed by the Health Insurance Fund of Macedonia (HIFM) to the Ministry of Finance.

In North Macedonia, the amount of funds for the health sector over the last ten years has reached six to eight percent of GDP, with a falling tendency.[22] When we speak of funds allocated to the health sector, we must distinguish between the funds dedicated to the Health Insurance Fund and the funds allocated to the Ministry of Health. Funds allocated from the state budget to the ministry as a rule are intended for the entire population, while the funds allocated to the Health Insurance Fund are provided for the purpose of purchasing medical services from health institutions and aimed at the recovery of insured people and their next of kin. In this case, the fund is presented as a buyer of healthcare services while public healthcare institutions, in some cases private ones also, appear as sellers (providers) of health services. The parties establish this agreement through a contract, where they clearly define the types and volume of healthcare services they should offer and their prices. The Fund is a healthcare institution which provides healthcare services and the recovery of its insured members through the payment of funds to healthcare providers on behalf of insured people who are the beneficiaries of these services.[23]

21　Budget of the Republic of Macedonia for 2018, https://vlada.mk/sites/default/files/dokumenti/budzeti/budzet_2018_.pdf (accessed February 10, 2019).
22　Maja Parnardjieva and Vladimir Dimkovski, Analysis of Public Health Care Expenditures for children in the Country (Skopje: Finance Think, 2008), 7.
23　Elizabeta Pacemska, Analysis and Control of the Financial Operations of Health Insurance Fund of Macedonia as a Prerequisite for Quality Health Care, 35.

On the other hand, private health insurance is made on a voluntary and a private basis by people who seek to obtain expanded health care for themselves and their family members. This medical insurance usually covers specialist medical, diagnostic and therapeutic health services in private healthcare institutions. Usually through this health insurance, people intend to cover those health services that are not performed by public healthcare institutions and are not covered by compulsory health care.[24] In order for a person to have a voluntary healthcare insurance and to use healthcare services from private healthcare institutions, the user must be insured in the compulsory healthcare service.[25] Through this model, the entities independently regulate their relationships through private insurance companies and private healthcare institutions.

4 Pension and Disability Insurance in the Republic of North Macedonia

Health insurance and pension and disability insurance aims to ensure minimum conditions for existence when an individual is unable to provide for themselves. Pension and disability insurance insures the person and his or her family members financially when they are unable to work due to age or disability. Individual pension insurance is primarily social and has no commercial intent.

Based on the provisions of the Constitution of North Macedonia, in the framework of social security for citizens, the rights to pension and disability insurance as basic human rights with which social security is guaranteed are also foreseen. Pension and disability insurance, as a system, represents the entirety of norms of both financial and administrative institutions that provide age and disability risk insurance. All these rights of a property character deriving from pension and disability insurance are rights that are related to the person and as such cannot be transferred to third parties through the legal actions of the parties, by inheritance or in any other form. The Law provides details on the category of insured people who are obliged to pay contributions for pension and disability insurance, such as private and public sector employees, people elected and appointed as holders of public functions, North

---

24 Law on Voluntary Health Insurance, Article 4, section 2, Official Gazette no. 145, 2012, http://zdravstvo.gov.mk/wp-content/uploads/2018/01/ZAKON-ZA-DOBROVOLNO-ZDRAVSTVENO-OSIGURUVANE-zakluchno-so-br.-192-od-2015.pdf (accessed March 21, 2019).
25 Ibid, Article 10, Section 2.

Macedonian nationals employed in international organizations, natural people who are engaged in agricultural activity and many other cases explicitly stated in the Law.[26] This obligation also includes foreign residents employed in North Macedonia or people exercising any kind of activity.

The newly reformed pension system in North Macedonia, after 2000, unlike the previous one, is based solely on generational solidarity. The pay-as-you-go principle is based on several new basic principles, such as private pension management, protecting the interests of all participants, financial and social security of members, participant rights depending on time and amount of the contributions paid, as well as the security and diversification of the invested funds.[27]

In Europe there are three types of social security systems, namely the Bismarck, the Scandinavian, and the Beveridge models. In Macedonia, the pension system has functioned on the PAYG system and Bismarck model of social security.[28] Also, these systems continue to be applied today in most countries worldwide. Each of these systems differs based on its characteristics and the circumstances of the country where it is implemented.[29]

---

[26] Law on Pension and Disability Insurance, Article 11, Official Gazette, no. 98, 2012, https://www.pravdiko.mk/wp-content/uploads/2013/11/Zakon-za-penziskoto-i-invalidskoto-osiguruvane-Prechisten-Tekst-11-04-2013.pdf (accessed February 8, 2019).

[27] Svetlana Atanasovska, Reform in the pension system and pension funds as institutional investors (Štip: University Goce Delcev, 2011), 58.

[28] Verce Mitkova, Pension System in The Republic of Macedonia with accent of The Third Pension Pillar in The Municipalities of South-Eastern Macedonia, (Štip: University Goce Delcev, 2014), http://eprints.ugd.edu.mk/15812/ (accessed March 15, 2019).

[29] The Bismarck model provides greater social security for workers' rights and is created by contributions of workers and employers. The Scandinavian model guarantees a safe retirement for citizens because the way of its creation is largely based on taxes and only part of it is supplemented by employee contributions. The Beveridge model created by William Beveridge, who established the British National Health Service, is provided through financing only from citizens' taxes and guarantees the minimum pension for each citizen. This system of pension and disability insurance is based on the principle of solidarity and reciprocity. The most widespread system in the world and Europe is the Pay-As-You-Go (PAYG) system, which is based on the principle of generational solidarity. According to this system, the currently working employees allocate funds from their contributions to retirement pensions for the purpose of paying pensions of current pensioners. So, even low-income people are provided with basic means for minimum standard of living. This system is very suitable for countries that have the young demographic structure and whose economy is growing. By the principle of reciprocity, we mean that the person pays when young and benefits from a pension when he or she retires. According to this principle, pension insurance also has the role of saving for the person him or herself, which means that he or she saves in their youth to have in his old age when he or she is in

The complex short- and long-term consequences of demographic changes, the most important of which is the (continuing) ageing of the population, can be more easily monitored and forecast for individual categories of public finance, as can the effects of modifications to the system of taxation and social security on the competitiveness and flexibility of the economy, and thus on growth.[30]

The main factors influencing the issue of the pension system are:
– demographic factors;
– social factors;
– economic factors.

Demographic factors include aging of the population, prolonged life expectancy due to improved healthcare and a low birth rate. As in most European countries, in North Macedonia also, the aging of the population and the increase in the number of elderly people for retirement is noted, in contrast to the number of young people who are able to work, whose number is constantly decreasing.

This can be clearly seen in Table 2.1 on how the number of retirees has steadily increased and the birth rate has decreased. For example, in 1980, the number of pensioners in Macedonia was 84,948, and the number of births was 39,784. In 1990, the number of pensioners in Macedonia was 166,224, and the number of births was 35,401. In 2000, the number of pensioners in Macedonia was 241,221, and the number of births was 26,168. In 2005, the number of pensioners in Macedonia was 272,740, and the number of births was 22,482. In 2010, the number of pensioners in Macedonia was 280,000, and the number of births slightly increased due to state measures which brought the number to 24,296. Finally, in 2017 the number of pensioners reached 307,610 and the number of births once again decreased to 21,754.

Among social factors, we can mention unemployment and poverty that may be due to age, and lack of educational and vocational training. This situation can be overcome by educating the elderly for their adaptation to the new labor market demands so that they are as active as they can be with legal changes according to their social needs.

---

need the most and this is done by the Pension Insurance Fund in the best way. Through these principles, pension insurance eliminates the risk of old age, disability and inability to work.

30 Miroslav Verbic, Modelling the Pension System in an Overlapping-Generations General Equilibrium Modeling Framework, 2007, https://mpra.ub.uni-muenchen.de/10350/ (accessed March 17, 2019).

TABLE 2.1 The number of pensioners and birth rate in North Macedonia

Year	Number of pensioners	Birth rate
1980	84,948	39,784
1990	166,224	35,401
2000	241,221	26,168
2005	272,740	22,482
2010	280,000	24,296
2017	307,610	21,754

SOURCE: MARYAN NIKOLOV, MIROLUB SHUKAROV, AND IVANA VELKOVSKA, REPORT ON THE PUBLICLY FUNDED PENSION SCHEME IN MACEDONIA (SKOPJE: CENTER FOR ECONOMIC ANALYSIS, 2017), HTTPS://CIVICAMOBILITAS.MK/WP-CONTENT/UPLOADS/2018/02/TSEA-ODRZHLIVOST-NA-PENZISKIOT-FOND-VO-MK-FINAL-2.PDF (ACCESSED MARCH 6, 2019).

Among economic factors, we can mention the recent intensive technology development which has enabled an increase of production and profits with a smaller number of workers, causing job losses and increasing unemployment. The rapid growth and adoption of AI and robotics will have uncertain, but potentially serious and long-lasting consequences on employment, wages and income distribution.[31] This factor mostly influences poor and developing countries, and North Macedonia is also part of the latter. Other factors affecting the sustainability of the pension system are demographic change, labor market movements and the reconciliation of pensions with economic potential.[32] All of the factors mentioned above, along with the extension of the active working age, the new age of retirement, and the dismissal of technological surplus during the transition phase in North Macedonia, caused an ever-increasing number of pensioners at the expense of employees. These circumstances also fueled the growth of the gray economy and the avoidance of

---

[31] Joël Blit, Samantha St. Amand and Joanna Wajda, Automation and the Future of Work: Scenarios and Policy Options (Waterloo: Centre for International Governance Innovation, 2018), https://www.cigionline.org/publications/automation-and-future-work-scenarios-and-policy-options (accessed February 6, 2019).

[32] Blagica Petreski and Pavle Gacov, Sustainability of the Pension System in Macedonia. A Comprehensive Analysis and Reform Proposal with MK-PENS – Dynamic Microsimulation Model, Policy Study 14, 2018, https://www.financethink.mk/wp-content/uploads/2018/06/Pension-analysis-EN.pdf (accessed March 7, 2019).

payment of contributions, all of these reflect negative effects on the Pension Fund budget. Because of this, the gap between revenues and expenditures has deepened, which can be overcome either with increased contributions or increased transfers from the state budget, which would be detrimental to the financing of other projects.[33] This is a global problem. Compared to 2017, the number of people over the age of 60 is expected to double by 2050 and triple by 2100, rising from 962 million in 2017 to 2.1 billion in 2050 and 3.1 billion in 2100. In Europe, this figure is 25% of the population over 60.[34] In North Macedonia, in the 1950s the average life expectancy of the population in the country was around 60 years old and now (2010) it has climbed to 76 years old for women and 72 years old for men and therefore the demographic criteria age population moves to 60 years old.[35] The solution to the long-term problem has imposed the need for deep reforms of the pension system by enabling a multi-lingual system which, in principle, also enables the privatization approach to these pillars. Figure 2.1 clearly shows how the average life expectancy increased 1.6 years from 2005 to 2015, increasing from 73.9 to 75.5 years old.[36]

The pension and disability insurance system in the Republic of North Macedonia has undergone a reform and crisis process after independence, like most countries transitioning from a country with a planned economy to a market economy have done. This is also because the country endured a crisis as a result of the collapse of the economy following the transition, wars and embargoes in the Balkan countries. This process also contributes to the early retirement of many employees and the increase in the number of the unemployed. Therefore, this situation imposed the need for reformation which started from 1993 and lasted until 2000 with the adoption of the Law on Pension and Disability Insurance, according to which for the first time the legal framework is provided for the organization of this system with three pillars.[37]

---

33 Svetlana Atanasovska, Reform in the Pension System and Pension Funds as Institutional Investors, 13.
34 United Nations, Department of Economic and Social Affairs, World Population Prospects: The 2017 Revision, https://www.un.org/development/desa/publications/world-population-prospects-the-2017-revision.html (accessed February 21, 2019).
35 Cane Koteski, Dusko Josheski, Zlatko Jakovlev, Nikola V. Dimitrov, and Snezana Bardarova, "Macedonia Demographic Aging", Journal of Earth Science and Engineering 4 (2014).
36 Maryan Nikolov, Mirolub Shukarov, and Ivana Velkovska, Report on the Publicly Funded Pension Scheme in Macedonia (Skopje: Center for Economic Analysis, 2017), 9, https://www.un.org/development/desa/publications/world-population-prospects-the-2017-revision.html (accessed March 6, 2019).
37 Verce Mitkova, Pension System In The Republic of Macedonia with Accent of The Third Pension Pillar in The Municipalities of South-Eastern Macedonia, 82.

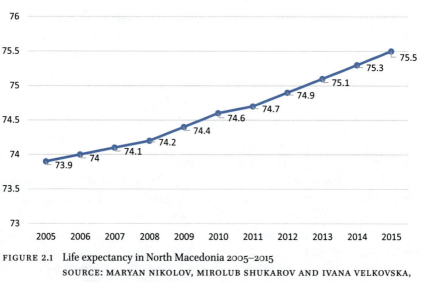

FIGURE 2.1 Life expectancy in North Macedonia 2005–2015
SOURCE: MARYAN NIKOLOV, MIROLUB SHUKAROV AND IVANA VELKOVSKA, REPORT ON THE PUBLICLY FUNDED PENSION SCHEME IN MACEDONIA (SKOPJE: CENTER FOR ECONOMIC ANALYSIS, 2017), 9, HTTPS:// CIVICAMOBILITAS.MK/WP-CONTENT/UPLOADS/2018/02/TSEA-ODRZHLIVOST -NA-PENZISKIOT-FOND-VO-MK-FINAL-2.PDF (ACCESSED MARCH 6, 2019).

This three-pillar retirement system also represents the World Bank's main agenda in promoting reforms in the pension system, which should be a combination of public and private pension funds. The entire pension and disability insurance system is based on the Law on Pension and Disability Insurance, which constitutes the basic law in this area and the provisions of other laws, by-laws and international acts ratified by the Republic of North Macedonia.

The rights that can be provided by pension and disability insurance are:
– the right to old-age pension, the right to disability pension;
– the right to professional rehabilitation and the right to adequate compensation;
– the right to a family pension;
– the right to compensation for bodily injuries;
– the right to a small pension value lump sum.[38]

The insured obtains the right to an old-age pension by the age of 64 (for men) and 62 years (for women) with at least 15 years of work experience. The insured person obtains the right to a disability pension when his or her work ability is

---

38   Law on Pension and Disability Insurance, Article 5, Official Gazette, no. 98, 2012.

permanently lost and the same cannot be cured through medical rehabilitation. People with health disabilities are divided into two categories by law:
- category I – when the work ability of the insured is reduced by more than 80% and there is permanent loss of working ability (general working inability);
- category II – when the workability of the insured is reduced by more than 50% and up to 80% (professional work disability).[39]

Factors that cause disability may vary, such as illness, injuries at work or after work or occupational diseases.

Based on the Strategic Plan 2018–2020 of Pension and Disability Fund in North Macedonia, the number of beneficiaries increases together with the amount paid. The number of retirement beneficiaries by the end of 2018 is expected to reach 320,300, while the amount of pensions to be allocated by the Fund amounts to 880 million euro (€ 880,000,000 million), which, compared the previous year, is 34 million euro higher. This figure is expected to increase until 2020, with the number of pensioners reaching 333,306, which according to the strategy means that this figure will increase by 13,000 new beneficiaries in the next two years, while the amount that will be needed to be allocated by the Fund will reach 100 million euros. If we compare the ratio of employees to the number of pensioners in North Macedonia, it shows that this ratio is 2 to 1, which means that for every two employees there is one pension beneficiary, based on the data of the State Statistical Office, where the number of employees in 2018 was 771,806. The successful functioning of the pension system based on the current system can only be achieved if the systemic dependency norm, the ratio of the number of employees and the number of pensioners will be 3–3.5 or more employees financing the pension of one pensioner.[40] If this ratio falls below 2.5:1, then the pension system will have difficulties in operation and in this case, it will be necessary to intervene to fill the gaps that will appear in the budget. Therefore, this report shows that the PAYG system based on solidarity of generations in North Macedonia is not sufficient for the future based on the demographic structure of our country. According to the Pension and Disability Insurance Fund of North Macedonia, at the end of 2018, there were 578,023 insured persons with compulsory pension and disability insurance and 86,360 obliged persons were registered. In 2018, from all types, the total number of pensions was 315,780. More than half of the pension beneficiaries

---

39 Pension System in North Macedonia, Finance Think, https://www.financethink.mk/en/pension-system-of-macedonia/ (accessed March 3, 2019).
40 Milena Svetislav Nikolic, Pension System Reform of the Republic of Serbia in Functions of their Sustainability, (Niš: University of Niš, 2017).

TABLE 2.2   Status of pension beneficiaries by paid pension, type, and the percentage of employment/unemployment rate in 2017 in North Macedonia

Type of pension	Number of beneficiaries
Family pension	76,052
Disability pension	37,465
Old-age pension	191,592
Total	**315,780**
Employment rate	44.1%
Unemployment rate	22.6%

SOURCE: BLAGICA PETRESKI AND PAVLE GACOV, SUSTAINABILITY OF THE PENSION SYSTEM IN MACEDONIA. A COMPREHENSIVE ANALYSIS AND REFORM PROPOSAL WITH MK-PENS – DYNAMIC MICROSIMULATION MODEL, POLICY STUDY 14, 2018, HTTPS://WWW.FINANCETHINK.MK/WP-CONTENT/UPLOADS/2018/06/PENSION-ANALYSIS-EN.PDF (ACCESSED MARCH 7, 2019).

in Northern Macedonia are on an old-age pension (Table 2.2). When looking at the percentage of insured persons who pay contributions compared to the number of uninsured (unemployment) persons this ratio is 2:1, similar to the ratio of insured persons to the number of pensioners.

The types of pensions recognized by the Law on Pension and Disability Insurance in Northern Macedonia, including Old-age Pension, Disability Pension, Family Pension, Agricultural Pension, and War Pension are listed in Table 2.3. The second column in this table shows the average amount in the national currency for each pension. The third column shows the percentage of pension beneficiaries by category. Moreover, Table 2.3. shows the agricultural pension provides lower income, while the war pension provides higher income. The largest percentage of pensions beneficiaries are those of the old age category, while the smallest number are those within the agricultural category.

More than half of the pension beneficiaries in Northern Macedonia are on an old-age pension (Table 2.3). When looking at the percentage of insured persons who pay contributions compared to the number of uninsured (unemployed) persons this ratio is 2:1, similar to the ratio of insured persons to the number of pensioners.

The pension and disability insurance system in North Macedonia consists of compulsory disability pension insurance on the basis of generation

TABLE 2.3 Average amount of pension and pensioners structure by pension type in 2017 in North Macedonia

Type of pension	Average amount	Pensioners structure
Family pension	11,331	24.20%
Disability pension	12,801	11.44%
Old-age pension	15,414	63.87%
Agricultural pension	7,033	0.07%
War pension	21,330	0.42%

SOURCE: ANETA DODEVSKA, ANALYSIS: PAYMENT OF PENSIONS WILL NEED OVER 1 BILLION EUROS, 2018, HTTPS://VISTINOMER.MK/ANALIZA-ZA-ISPLATA-NA-PENZII-KE-BIDAT-POTREBNI-POVEKE-OD-1-MILIJARADA-EVRA/ (ACCESSED FEBRUARY 5, 2019).

solidarity (first pillar), compulsory capital financing of pension insurance (second pillar), and voluntary capital financing of pension insurance (third pillar).[41] Through the first pillar, part of the pension is provided for old age or disability, family pension due to death and a physical disability pension. The second pillar provides the supplementary part of pension insurance in the case of old age where the person receives an old-age pension depending on the level of contributions and the compensation each person earns based on the market economy. The second pillar is also created through compulsory pension insurance based on the personal capital savings of the insured in their individual account. The second pillar pension is dependent on the accumulated contributions from salaries. The third pillar is only voluntary and depends on the person's desire to create personal capital savings for the future. This pillar is characteristic of including all people who want to secure greater independence and security than provided by the first and second pillars. In the second and third pillar, all paid contributions and interests are accumulated in the individual account of the insured person through capital financing until their retirement. With this method, each person participates in their pension, and this is not dependent on the contributions of other generations.

---

41   Law on Pension and Disability Insurance, Article 2, Official Gazette, no. 98, 2012.

All people who were insured on any basis in single-pillar system before January 1, 2003 had the right to join the second pension pillar, while people who were employed after that date had a membership obligation in the second pillar. Voluntary pension funds were established in 2009 and started to function on January 1, 2010 and the same are funded through a capital investment system in the form of financing.

Based on the Law on Pension and Disability Insurance of the Republic of North Macedonia, we present in a tabular form the types of rights from pension and disability insurance and the conditions how to get to them.

Table 2.4 shows the types and conditions of retirement that a person can receive, depending on age, sex, and the relation to a deceased family member. Others have also set forth the conditions on which family members are entitled to family pension benefits and, in the latter case, disability benefits which may be used by the insured person in the event of accidental disability or illness.

TABLE 2.4   Terms and conditions for pension and disability insurance

Type of pension	Income and definition of rights	Pension value
Old-age pension	64 (men) and 62 (women) years of age At least 15 years of work experience.	Pension basis is determined by the average valorized monthly salaries that the insured has earned during their working time. The amount of the pension is determined by the retirement base, in a certain percentage depending on the length of the pension work experience. Depending on whether the insurer is in both pillars or only in the first, different rates of calculation apply.

TABLE 2.4 Types of terms and conditions for pension and disability insurance (*cont.*)

Type of pension	Income and definition of rights	Pension value
Family pension	Family members of the insured deceased person: spouse, children and parents who he/she supported. They are entitled to a family pension if the insured person is deceased: has completed at least five years of work experience or at least ten years of work experience, has fulfilled the conditions for retirement or disability pension or has been a retirement or disability pension beneficiary. The spouse has the right to use the family pension after the age of 50. The child obtains the right to a family pension until he reaches 15 years of age and if he/she continues education, up to the age of 26.	The value of pension is determined by the percentage of the old-age or disability pension that the insured would have at the time of death, i.e.: 70% for a family member and 10% for each prospective member, but not more than 100%.
Disability pension	Disability impaired by work injuries or occupational diseases – regardless of the length of retirement work experience Disability caused by injury or illness at work, provided that on the day of the disability the person fulfills certain conditions regarding the old age and the completion of the years of work experience.	80% of the pension basis when the disability is caused during work injury or occupational disease. Pension basis depending on length of retirement work experience and life expectancy when disability is caused during work injury or illness.

SOURCE: LAW ON PENSION AND DISABILITY INSURANCE, OFFICIAL GAZETTE, NO.98, 2012, ARTICLE 11. HTTPS://WWW.PRAVDIKO.MK/WP-CONTENT/UPLOADS/2013/11/ZAKON-ZA-PENZISKOTO-I-INVALIDSKOTO-OSIGURUVANE-PRECHISTEN-TEKST-11-04-2013.PDF (ACCESSED FEBRUARY 8, 2019); BLAGICA PETRESKI AND PAVLE GACOV, SUSTAINABILITY OF THE PENSION SYSTEM IN MACEDONIA. A COMPREHENSIVE ANALYSIS AND REFORM PROPOSAL WITH MK-PENS – DYNAMIC MICROSIMULATION MODEL, POLICY STUDY 14, 2018, HTTPS://WWW.FINANCETHINK.MK/WP-CONTENT/UPLOADS/2018/06/PENSION-ANALYSIS-EN.PDF (ACCESSED MARCH 7, 2019).

However regardless of the retirement age provided for by the law, men at 64 and women at 62, a certain category of people acquire this right earlier as a result of accelerated work experience (reduced service years required for retirement), disability pension and family pension. The work experience is normally recognized for people employed at the Ministry of the Interior, employees in penitentiary and correctional institutions, and educational and rehabilitation houses and some other sectors of the economy that severely affect the health and skills of employees and those jobs that because of the nature and importance of work reduces the physiological functions of the body to such an extent that the worker becomes incapable of further pursuit of the same job.

The Disability Pension Fund budget is created by the rate of contributions paid by employers to employees. According to the law, this contribution rate this year is 18.4% for the first pillar, of which 6% goes to the second pillar for the insured on this pillar. The third pillar depends on the will and the agreement of the insured with Voluntary Pension Funds. The funds deposited in the third pillar are stored in the bank, which in this case is presented as a guardian of voluntary pension funds in North Macedonia.

The contributions payment rate in North Macedonia is paid by the employer and has oscillated over number of years. It is now expected to increase slightly due to the deficit in the Disability Pension Fund because of the low rate of contributions and structural changes that occurred in the pension system in 2006 when it transitioned from the single pillar to multi-pillar system. In 2006, the contribution rate was 21.2%, in 2009 19%, in 2010 18%, and now in 2019 it is 18.4%. From 2020, it will be 18.8%.[42]

The level of realization of rights from disability pension insurance depends on the level of the person's income, as the contribution percentage increases symmetrically with increasing salary, and the way of investment, whether the insured pays only into the first pillar, into the first and the second pillars, or into all three pillars. At the time of retirement of the person due to age, after the first pillar pension is realized, part of the second pillar fund is transferred to the competent institution for the granting of pensions and the pension is given to the citizen in total. The realization of the right to any form of pension and disability insurance is made at the request of the insured party or by family members, who are insured under his or her name if the insured has passed away, addressed at the Pension and Disability Fund of North Macedonia. In each of the forms of retirement, whether old-age, disability, or family, the insured or his or her family members have the right to use the pension equally

---

42 Svetlana Atanasovska, Reform in the Pension System and Pension Funds as Institutional Investors, 45.

from all three pillars, depending on the contributions they have deposited. All details of the parties' procedural actions are set out in the provisions of the Law on Pension and Disability Insurance.

This way of organizing the pension system in North Macedonia allows greater security due to diversity in case of danger, since funding is made in two or three pillars and due to the parallel existence of compulsory and voluntary insurance. This system also guarantees the solvency of pensions due to increased savings and investment opportunities in case of economic growth.

The challenges of pension and disability insurance are demographic factors that are followed by constant aging of the population and increased life expectancy, the low birth rate; the informal economy and the mass exodus of young people capable of working in the West. In the 2017 report, the World Bank warns North Macedonia that the Fund's budget is at risk because of the lack of funds and opening of new government-subsidized jobs. According to this report, 89% of new employers are exempt from the obligation to pay contributions to new employees. In recent years, the percentage poured into the Fund from the state budget amounts to 46%, which implies a large dependence on the Central Budget Fund. Informal employment comprises 18.5% of all employment in 2016 in North Macedonia (World Bank / WIIW, 2018) and the informal sector contributes 17% of GDP (EC, 2018).[43] This figure in 2016 among young people aged 15–24 is 34.4%. Informality and job subsidies affect the non-payment of taxes and contributions, thus increasing the fiscal burden of the economy.

The prospect of pension system security should be seen in the pay-as-you-go system based on the solidarity of generations in a fully funded or capitalized system, according to which the capital funded for pension insurance has an investment function. Another factor that can increase the safety of the functioning of the pension system is the increase of the retirement age to correspond to the increase in life expectancy or even the increase of the percentage rate of contributions. Only a combination of concrete measures represents a guarantee for the long-term security of this pension insurance system.

---

43 OECD/ETF/EU/EBRD, SME Policy Index: Western Balkans and Turkey 2019: Assessing the Implementation of the Small Business Act for Europe (Paris: OECD Publishing), 744, https://www.oecd-ilibrary.org/development/sme-policy-index-western-balkans-and-turkey-2019_g2g9fa9a en;jsessionid=7-SGYZgUwgkScQTxO_tk-DOs.ip-10-240-5-176 (accessed February 18, 2019).

5 Conclusion

Social security is an organized government activity through which social assistance is provided to people in the event of an economic or health risk that may arise, such as illness, unemployment, old age, etc. Social insurance differs from other forms of insurance because payment for this type of insurance is mandatory. North Macedonia has completed its social security legislation for its citizens, and this resembles most countries of the region and Europe. Among the most important forms of social insurance are healthcare insurance and disability pension insurance. The most widespread healthcare system in Europe and in the world where Macedonia is situated is the Bismarck Model, which was first set up by Otto von Bismarck in the nineteenth century. In this model, healthcare insurance is based on social security where a portion of the contributions are deducted from employee salaries as part of healthcare insurance and another part from employers. According to the Constitution, every citizen is guaranteed the right to healthcare protection and every citizen has the right and obligation to preserve and improve his or her health and the health of others. Healthcare insurance in Macedonia, as in most Western countries, is based on compulsory and voluntary insurance. The healthcare insurance system in Macedonia covers all outpatient and hospital services, ranging from prevention, diagnosis, recovery and rehabilitation of patients. Compulsory healthcare insurance is provided through the "Health Insurance Fund" as a legal obligation, while the voluntary one is carried out through insurance companies.

Pension and disability insurance insures the person and his or her family financially when they are unable to work due to age or disability. The Bismarck model provides greater social security for workers' rights and is created by contributions of workers and employers. The most widespread system in the world and Europe is the Pay-As-You-Go (PAYG) system, which is based on the principle of generational solidarity. The main factors affecting the pension system issue are demographic factors, social factors and economic factors. The right to old-age pension is obtained by the insured when turning 64 (for men) and 62 years (for women) with at least 15 years of work experience. The system of pension and disability insurance in North Macedonia consists of compulsory disability pension insurance on the basis of generational solidarity (first pillar), compulsory capital financing of pension insurance (second pillar) and voluntary capital financing of pension insurance (third pillar). The Disability Pension Fund budget is created by the rate of contributions paid by employers to employees. The challenges of pension and disability insurance are demographic factors that are followed by constant aging of the population and increased life expectancy, the low birth rate, the informal economy and the mass exodus of young people capable of working in the West.

Based on the analysis of this study, it has been concluded that the health insurance system has been continuously undergoing reforms in order to increase the quality of medical services and provide better accessibility to patients. We currently lack timely diagnostics of rare diseases and their ongoing treatment. This is due to the fact that the state has a duty to provide health protection to all its citizens. In cases when there are rare diseases or more complicated care is required that cannot be given in the country, the Health Insurance Fund is obligated to cover all medical expenses and patient therapy for treatment abroad. These situations are usually very costly, which greatly increases the costs of the Fund. I recommend that, despite the reforms, a continued supply of innovative medical technology combined with the training of medical professionals for the use of these technologies and the latest medical methods. Health policies should be focused in this direction.

Also, due to the increasing deficiency between income contributions from insured persons and the costs of paying pensions, I recommend that the policy be focused on generating new jobs. This can only happen by implementing long-term investment strategies in the education sector, which subsequently guarantee the development of other sectors of industry. In addition to this positive effect on the sustainability of the Pension and Disability Fund, it ensures that the wages of employed persons will rise and their pension contributions will as well.

Bibliography

Amendments to the Law on Mandatory Social Security Insurance Contributions, no. 08-7421/1 (2018).

Atanasovska, Svetlana. Reform in the Pension System and Pension Funds as Institutional Investors. Štip, University Goce Delcev, 2011.

Blit, Joël, Samantha St. Amand and Joanna Wajda. Automation and the Future of Work: Scenarios and Policy Options. Waterloo: Centre for International Governance Innovation, 2018. Accessed February 6, 2019. https://www.cigionline.org/publications/automation-and-future-work-scenarios-and-policy-options/.

Budget of the Republic of Macedonia for 2018. Accessed February 10, 2019. https://vlada.mk/sites/default/files/dokumenti/budzeti/budzet_2018_.pdf.

Constitution of the Republic of North Macedonia. Official Gazette, no. 52/91, 1991. Accessed March 6, 2019. https://www.sobranie.mk/the-constitution-of-the-republic-of-macedonia-ns_article-constitution-of-the-republic-of-north-macedonia.nspx.

Dodevska, Aneta. Analysis: Payment of Pensions will Need over 1 Billion Euros. 2018. Accessed February 5, 2019. https://vistinomer.mk/analiza-za-isplata-na-penzii-ke-bidat-potrebni-poveke-od-1-milijarada-evra/.

Finance Think. Pension system in North Macedonia. Accessed March 3, 2019. https://www.financethink.mk/en/pension-system-of-macedonia/.

Glavince, Nikola. "Legal Solution Regarding Life Insurance", Economy and Business, no. 233 (2017).

Isaacs, Stuart, David Blundell, Anne Foley, Norman Ginsburg, Brian McDonough, Daniel Silverstone, and Tara Young. Social Problems in the UK. Oxon: Routledge, 2015.

Koteski, Cane, Dusko Josheski, Zlatko Jakovlev, Nikola V. Dimitrov, and Snezana Bardarova. "Macedonia Demographic Aging". Journal of Earth Science and Engineering 4 (2014): 445–454.

Law on Health Insurance. Official Gazette, no. 07–12961, 2010. Accessed March 12, 2019. https://www.refworld.org/pdfid/5aa125974.pdf.

Law on Health Protection. Official Gazette, no. 07–1704/1, 2012. Accessed March 18, 2019. https://www.refworld.org/pdfid/54edef434.pdf.

Law on Insurance Supervision. Official Gazette, no. 30 (2012). Accessed March 10, 2019. https://finance.gov.mk/wp-content/uploads/2009/05/LAW-ON-INSURANCE-SUPERVISION-2015.pdf.

Law on Pension and Disability Insurance. Official Gazette, no. 98, 2012. Accessed February 8, 2019. https://www.pravdiko.mk/wp-content/uploads/2013/11/Zakon-za-penziskoto-i-invalidskoto-osiguruvane-Prechisten-Tekst-11-04-2013.pdf.

Law on Voluntary Health Insurance. Official Gazette, no. 145, 2012. Accessed March 21, 2019. http://zdravstvo.gov.mk/wp-content/uploads/2018/01/ZAKON-ZA-DOBROVOLNO-ZDRAVSTVENO-OSIGURUVANE-zakluchno-so-br.-192-od-2015.pdf.

Mitkova, Verce. Pension System in The Republic of Macedonia with Accent of The Third Pension Pillar in The Municipalities of South-Eastern Macedonia. Štip: Universitet Goce Delcev, 2014. Accessed March 15, 2019. http://eprints.ugd.edu.mk/15812/.

Nikolic, Milena Svetislav. Pension System Reform of the Republic of Serbia in Functions of their Sustainability. Niš: University of Niš, 2017.

Nikolov, Maryan, Mirolub Shukarov, and Ivana Velkovska. Report on the Publicly Funded Pension Scheme in Macedonia. Skopje: Center for Economic Analysis, 2017. Accessed March 6, 2019. https://www.un.org/development/desa/publications/world-population-prospects-the-2017-revision.html.

Normand, Charles, and Axel Weber. Social Health Insurance: A Guidebook for Planning. Geneva: WHO Library, 1994.

OECD/ETF/EU/EBRD. SME Policy Index: Western Balkans and Turkey 2019: Assessing the Implementation of the Small Business Act for Europe. Paris: OECD Publishing. Accessed February 18, 2019. https://www.oecd-ilibrary.org/development/sme-policy-index-western-balkans-and-turkey-2019_g2g9fa9a-en.

Pacemska, Elizabeta. Analysis and Control of the Financial Operations of Health Insurance Fund of Macedonia as a Prerequisite for Quality Health Care. Štip: Faculty of economics, 2013.

Parnardjieva, Maja, and Vladimir Dimkovski. Analysis of Public Health Care Expenditures for Children in the Country. Economic Research and Policy Institute, Skopje, 2008.

Petreski, Blagica, and Pavle Gacov. Sustainability of the Pension System in Macedonia. A Comprehensive Analysis and Reform Proposal with MK-PENS – Dynamic Microsimulation Model, Policy Study 14, 2018. Accessed March 7, 2019. https://www.financethink.mk/wp-content/uploads/2018/06/Pension-analysis-EN.pdf.

Rulebook on the Use of Health Services of Insured Persons Abroad. Official Gazette, no. 105, 2011. Accessed December 8, 2017.

United Nations, Department of Economic and Social Affairs. World Population Prospects: The 2017 Revision, 2017. Accessed February 21, 2019. https://www.un.org/development/desa/publications/world-population-prospects-the-2017-revision.html.

Universal Declaration of Human Rights of United Nations, 1948–1998. New York: United Nations Department of Public Information.

US Government Accountability Office. Social Security's Future. Washington DC: October 2015.

Verbic, Miroslav. "Modelling the Pension System in an Overlapping-Generations General Equilibrium Modeling Framework", 2007. Accessed March 17, 2019. https://mpra.ub.uni-muenchen.de/10350/.

World Health Organization. The World Health Report 2000. Health Systems: Improving Performance. Geneva: World Health Organization, 2000. Accessed February 23, 2019. https://www.who.int/whr/2000/en/whr00_en.pdf?ua=1.

Xhumari, Merita. The Process and Institutions of Social Policy. Tirana: ABC, 2009.

CHAPTER 3

Poverty as a Social Phenomenon in the Republic of North Macedonia

Kire Sharlamanov and Katerina Mitevska Petrusheva

1   Introduction

Poverty is a feature of social stratification and a social problem that any well-organized state tries to reduce by various means and policies. Usually, people living in poverty are the lowest strata in social stratification in a society. This chapter attempts to make an analysis of poverty as a social phenomenon in the Republic of North Macedonia. The very term poverty is often used and there are many definitions of it. Hence, to make it clear what exactly we mean when we use the term poverty, we first define it. In order to understand the dimensions of poverty in the Republic of North Macedonia and its amplitudes over time, we conduct an analysis of the evolution of the poverty rate and the methodology after which it is calculated in the period of the transition of the socio-economic system from the 1990s to the present. In order to explain the amplitudes of poverty over this time period, we analyze the reasons that cause it. Of course, life in poverty has serious social consequences that we attempt to point out, including social exclusion and material deprivation. A key place in this chapter is held by the analysis of the structure of poverty in the Republic of North Macedonia. Several structural aspects of poverty are analyzed here: the period when it occurs, the number of family members affected, unemployment and education. Each country tends to create a society of equal opportunities and with as low a poverty rate as possible. Hence, countries around the world are taking various steps to reduce poverty. In this chapter, we analyzed the system of social protection in the Republic of North Macedonia and the policies and measures taken to reduce poverty.

Although poverty is one of the greatest social problems, it is difficult to find studies that analyze poverty in the Republic of North Macedonia in depth and multi-dimensionally. It is particularly difficult to find studies that analyze policies and measures to reduce poverty. Hence, the aim of this chapter is to offer a comprehensive analysis of the poverty in the Republic of North Macedonia, to analyze the factors that cause it and identify the policies and measures that reduce it. The research question we are trying to answer is which policies and measures were most effective in the fight to reduce poverty in the Republic of North Macedonia. Secondary sources of information and a combination of qualitative and quantitative methodology were used in order to achieve the goals of our research. The most important authors who have written about poverty in the Republic of North Macedonia in the past twenty years have been taken into consideration, analyzed, compared and placed in an appropriate context. Particular attention is paid to the data published by the State Statistical Office of the Republic of North Macedonia, as well as the methodology used by this institution.

2 Defining Poverty

Poverty is a complex multi-dimensional issue that depends on many aspects of functioning in society and directly affects violation of the basic human right for a decent life, social exclusion and the inability to enjoy the basic rights of health care, education, and employment. Poverty as a phenomenon is not unknown to the overall historical development of humankind. In the world, 1.3 million people, or 20.6% of the total population, live in extreme poverty, or with $ 1.25 per day or less.[1]

If in the past, poverty has been accepted as a normal social phenomenon, today, especially if it is widespread, attempts at its reduction are made, through raising public awareness and implementation of appropriate policies. For every sociologist, the existence of poverty is a sign of social stratification and social inequalities in society.

Every serious analysis shows that poverty is primarily related to a lack of resources, opportunities, power, and security. To be poor means to have no access to resources or to power over the resources that can maintain a decent standard of living or to raise it. To be poor also means not having possibilities to exploit the resources in a powerful manner, not having power to make or implement necessary decisions, and experiencing social and physical insecurity. Poverty restricts the possibilities of individuals to provide the conditions for a decent life and existence.[2]

Although there are many definitions of poverty, it seems that the most commonly accepted is the one that says poverty is when individuals cannot meet

---

[1] Marija Bashevska, Policies on the Labor Market and Poverty in Macedonia: 2008–13 (Skopje: Leftist Movement Solidarity, 2014), 48.
[2] Biljana Petroski and Emelj Tuna, Multidimensional Poverty Analysis: Report of Macedonia (Skopje: Federation of Farmers of Republic of Macedonia, 2017), 21.

their basic living needs. The definition of poverty given by Eurostat, and which is accepted by the State Statistical Office of the Republic of North Macedonia, says that " (…) as poor are considered all persons, families, and groups of people whose resources (material, cultural and social) are at a level, which excludes them from the minimum acceptable way of living in the country of residence".[3]

In general, a distinction between the absolute and the relative poverty rate can be made. The absolute rate of poverty is the lack of a sufficient amount of food, water and other needs for survival. Regardless of the state in which a person lives, when he/she does not have the resources that provide basic existence, he/she belongs to the group of persons living in absolute poverty. As a criterion for absolute poverty, the methodology used by several international organizations, such as the World Bank, the International Monetary Fund and the United Nations, says that poverty is living with a less than one dollar per day.[4]

In contrast, one can define relative poverty as when individuals, families or groups lack sufficient resources to consume a diet, engage in social activities, or enjoy living conditions that are commonplace for the society that they live in. The boundary separating those in poverty from others living in a given society is called the poverty line. This can be defined either in terms of income or in terms of a particular standard of living, whereby the definition based on income has been the more commonly used one in the past several decades. A problem that arises here, however, is the difference between income and standard of living in different countries. A monthly income of € 1000, for example, places a person in a very different social status in developing countries compared to developed countries. Where in a highly developed country, a person with a monthly income of €1000 would most likely be below the poverty line, whereas in many developing countries, this income would place a person in the middle class. Thus, the average income for a given country must be considered when calculating poverty. The percentage of people with a monthly income that is less than 70% of the median income in a given country or region is the relative poverty rate.

In addition to absolute and relative poverty, we can also speak about the rate of subjective poverty, which covers the subjective attitude of the person in terms of whether he/she lives in poverty or not.[5]

---

3 Marjan Petrevski and Nikica Mojsovska-Blazevski, Overhaul of the Social Assistance System in Macedonia: Stimulating the Effects of Introducing Guaranteed Minimum Income (GMI) Scheme (Skopje: Finance Think, 2019), 7.
4 Report on the Progress Toward the Millennium Development Goals (Skopje: Government of Republic of Macedonia, 2009), 18.
5 Blagica Novkovska, "Measurement of Welfare in Transition Countries: Conditions and the Perspective in the Republic of Macedonia", Paper Presented at 27th Conference of International Association for Research in Income and Wealth, Djurgarden, Sweden 2002.

3 Poverty Rates in the Republic of North Macedonia

The first experimental calculations of poverty in the Republic of Macedonia date back to 1994.[6] Prior to the introduction of the EU-SILC methodology, the relative poverty line was used to calculate the poverty rate in Macedonia, defined as the necessary level for survival. In the period from 1994–96, the rate of relative poverty was set at 60% of the median equivalent household expenditures.[7] During the period from 1997–2010, the standard for poverty was set at 70% of the median equivalent household expenditure. The use of different benchmarks in calculating the poverty rate in the Republic of Macedonia from those in the EU was a political decision in order to show a lower poverty rate. The calculation of poverty was based on the costs, taking into consideration the size of the grey labor market and situation in which the incomes of many citizens were not recorded.[8]

The Survey on Income and Living Conditions (SILC), following EU recommendations, was conducted in the Republic of Macedonia by the State Statistical Office. The aim of this research was to produce results that would be comparable to those from other EU countries. As Nolev states,[9] the plans of the State Statistical Office, which were realized, were for SILC to be used as a pilot survey, for the first time to be conducted in 2009, in order to test the model and the sample of the survey. Starting in 2010, SILC was implemented in regular statistical surveys of the State Statistical Office. According to SILC, it was determined that poverty is measured based on the incomes and the poverty line to be 60% of the median equivalent income.

The results of the survey in 2010 showed that poverty in Macedonia is at a quite high level for the year 2010 – 30.9%. In 2012 it decreased to 27%, which is significantly more than the average for the European Union, which was 16.9% in 2012. The poverty rate in the Republic of North Macedonia is quite high compared with the other countries in the region, such as Serbia (24.6%), Greece (23.1%), Romania (21.2%), Bulgaria (21.2%), and Croatia (20.5%). Factors that contributed to the high poverty rate in North Macedonia are the ongoing high poverty rates since the period of the country's independence and the high unemployment rate, along with the low rates of development after independence (Table 3.1).[10]

---

6 Report on the Progress Toward the Millennium Development Goals, 17.
7 Zdravo Saveski, Artan Sadiku and Kire Vasilev, Wealth and Poverty in Macedonia (Skopje: Solidarnost, 2013), 9.
8 Maja Gerovska-Mitev, "Poverty and Social Exclusion in Macedonia, Serbia and Croatia: Status and Policy Responses", Review of Social Policy, 22, no. 1 (2015): 82.
9 Spase Nolev, "Measurement of the Standard of Living in Republic of Macedonia", Review for Social Policy, 1, no. 2 (2008): 181.
10 Maja Gerovska-Mitev, "Poverty and Social Exclusion in Macedonia, Serbia and Croatia: Status and Policy Responses": 82.

TABLE 3.1 Poverty rate in the Republic of North Macedonia

Year	Poverty rate	Index of depth of poverty
1994	9.0	–
1995	16.2	–
1996	18.3	–
1997	19.4	4.6
1998	20.7	5.1
1999	21.0	5.7
2000	22.3	6.0
2001	22.7	5.4
2002	30.2	9.3
2003	30.2	9.4
2004	29.6	9.4
2005	30.0	9.7
2006	29.8	9.9
2007	29.4	9.7
2008	28.7	9.2
2009	31.1	10.1
2010	30.9	10.9
2011	30.4	9.3
2012	26.2	–
2013	24.2	–
2014	22.1	–
2015	21.5	–
2016	21.9	–
2017	22.2	–

SOURCE: STATE STATISTICAL OFFICE OF THE REPUBLIC OF MACEDONIA. (THE POVERTY RATE CALCULATED IN THIS TABLE UNTIL 1996 IS BASED ON 60% OF THE MEDIAN EQUIVALENT EXPENDITURE, FROM 1997 TO 2011 IS CALCULATED AT 70% OF THE MEDIAN EQUIVALENT EXPENDITURES, AND FROM 2012 TO 60% OF THE MEDIAN EQUIVALENT INCOME). THE DATA IN THE TABLE FOR THE PERIOD 1994–96 IS TAKEN FROM NATIONAL STRATEGY FOR POVERTY REDUCTION IN THE REPUBLIC OF MACEDONIA (2002):6.

As can be seen, the poverty rate in the Republic of North Macedonia shows constant growth from 1997 until 2002. A large increase in the poverty rate is observed between 2001, when the poverty rate was 22.7%, and 2002 when the poverty rate was 30.2%. This situation occurred for two reasons. The first was the change in the approach in calculating the poverty rate. The second were the effects of the conflict in Macedonia in 2001. Regarding the change in approach, this involved a change in the manner of data collection: initially, this was done with the use of questionnaires four times a year, which was then changed to daily diaries, collected once a year. In that period, the sample of households included in the Household Consumer Survey was also changed from 1,000 to 5,040. The depth of poverty from 1997 until 2006 was increasing constantly, which indicates that the poor are increasingly moving away from the standard of living of the rest of society.[11] Otherwise, the poverty depth index measures the intensity of poverty and shows how far the poorest people are below the poverty line. In 2010, there was an interesting occurrence. While the poverty rate did fall compared to the previous year, the depth of poverty grew. While the number of people below the poverty line may have fallen, the gap between them and the rest of society grew.[12]

For the substantial reduction of poverty in 2012, the biggest in the history of the Republic of Macedonia, a significant contribution was made by the change in the methodology used, as the poverty rate for the year 2012 was not calculated at 70% of the equivalent median expenditure, but at 60% of the equivalent median income. Yet the tendency of decreasing of poverty also continued for the next two years by 2% per year, which makes for a trend during a period of three years of poverty reduction, in total by 8.3%. For this reduction of poverty, some role was played by the introduction of a minimum gross salary, which was defined as 39.6% of the average gross salary in the Republic of North Macedonia. Since the minimum wage is a percentage of the average wage, any increase in the average wage in the Republic of Macedonia will also increase the minimum wage. The expectations were that the introduction of the minimum wage would have an impact on increasing the salaries of 65,000 workers, which for a relatively small country like the Republic of North Macedonia is a significant number.[13] The poverty rate prior to and

---

11   Report on the Progress Toward the Millennium Development Goals, 18.
12   Sustainable Development (Skopje: State Statistical Office, 2011), 74.
13   Maja Gerovska – Mitev, Material Deprivation, Poverty and Social Exclusion in Republic of Macedonia (Skopje, Friedrich Ebert Foundation, 2012A), 19.

after social transfers are paid can be one way to measure the success of social policy in a given country. In 2013, before social transfers, the poverty rate in the Republic of North Macedonia stood at 41%; after social transfers were made, it was 24.2%.[14] In the following year, the poverty rate before social transfers was 41.7%, i.e., 0.7% higher than the year before, but the rate after social transfers was in fact lower at 22.1%.[15] While this does indicate that social protection policy is effective, it does also indicate how people are dependent on the state (Table 3.2).

Although the poverty rate in 2017 was significantly reduced compared to 2010, when it was 30.9%, it was still at a higher level than the European Union average, but also than the developing countries in the region. There are also

TABLE 3.2 Risk of poverty, depending on the number of household members and social transfers

Year	2013	2014	2015	2016	2017
At risk of poverty rate, % of population	24.3	22.1	21.5	21.9	22.2
Number of persons below at risk of poverty threshold, in thousand persons	500.4	457.2	445.2	453.2	460.3
At risk of poverty thresholds of single person household – annual equivalent income in denars	70,275	71,925	78,362	82,560	90,120
At risk of poverty thresholds of four person households (2 adults and 2 children aged less than 14) – annual equivalent income in denars	147,578	151,043	164,560	173,376	189,252
At risk of poverty rate before social transfers and before pensions, % of population	41.0	41.7	40.5	41.6	40.7
Inequality of income distribution S80/S20, %	8.4	7.2	6.6	6.6	6.4
Inequality of income distribution, Gini coefficient, %	37.0	35.2	33.7	33.6	32.5

SOURCE: ECONOMIC REFORM PROGRAM 2019–21 (SKOPJE: MINISTRY OF FINANCE, 2019), 41.

---

14 Sustainable Development (Skopje: State Statistical Office, 2015), 71.
15 Sustainable Development (Skopje: State Statistical Office, 2016), 73.

some doubts about the sustainability and the possible reduction of this level of poverty in the country. Substantial reforms are needed in order for the poverty rate to be below 16% by 2020.[16]

4 Reasons for Poverty in the Republic of North Macedonia

Historically, the Republic of Macedonia, even in the time of the former Yugoslavia, lagged behind the other republics of the former Yugoslavia, in economic development and the level of the standard of living, which is still reflected in the poverty rate in the Republic of North Macedonia.

Recent factors which contributed to the increase in the historical poverty rate in the Republic of North Macedonia are the unsuccessful economic transition (economically inefficient and slow process of privatization), which resulted in the closure of many enterprises and job loss for their employees.[17]

Some objective circumstances in the Republic of North Macedonia in the 1990s also influenced the increase in the poverty rate, such as military conflicts in the region, as well as the conflict in Macedonia, the economic embargoes that the United Nations imposed on some of the country's neighbors, but also the Greek economic embargo of Macedonia.

However, the most important factor for the rise in the poverty rate in Macedonia seems to be the inadequate economic policies, which needed to produce rapid economic growth and employment, and inadequate social policies, needed to help groups at social risk. An additional factor, of course, might be the social stratification that emerged after the transition. In 2011, 20% of the population with the highest income earned twelve times more than the 20% with the lowest income.[18] In 2013, the 20% of the population with highest-income earned 8.4 times more than the lowest-earning 20%. In 2014, the 20% of the population with the highest income earned slightly less than 7.2 times more than the 20% of the population with the lowest income.[19]

In 1998, the richest 20% of the population received 36.7% of total income, while the poorest 20% of the population received 8.5% of the total income.

---

16 Economic Reform Program 2019–2021 (Skopje: Ministry of Finance, 2019), 41.
17 National Strategy for Poverty Reduction in the Republic of Macedonia (Skopje: Ministry of Finance, 2002), 29.
18 Sustainable Development (Skopje: State Statistical Office, 2014), 76.
19 Sustainable Development (Skopje: State Statistical Office, 2016), 78.

This difference became more obvious in 2010, when the richest 20% of the population received 49% of the total income, while the poorest 20% of the population received 4.9% of the total income. An indicator of the growth of inequality in Macedonian society is also the Gini coefficient. This coefficient, measured by the World Bank, was 28.1 in 2010, while in 2010 it was 43.6. The World Bank's data from 2013 show that the Republic of Macedonia had the greatest inequality in the distribution of income compared to other countries in the region.[20]

5   Poverty, Social Exclusion and Material Deprivation

Poverty represents a violation of human rights because it excludes the persons who lack resources and income from public and social life. Social exclusion and poverty create a circle which perpetuates constantly, locking the most vulnerable members of society. Such exclusion affects the dignity, sense of trust, and life of people. This is a situation that prevents people from fulfilling their guaranteed rights to education, employment, access to quality health care, etc.[21]

The low standard of living also generally reflects the material deprivation of the population. For example, according to data from the State Statistical Office, as much as 72.2% of the population in the Republic of North Macedonia could not afford a week of vacation away from home, and for 56.9% of the population a meal with meat, fish, or vegetarian equivalent every other day was not something they could afford.[22]

As an indicator of material deprivation, the State Statistical Office takes persons that are seriously disadvantaged. Seriously disadvantaged persons are those who lack the means to meet at least four of the following eight needs:
– to pay rent or utility bills;
– to adequately warm up the home;
– to have a meal with meat or fish every second day;
– to have one-week vacation during the year;

---

20   Marija Bashevska, Policies on the Labor Market and Poverty in Macedonia: 2008–13, 48.
21   Report on Poverty and Social Exclusion in the Republic of Macedonia for 2010 (Skopje: Macedonian Platform Against Poverty 2011), 7.
22   Maja Gerovska-Mitev, "Poverty and Social Exclusion in Macedonia, Serbia and Croatia: Status and Policy Responses": 85.

- car;
- washing machine;
- color TV;
- phone.

The part of the population who cannot afford to satisfy four of the eight above-listed needs in 2005 was reduced from 55.9% to 40.6% in 2010, only to rise again in 2011.[23] In the Survey on the Income and Living Conditions, conducted by the State Statistical Office for 2013, one additional need was added – dealing with an unexpected expense – which showed that 37.7% of the population was seriously materially disadvantaged.[24] For 2014, the number of persons who were seriously materially disadvantaged decreased to 35.7%.[25]

The data from the study of material deprivation, conducted on a representative sample of 1,602 participants in 2011, which includes the same nine basic needs measured by the State Statistical Office, shows that 30.8% of the population was materially deprived, because they could not satisfy four or more of the listed nine basic needs, 22% of households could satisfy all nine basic needs, and 78% of households in the Republic of Macedonia could not provide some of the basic needs for a decent life. In addition, the majority of households, or 54.2%, could not afford a one-week vacation away from home, 49.9% could not pay unexpected expenses and 39.3% could not afford a meal with meat or fish for themselves every other day of the week.[26]

6 Structure of Poverty in the Republic of North Macedonia

According to the National Strategy for Poverty Reduction in the Republic of Macedonia, households living in poverty in the Republic of Macedonia are divided into three groups:
- traditionally poor – this group includes rural, agricultural household and is characterized by a low level of education of members of the household and low potential for economic activity, usually in agriculture;

---

23 Sustainable Development (Skopje: State Statistical Office, 2012), 71.
24 Sustainable Development (Skopje: State Statistical Office, 2015), 75.
25 Sustainable Development (Skopje: State Statistical Office, 2016), 77.
26 Maja Gerovska-Mitev, Material Deprivation, Poverty and Social Exclusion in the Republic of Macedonia, 29.

- newly poor, losers of the transition – people who in the process of transformation of social capital and privatization of enterprises have lost their jobs, usually live in the cities, and none or only one of the members of the household is employed;
- chronically poor – this is the most endangered group of people living in poverty and includes elderly people, the disabled and agricultural households without a permanent source of income.[27]

Regarding the age structure of the population, the group exposed to the highest risk of falling into poverty are the youngest under 18 years old, unlike in Croatia, for example, where the most at-risk group is those older than 65. Regarding families, the most vulnerable to poverty are the families with more children, unlike in Croatia, where those at the highest risk of falling into poverty are women in one-person families.[28] The Report of the Republic of Macedonia for the Progress in achieving the Millennium Objectives[29] points out that in 2007, the highest poverty rate was among people aged from 40 years up to 59 years. For this group of people, the poverty rate was 30.1%, which was 57% of the overall poverty structure in Macedonia for this year. In 2013, the highest risk of poverty was again noted for the youngest under 18 years and that risk is 30.9%. The risk of poverty is the lowest in people older than 65, who live on pensions and other social transfers.[30] Analysis of data from the State Statistical Office shows that poverty is closely related to several parameters (Table 3.3, 3.4, 3.5):

TABLE 3.3   Percentage of unemployed out of people that are living in poverty

Year	2010	2011	2012	2013	2014	2015	2016	2017
Percentage of unemployed out of people who are living in poverty.	44.8	46.0	–	43.7	40.4	39.7	41.1	38.7

SOURCE: SUSTAINABLE DEVELOPMENT 2010–2018.

---

27 National Strategy for Poverty Reduction in The Republic of Macedonia (Skopje: Ministry of Finance, 2002), 28.
28 Maja Gerovska-Mitev, "Poverty and Social Exclusion in Macedonia, Serbia and Croatia: Status and Policy Responses": 85.
29 Report on the Progress Toward the Millennium Development Goals, 21.
30 Sustainable Development (Skopje: State Statistical Office, 2015), 71.

- unemployment: many of the families with one or more unemployed members live in poverty. The data of the State Statistical Office for 2010 show that 44.8% of all poor people in the Republic of Macedonia were unemployed;
- the number of household members: a higher number of household members increases the risk of falling into poverty. The data from the State Statistical Office for 2010 show that 47.3% of the poor people in the Republic of Macedonia lived in a household with five or more members;
- the level of education: a higher percentage of the household in which the head of the household has not completed elementary education, live in poverty. State Statistical Office data for 2010 shows that 54.7% of the poor lived in households in which the head of the household had completed elementary education.

TABLE 3.4   Percentage of poverty of persons living in households with five or more members

Year	2010	2011	2012	2013	2014
Percentage of those who live in household with five or more members out of people that are living in poverty. From 2013, the percentage of those that live in household with three or more dependent persons out of people that are living in poverty is calculated.	47.3	48.5	–	49.9	51.3

SOURCE: SUSTAINABLE DEVELOPMENT 2010–2016.

TABLE 3.5   Percentage of household where the head of the household has no education or primary education

Year	2010	2011	2012	2013	2014	2015	2016
Percentage of household where the head of the household has no education or only elementary education out of the total number of the people that are living in poverty in the Republic of Macedonia.	54.7	54.6	–	–	–	–	–

SOURCE: SUSTAINABLE DEVELOPMENT 2010–2012.

Analyzing the data for the poverty rate in the Republic of Macedonia, it can be noticed that the number of household members has an impact on poverty. The poverty rate of households with six or more members is significantly higher than the rate of households with a lower number of members. In some years it exceeds 40%, and in 2003 it reaches 43.6% (Table 3.6).

An important factor that affects an increase in the poverty rate is unemployment. The poverty rate for the unemployed in 1996 was 26% and a constant increase can be noted until 2005, when it reaches 41.5%, and in the next two years, it starts to decrease (Table 3.7).

TABLE 3.6   Relative poverty according to the number of household members (1997–2007)

Year	1997	1998	1999	2000	2001	2002	2003	2004	2005	2006	2007
Total	19.0	20.7	21.0	22.3	22.7	30.2	30.2	29.6	30.0	29.8	26.4
1 member	6.3	11.1	16.5	14.5	5.6	30.4	25.2	20.2	19.6	24.3	26.9
2 members	17.0	16.4	15.6	16.6	18.0	25.4	20.6	16.5	20.8	23.9	24.2
3 members	15.8	12.9	16.6	13.5	9.2	20.2	22.9	22.5	21.6	17.4	18.8
4 members	18.0	20.4	20.6	20.9	14.4	27.3	28.6	23.5	22.1	21.4	25.6
5 members	17.4	29.5	23.8	33.6	19.6	33.8	35.5	29.5	31.0	29.9	30.6
6 and more members	31.5	30.0	29.0	27.5	29.5	38.6	43.6	42.5	37.5	38.8	37.5

SOURCE: STATE STATISTICAL OFFICE 1997–2007, HTTP://WWW.STAT.GOV.MK/PRETHODNISOOPSTENIJAOBLAST.ASPX?ID=37 (ACCESSED NOVEMBER 20, 2018).

TABLE 3.7   Relative poverty according to the economic status of members of the household (1997–2007)

Year	1997	1998	1999	2000	2001	2002	2003	2004	2005	2006	2007
Unemployed	26.0	29.0	31.2	32.6	35.5	37.5	36.2	39.0	41.5	40.9	39.1
1 employed	19.2	22.1	21.2	22.2	21.0	28.0	29.3	27.8	28.2	28.1	30.7
2 and more employed	9.8	7.3	7.3	6.8	9.9	18.7	18.9	18.1	16.8	18.5	17.2

SOURCE: STATE STATISTICAL OFFICE 1997–2007, HTTP://WWW.STAT.GOV.MK/PRETHODNISOOPSTENIJAOBLAST.ASPX?ID=37 (ACCESSED NOVEMBER 20, 2018).

The level of education is also a significant factor contributing to the increase in the poverty rate (Table 3.8). Households headed by people who lack a primary education showed a considerably different rate, 53.7% of these lived in poverty in 2007. As for the households run by people with higher education, only 11.0% lived in poverty in 2007. A trend of rising poverty is also visible from 1997 to 2007 in all categories of households, but that trend is greatest among households run by persons without an education. While in 1997, 34.4% of these families lived in poverty, in 2007 – 53.7% of these households lived in poverty, which is an increase in poverty in this category of families by almost 20%.

The statistics show that households with children are more exposed to poverty than households without children. The poverty rate for households with children from 1997 until 2005 is in constant growth, and then decreases from 2005 to 2007. In 2007, the poverty rate among married couples with children was 27.1%, and among other households with children 33.4%, which is significantly higher than the poverty rate of households without children and aged households.[31] The data also shows that the poverty rate is higher in rural areas.

TABLE 3.8   Relative poverty according to the level of education of the head of the household (1997–2007)

Year	1997	1998	1999	2000	2001	2002	2003	2004	2005	2006	2007
No education	34.4	38.9	37.5	42.6	45.8	41.4	51.4	57.9	46.8	53.9	53.7
Uncompleted elementary education	26.6	28.8	30.3	34.2	35.0	35.7	32.8	32.8	39.9	37.6	37.7
Elementary education	28.0	21.8	30.6	30.4	25.7	37.7	37.6	38.4	38.2	39.8	37.4
Secondary education	11.2	16.9	13.6	14.0	12.1	24.3	24.4	22.9	23.4	22.8	23.6
Post-secondary education	8.2	1.9	6.2	9.4	13.5	14.2	19.0	17.4	17.6	17.4	17.4
Higher education	1.4	5.3	0.0	3.7	3.6	10.1	12.1	9.1	7.3	8.9	11.0

SOURCE: STATE STATISTICAL OFFICE 1997–2007, HTTP://WWW.STAT.GOV.MK/PRETHODNISOOPSTENIJAOBLAST.ASPX?ID=37 (ACCESSED NOVEMBER 20, 2018).

---

31   Report on the Progress Toward the Millennium Development Goals, 21.

In 2007, 31% of this population lived in poverty, in contrast to urban areas where the poverty rate was 28.7% and the City of Skopje in which the poverty rate was 28.4%.[32]

7 The System of Social Security in the Republic of North Macedonia

Similarly, to other European countries, the Republic of North Macedonia has a complex system of social security that includes:
- contributory benefits (pensions, disability insurance, and health insurance);
- active and passive labor market programs;
- social assistance programs for protecting income and consumption for the poor. The passive measures provide compensation for unemployment, depending on the amount of time that the person had previously worked. Considering that about 80% of people in the Republic of North Macedonia are long-term unemployed, in 2012 this measure was used for 9% of the unemployed. Also, it should be taken into consideration that the benefits of this measure can be used for a relatively short time.[33]

The social assistance system in the Republic of North Macedonia is not universal, but rather it is focused on certain vulnerable groups in society, such as the unemployed and people with disabilities. Additionally, this system is fragmented and consists of a large number of programs, rather than one harmonized and detailed program. The entire system consists of sixteen benefit schemes and two programs. Among the schemes, eleven are social, and five are related to child protection. The biggest one in the social assistance system is social financial assistance (SFA). Other programs include permanent social assistance (for those who are permanently incapable of work, disabled and elderly), cash assistance for orphans, child allowance, benefits for caregivers, one-time cash benefits, salary supplement – for a family member who cannot work full-time because he/she takes care of a child with disabilities, housing, and health insurance benefits. In the last few years, the Government has implemented new measures for social protection, although they were essentially part of the demographic policy.[34]

---

32 Ibid.
33 Marjan Petrevski and Nikica Mojsovska-Blazevski, Overhaul of the Social Assistance System in Macedonia: Stimulating the Effects of Introducing Guaranteed Minimum Income (GMI) Scheme (Skopje: Finance Think, 2019), 5; Suzana Bornarova, "Development of the Social Protection System in Macedonia: Social Policy Making and Social Progress", in Welfare State in Transition: 20 Years After Yugoslav Welfare System, ed. Marija Stambolieva, Stefan Dehnert (Sofia: Friedrich Ebert Foundation, 2011), 138.
34 Marjan Petrevski and Nikica Mojsovska-Blazevski, Overhaul of the Social Assistance System in Macedonia: Stimulating the Effects of Introducing Guaranteed Minimum Income (GMI) Scheme, 5.

The social financial system (SFA) is the most important program in the social assistance system. It includes support for poor households. In this program are included families whose members are able to work but cannot provide material security. This measure provides a material benefit of 115 euros per month, for families with up to five members. Families that independently reach the income level projected by this program, lose the right to be included in it further.[35]

The Republic of North Macedonia devoted 0.99 of GDP in 2016 to social assistance programs (including SFA, child and family protection, non-contributory disability benefits). Only 0.17% of GDP was spent on SFA spent, but in the last few years, a much greater part is spent on the third child allowance or 0.37% of GDP.[36]

It has been remarked that the social assistance system does not motivate people to be active in the labor market and to actively seek work. Although there are certain measures such as reducing social financial assistance by 50% after the third year of its use, as well as the loss of the right to social financial assistance if the person refuses to participate in public works organized by local communities, it seems that these measures do not have enough influence to motivate people using social financial assistance to be proactive in the labor market.[37]

There are at least two arguments that the system for social protection needs to be reformed. The first is the small contribution this system has on reducing the poverty in the long term. The second argument is the insufficient budget of the social assistance programs.[38]

8   Poverty Reduction Policies in the Republic of North Macedonia

The first documents referring to the policy of dealing with poverty by the Government of the Republic of Macedonia were created in 2001 through the Strategy for Poverty Reduction.[39] Although previously there was no such document, the Government of the Republic of Macedonia still conducted an active policy of poverty reduction. As a case in point, 30% of the arrangement that the Government of the Republic of Macedonia signed with the International Monetary Fund in December 2000 referred to the Poverty Reduction and Growth Facility.[40]

---

35   Ibid.
36   Ibid.
37   Ibid., 6.
38   Ibid., 7.
39   Report on the Progress Toward the Millennium Development Goals, 17.
40   National Strategy for Poverty Reduction in the Republic of Macedonia, 28.

The progress toward achieving the millenium development goals was noted; however, given current trends, achieving the stated goals would be impossible, namely to reduce poverty to 9.5% by 2015.[41] Therefore, this Report urges that the goals for poverty reduction should be revised and made more realistic. Further, the report calls for the implementation of several policies that would reduce poverty:
- stimulating accelerated and sustained economic growth together with the implementation of active employment policies;
- steps to promote social inclusion of multi-member households, households without any employed person, households in which the head of the household is without education (or has uncompleted elementary education), households with children and households living in rural areas;
- better targeting of social transfers toward target groups and application of the policy of social benefits, which will enable the users to achieve a better standard of living.

Legislative reform, reform of institutional capacities and increased participation of citizens in efforts to reform the social protection system are some measures that can be taken to reduce poverty. Important in this would be associations such as the Macedonian Platform against Poverty a Union of more than 40 citizen associations and researchers.[42] The Strategy for the Reduction of Poverty and Social Exclusion, adopted in 2010, and revised in 2013, in order to get closer to the goals and guidelines of the European Union Strategy – Europe 2020 serves as the basis in the fight against poverty. The Strategy has foreseen reducing poverty through measures and activities in the following areas: employment and strengthening of entrepreneurship; adapting education to the labor market; social and child protection and creation of a new social model; promoting health care and long-term care; transport, communications, and housing; activation and strengthening of the local authorities and support for vulnerable groups.[43] Although the Strategy for Reduction of Poverty and Social Exclusion is the only document that directly addresses the situation of vulnerable groups and represents placing a priority on their comprehensive inclusion in the measures and services of the system for social protection, according to Gerovska-Mitev, there is no evidence of any practical measures of implementing this strategy.[44]

41　Report on the Progress Toward the Millennium Development Goals, 25.
42　Ibid., 7.
43　National Strategy for Reduction of Poverty and Social Exclusion in the Republic of Macedonia 2010–20, Revisited (Skopje: Ministry of Finance, 2013), 3.
44　Maja Gerovska-Mitev, "Poverty and Social Exclusion in Macedonia, Serbia and Croatia: Status and Policy Responses": 85.

In addition to the strategy, the National Program for Development of Social Protection 2011–2025 was adopted. This program identifies the priority areas on which the changes for the improvement of social protection should be focused. In the National Employment Strategy of 2015, there is a chapter referring to the reduction of poverty and social inclusion. The European Commission's 2013 Progress Report on Macedonia underlines that progress in implementing the national strategy for poverty and social inclusion 2010–2020 is limited. That is, poverty remains at a high level, and the implementation of the policies and strategic plans that have been adopted is not satisfactory, hindered by the lack of institutional capacity and financial resources. Remarks on the insufficient institutional capacity were also included in the analysis of the implementation of the Law on Social Protection. The amount of budget funds projected for measures for alleviation of poverty in 2013 is 0.13% of budget expenditures, which is a decrease of 0.2% of the funds projected for this purpose in 2008.[45]

It can be said that the government's economic doctrine until the year 2016 served as a policy for preventing poverty. The economic policies of the government relied on direct foreign investment, hoping that it would help in reducing unemployment and poverty rate; active employment measures by targeting a limited number of unemployed people; passive measures of social transfers for the unemployed and people with low incomes. According to Gerovska-Mitev, these passive measures do not cover all the citizens living in poverty, while the active measures receive insufficient financial support at only 0.11% of GDP, to make significant changes in the fight against poverty.[46] Some measures fail to address actual problems found in practice. As a case in point, the group that is most vulnerable, according to indicators, are families that have more than three children, and yet the amount of social assistance provided does not rise in proportion to the number of children a family has.

The Strategy of Poverty Reduction predicts a reduction of poverty to 20.6% by 2020. In addition, the expectations are that this should be more as a result of an increase in the percentage of people with higher education and in employment than through direct measures for poverty reduction.[47] In addition, Gerovska-Mitev states that it is problematic to link the objectives with specific policies, or more precisely, it is difficult to find a link between objectives and the measures.[48] One of the weaknesses of the strategy for the alleviation

---

45 Marija Bashevska, Policies on the Labor Market and Poverty in Macedonia: 2008–13 (Skopje: Leftist Movement Solidarity, 2014), 48.
46 Maja Gerovska-Mitev, "Poverty and Social Exclusion in Macedonia, Serbia and Croatia: Status and Policy Responses": 87.
47 Ibid, 89.
48 Ibid.

of poverty is that there is no revision of the goals related to the dynamics of achieving them and the changes over a certain period of time.

In 2017, the government adopted a program of economic reform, which also includes measures for reducing poverty. This program concludes that the system for social protection is at a stage when important reforms are needed that will increase the efficacy of the system for social protection and the benefits for its users. The program concludes that the existing system for social protection is ineffective and deepens inequality in society. The services provided by the system do not correspond to the needs of individuals, and hence non-institutionalization, decentralization, and pluralization of the social security system are recommended.[49]

Although the Law on Social Protection allows pluralization of the institutions and organizations that provide social services, in practice such services are provided only by state institutions. There is a lack of initiatives from municipalities to establish a system of supplemental social protection. There is also a lack of initiative and activities by local communities in the implementation of policies in this area. It can be concluded that there is a lack of private initiative in this sector, primarily because the state has not defined the goals of certain services. There is also insufficient involvement of the private sector in the area of social protection.[50] Hence, in 2018, the national strategy for deinstitutionalization 2018–2027 was adopted.[51]

The measures planned by the Ministry of Labor and Social Policy include a full reform of the system for social protection for children. The aim of this reform is to harmonize the amount of financial assistance with the real needs of people living in poverty. It significantly increased financial support for these individuals. At the same time, people living in poverty will be able to continue and complete their education in order to become competitive on the labor market.[52] In order to reduce child poverty, easier access to the child allowance will be provided. This reform enabled families to obtain a child allowance if they have low income and if no family member is employed. The practice in the Republic of North Macedonia was that the right to a child allowance belongs to low-income families, in which at least one family member is employed. One of the novelties implemented with the reform of the system for social protection is an education allowance for children who regularly attend a primary school.

---

49 Economic Reform Program 2019–21 (Skopje: Ministry of Finance 2019), 41.
50 Ibid.
51 European Commission, Communication with EU Enlargement Policy – North Macedonia Report 2019 (Brussels: European Commission, 2019), 80.
52 Ibid., 41.

Its aim is to prevent children living in poverty from dropping out of primary education.[53]

The EU's report on the Republic of North Macedonia 2017 concludes that poverty remains a serious social issue in the Republic of North Macedonia. It points out that there are not enough financial resources for the implementation of the social reform program. In the Report, a hope is expressed that the new Law on Social Security, which is in the process of preparation, will contribute to poverty reduction. According to this Law, minimum financial assistance should be provided to all unemployed people, but also the focus is on people who are employed, but still living in poverty, or at risk of falling into the group of people living in poverty. The data show that 9% of the employed and 7% of pensioners live at risk of falling into poverty. The new Law on Social Protection also projects the possibility of a social pension, for persons older than 64, and which on no basis can fulfill the right to a pension or any other income. However, the report concluded that the activities and measures which have been undertaken to reduce poverty are insufficient. The social protection for children with disabilities is insufficient and should be aligned with the UN Convention on the Rights of Persons with Disabilities.[54]

9   Conclusion

This chapter shows that poverty in the Republic of North Macedonia is a significant, chronic and dynamic social problem. It is significant because there is a high poverty rate, chronic because the high percentage of poverty has existed over a longer period of time and dynamic because, over time and depending on the social context, the rate of poverty changes. Data from the State Statistical Office shows that there was a steady increase in poverty during the transition to 2001. However, the poverty rose dramatically in 2002 shortly after the armed conflict that the country faced. Thus, the poverty rate in 2001 was 22.7%, and in the following 2002 it was 30.2%. It took great effort and thirteen years for the poverty rate to return to 21.5% in 2015.

Our research has shown that in the Republic of North Macedonia there is great social inequality in the income and wealth that is associated with that significant part of the population which lives in poverty. The most important

---

53   Ibid.
54   European Commission, Communication with EU Enlargement Policy – North Macedonia Report 2019, 78–80.

social factors causing poverty are unemployment, education and the number of family members in a household.

It seems that the policies that are being taken and the measures that are being implemented in the struggle for poverty reduction are inconsistent and reflect the ideological orientation of the political parties that are in power at a given point in time. While at one point liberal economic and labor market policies are pursued, at other times, interventionist economic policies are pursued by asserting the welfare state, introducing a minimum wage, increasing it, and so on. This policy mix has given some results in reducing poverty. However, given that poverty in 2002 was extremely high and that although poverty has been reduced, it is still higher compared to the countries of the European Union and the countries of the region. It can be said that the results achieved in the fight against poverty in the Republic of North Macedonia are modest.

Bibliography

Bashevska, Marija. Policies on the Labor Market and Poverty in Macedonia: 2008–13. Skopje: Leftist Movement Solidarity, 2014.

Bornarova, Suzana. "Development of the Social Protection System in Macedonia: Social Policy Making and Social Progress". In Welfare State in Transition: 20 Years after Yugoslav Welfare System, edited by Marija Stambolieva, Stefan Dehnert. Sofia: Friedrich Ebert, 2011.

Economic Reform Program 2019–21. Skopje: Ministry of Finance, 2019.

Eftimovski, Dimitar. "Measuring Quality of Life in Macedonia – Using Human Development Indicators". Zbornik Radova, Ekonomski Fakultet, Rijeka 24, no. 2 (2006): 257–272.

European Commission. Communication with EU Enlargement Policy – North Macedonia Report 2019. Brussels, 2019.

Gerovska-Mitev, Maja. Material Deprivation, Poverty and Social Exclusion in Republic of Macedonia. Skopje: Friedrich Ebert Foundation, 2012A.

Gerovska-Mitev, Maja. "Poverty and Social Exclusion in Macedonia, Serbia and Croatia: Status and Policy Responses". Review of Social Policy 22, no. 1 (2015): 81–94.

Gerovska-Mitev, Maja. Report for Poverty and Social Exclusion in the Republic of Macedonia in 2011. Skopje: Macedonian Platform against Poverty, Institute for Human Rights, 2012.

National Strategy for Poverty Reduction in the Republic of Macedonia. Skopje: Ministry of Finance, 2002.

National Strategy for Reduction of Poverty and Social Exclusion in the Republic of Macedonia 2010–2020 – Revised. Skopje: Ministry of Finance of the Republic of Macedonia, 2013.

National Strategy Reduction of Poverty and Social Exclusion in the Republic of Macedonia 2010 – 2020. Skopje, Ministry for Finance of the Republic of Macedonia, 2010.

Nolev, Stase. "Measurement of Standard of Living in the Republic of Macedonia". Review for Social Policy 1, no. 2 (2008).

Novkovska, Blagica. Measurement of Welfare in Transition Countries: Conditions and the Perspective in the Republic of Macedonia, Paper Presented at 27th Conference of International Association for Research in Income and Wealth. Djurgarden, Sweden, 2002.

Petrevski, Marjan and Nikica Mojsoska-Blazeski. Overhaul of the Social Assistance System in Macedonia: Stimulating the Effects of Introducing Guaranteed Minimum Income (GMI) Scheme. Skopje, Finance Think, 2019.

Petrovska, Biljana and Tuna Emelj. Multidimensional Poverty Analysis: Report of Macedonia. Skopje: Federation of Farmers of Republic of Macedonia, 2017.

Report on Poverty and Social Exclusion in Republic of Macedonia for 2010. Skopje: Macedonian Platform Against Poverty, 2011.

Report on the Progress Toward the Millennium Development Goals. Skopje, Government of Republic of Macedonia, 2009.

Saveski, Zdravko, Artan Sadiku, and Kire Vasilev. Wealth and Poverty in Macedonia Skopje: Solidarnost, 2013.

State Statistical Office 1997–2007. Accessed November 20, 2018. http://www.stat.gov.mk/PrethodniSoopstenijaOblast.aspx?id=37.

Sustainable Development. Skopje: State Statistical Office, 2010.

Sustainable Development. Skopje: State Statistical Office, 2011.

Sustainable Development. Skopje: State Statistical Office, 2012.

Sustainable Development. Skopje: State Statistical Office, 2013.

Sustainable Development. Skopje: State Statistical Office, 2014.

Sustainable Development: Skopje: State Statistical Office, 2015.

Sustainable Development. Skopje: State Statistical Office, 2016.

Sustainable Development. Skopje: State Statistical Office, 2017.

Sustainable Development. Skopje: State Statistical Office, 2018.

CHAPTER 4

Unemployment in the Republic of North Macedonia: Characteristics and Perspectives

Kire Sharlamanov and Katerina Mitevska Petrusheva

1   Introduction

High unemployment rates have serious social consequences as it is not only individuals who experience this social problem directly, but also society as a whole. High unemployment rates over a long period of time usually indicate problems with the efficiency of the economic system in a country, an inadequate connection between the economic and the education system, and dysfunction in the labor market. This chapter attempts to analyze unemployment in the Republic of North Macedonia. To do so, the meaning of the term "unemployment" is defined followed by a legal analysis of unemployment and the right to work as defined in Macedonian legislation and international organizations. To get an idea of the extent and structure of unemployment in the Republic of North Macedonia, we will review the unemployment rate from the 1970s to the present. To eventually make recommendations on possible policies and measures that could be applied to reduce unemployment, this chapter also analyzes the reasons for the high unemployment rate in the Republic of North Macedonia, the consequences of unemployment, the relationship between economic growth and unemployment, and labor market policies.

The aim of this chapter is to analyze unemployment in the Republic of North Macedonia, its consequences, and to point out possible ways of reducing it. The research questions are as follows: What are the reasons for the permanent long-term unemployment rate in the Republic of North Macedonia? What are the measures that are being taken to reduce it? The methodology used to answer these questions is analysis of secondary information from the most relevant institutions and authors that have studied this issue over the last 30 years.

2   Defining 'Unemployment'

Unemployment, especially high unemployment, is an undesirable phenomenon in almost every country in the world. Although there is no country in which the entire active population is employed, there are big differences in the level of employment. In some countries, unemployment is much higher than in others. Unemployment in the range 3–4% can have a positive impact both globally and individually. Within this framework, it can boost labor flexibility, increase productivity, and formulate appropriate behavior that increases the quality of work in order to stimulate education and improve the discipline of the labor force.[1] Employment is a productive and socially desirable achievement of the labor force. It represents an existential basis on which the financial, social security and social status of individuals are built. Unemployment represents the number of individuals who are willing and able to work for remuneration but cannot find a job.

According to the International Labor Organization (ILO), 'unemployed' is defined as all persons who have not undertaken any activity for a period longer than one hour, are available for employment and are actively searching for work. The underemployed are considered all individuals who are only partially employed, do not work full time, or have insufficient income for normal existence. The difference between unemployment and underemployment should be outlined. According to the International Labor Organization, unlike unemployment, underemployment means persons who work less than 35 hours a week but want to work more, who are overqualified for a given job, who feel insecurity in the workplace, who are not paid enough for the job they do, who do not have the required safety conditions at work and who, despite their willingness, work part-time.[2] Because this is too a broad definition, in this paper we are using the internationally accepted definition of unemployment based on three criteria. According to this definition, persons who are considered unemployed are in the age range in which they can be in the economically active population, and who in the long term are:

– unemployed – persons who are not in paid employment or self-employed;
– currently available for work – persons available for paid employment or self-employment;
– seeking employment – persons who express interest and are actively searching for employment or self-employment.

The indicator commonly used to show unemployment is the unemployment rate, which reflects the share of the unemployed in the total labor force, which

---

[1] Elena Mitreva, Application of Economic and Mathematical Models for Estimation of Youth Unemployment in the Republic of Macedonia (Stip: University Goce Delcev, 2015), 5.
[2] Blagica Petreski et al., "Analysis of Youth Unemployment in the Republic of North Macedonia, Monte Negro and Serbia", Finance Think, Polity Study, no. 22 (2019): 6.

is the sum of employed persons and unemployed persons, i.e., the active population.

Unemployment, especially if it is widespread, is a serious issue with considerable social consequences for both unemployed persons and society as a whole.[3] A high unemployment rate can cause a loss of economic potential, degradation of qualifications,[4] loss of prestige and social status, discouragement and loss of motivation of unemployed persons. There are many different types of unemployment: voluntary unemployment, involuntary unemployment, frictional unemployment, cyclical unemployment, seasonal unemployment, technological unemployment, structural unemployment and hidden unemployment.[5] These types of unemployment can be defined as follows:

- Voluntary unemployment is unemployment among people who want to get a good job and a high salary and do not plan to work for a low salary in a poor job.
- Involuntary unemployment is unemployment among people who are willing to work but cannot find a job at all.
- Frictional unemployment is unemployment that occurs when individuals change their job or profession.
- Cyclical unemployment relates to when the demand for particular goods and services decreases at certain time intervals.
- Seasonal unemployment is experienced by people who work at certain intervals in the year, i.e., in a particular season, but do not work for the rest of the year. Economic sectors that experience seasonal unemployment are tourism, construction and agriculture.
- Technological unemployment occurs as a result of mechanization that replaces the physical labor force. This kind of unemployment arises with technological progress and innovations that are implemented in production processes.
- Structural unemployment is unemployment that arises when the economy stagnates for a long period of time and is unable to create new jobs; it can also arise as a result of an inadequate labor market structure, inadequate geographical distribution of the labor force, and inadequate professional structure and skills in the labor market.

---

3 Jorde Jakimovski, "Unemployment as a Complex and Serious Personal and Social Issue", Skola Biznisa, no. 1 (2010): 73.
4 When individuals do not practice the knowledge and skills acquired in the educational process, they begin to forget them.
5 Ozonur Bayram Soylu, Ismail Cakmak and Fatih Okur, "Economic Growth and Unemployment Issue: Panel Data Analysis in Eastern European Countries", Journal of International Studies 11, no. 1 (2018): 94.

– Hidden unemployment consists of people who are formally employed but do not have any role in the process of production or in the provision of services, that is, their productivity rate is close to zero.[6]

3 Legal Framework and Unemployment

The right to work is one of the fundamental human rights guaranteed by the Constitution of the Republic of North Macedonia and numerous international documents which, after ratification, have become part of domestic legislation. In the Constitution of the Republic of North Macedonia, in the part entitled "Economic, social and cultural rights", Article 32 guarantees the right to work. According to this article, "Everyone has the right to work, the right of free choice of work, protection at work, as well as material assistance while unemployed". Everyone under equal conditions has the right to any job if the prescribed criteria are fulfilled. This means that everyone has the right to work under the same conditions without discrimination on the grounds of sex, nationality or religion. Each employee has the right to remuneration for the work he/she does.[7]

Many laws related to the right to employment, the rights of the employee, employers, state agencies, equal treatment to employees and prohibition of discrimination, etc. are obligatory according to several conventions of the International Labor Organization and EU directives. So far, the Republic of North Macedonia has ratified 74 IRO conventions and many EU directives.[8] In addition to laws, the labor market in the Republic of Macedonia is also regulated by several government documents such as the National Employment Strategy of the Republic of Macedonia 2016–2020, the Operational plan of programs and measures for employment and services in the labor force market, and the Action Plan for Youth Employment 2016–2020.[9] Also, the social security policy allows unemployed people to receive social assistance in order to facilitate their existential needs. Any person who has worked without interruption for at least 9 months has the right to unemployment benefits.[10]

---

6   Ibid.
7   Constitution of the Republic of North Macedonia (Skopje: Parliament of the Republic of North Macedonia, 2018), 6.
8   Blagica Petrevski and Despina Tumanovska, Active Labor Market Policies: Challenge for Macedonian Labor Market (Skopje: Finance Think – Economic Research and Policy Institute, 2016), 7.
9   Ministry of Labour and Social Policy, http://www.mtsp.gov.mk/ (accessed May 9, 2017).
10 Blagica Petreski and Despina Tumanovska. Active Labour Market Policies: Challenge for Macedonian Labour Market. Skopje: Finance Think – Economic Research and Policy Institute, 2016, 8.

A key institution that mediates labor demand and supply in the Republic of North Macedonia is the Employment Service Agency; this is responsible for mediating in the process of employment, promotion of employment, professional orientation, and insurance in the case of unemployment; it is also responsible for developing analytical and professional materials and informing the public about the labor market.[11]

4 Overview of Unemployment in the Republic of North Macedonia from the Time of Socialism to the Transition

A high rate of unemployment is one of the most serious economic, social and political issues in every country where it occurs, including the Republic of North Macedonia. Unemployment in North Macedonia has been a long-term and structural problem. Although it has occasionally varied, it has had very high rates since the 1970s. In 1960 the unemployment rate was 12.8%,[12] but in the 1970s it grew significantly to almost 20% and remained at the same rate until the 1990s. (Table 4.1). It can be said that in this period the unemployment rate was high but stable. In 1991, when the process of independence of the Republic of Macedonia started, the unemployment rate was 24%, which was significantly higher than some other countries within the former Yugoslavia, such as Croatia, where the unemployment rate was 8%.[13] At the same time, the gross domestic product in the Republic of Macedonia in the period 1959–1989 was among the lowest in comparison to other countries within the former Yugoslavia.[14]

---

11 Ibid.
12 Blagica Novkovska, Measuring Non-Standard and Informal Employment in the Republic of Macedonia, (Harvard, Kennedy School of Government, Harvard University, Paper presented at the Workshop on Measurement Informal Employment in Developed Countries WIEGO, 2008), 2.
13 Sasho Kjosev, "Unemployment in the Republic of Macedonia: Specifics and Possible Solutions", Economic and Organization 4, no. 2, (2007): 153; Aleksandar Kostadinov, Labour Market Policies in Republic of Macedonia (Skopje: Centre for Economic Analysis, 2009), 3; Suzana Saveska and Ron Brown, Unemployment in the Republic of Macedonia: Policy Opinion for Employment Growth (Sofia: Paper Presented at NISPAcee Annual Conference: Improving Relations between Academicians and the Public, 25–27 March, 1999), 4.
14 Suzana Saveska and Ron Brown, Unemployment in the Republic of Macedonia: Policy Opinion for Employment Growth, 3; Jeton Zuka, The High Rate of Unemployment in the Republic of Macedonia (Beograd: Paper Presented at ERAZ Conference, 2015), 1.

TABLE 4.1 Overview of the number of unemployed persons from 1976 to 1990

Year	Number of unemployed persons	%
1976	98,114	22.04%
1980	117,151	21.82%
1985	135,857	21.65%
1990	156,323	23.55%

SOURCE: SAVESKA SUZANA AND BROWN RON, UNEMPLOYMENT IN THE REPUBLIC OF MACEDONIA: POLICY OPINION FOR EMPLOYMENT GROWTH (SOFIA: IMPROVING RELATIONS BETWEEN THE ACADEMICIAN AND THE PUBLIC, 1999), 4.

The unfavorable economic conditions in the 1990s caused by the loss of traditional markets in the war-affected region, hyperinflation, the embargo on Serbia from the United Nations and Greece's embargo on Macedonia further reduced the economic opportunities and increased unemployment, thereby creating a space for social tension and irrational solutions to these problems. Therefore, in 1991 468,372 people were employed in the Republic of Macedonia, of which 381,924 (81.5%) worked in the "economic activities" sector, while 86,448 (18.5%) worked in the sector of "non-economic activities". By 1996 the number of employees had fallen by 33.02% compared to 1990. Namely, 339,824 persons were employed in 1996, out of which 255,659 (75.23%) worked in the sector of "economic activities", while 84,165 (77%) worked in "non-economic activities". Based on this, it can be said that besides the big decline of employment in this period, there was also a less favorable structure of employees.[15] Privatization and restructuring of enterprises were the main elements of the transition process, but the manner in which these were carried out also had serious implications for the employment rate. Companies that were unprofitable were liquidated and therefore a significant number of people lost their jobs. For other enterprises, privatization meant using the labor force more rationally, which meant increasing employee productivity and laying off workers.[16]

---

[15] Suzana Saveska and Ron Brown, Unemployment in the Republic of Macedonia: Policy Opinion for Employment Growth, 5.

[16] Josrde Jakımovskı, "Unemployment as a Complex and Serious Personal and Social Issue", Skola Biznisa, no. 1 (2010): 77.

The private sector, which was not well enough developed in that period, could not absorb the labor force surplus that emerged after the process of privatization. The decline in economic activity at the time of the transition was reflected in the growth of unemployment. Thus, after the end of the transition process, the Republic of Macedonia was among the countries with the highest unemployment rate. The transition had the most difficult consequences for low-skilled workers and women.[17] In the late 1990s, at the end of the transition, the rate of unemployment in the Republic of Macedonia was the highest in Europe.[18] The rise in unemployment has reversed since 2005, since when we can notice a constant decline in the unemployment rate; however, compared to other countries from the region and the EU average, this rate is still very high.

5   Reasons for the High Unemployment Rate

Besides the consistent relatively high rate of unemployment, the process of transition, after which the unemployment rate significantly increased, as well as objective factors such as the socio-historical context and military conflicts in the region, significant subjective factors which affected the high unemployment rate in the Republic of North Macedonia are determined by Kjosev as the following: reduction of economic activities in certain sectors and the lack of dynamism in replacing them with others; the weak export economy; the low level of foreign direct investments; the large informal economy; the inefficient labor force market and policies designed to solve this issue; rigid legislation in the labor force market and legal insecurity, namely the frequently changing laws.[19]

One of the reasons for the high unemployment rate was the inflexibility of the labor force. Micevska, Eftimovski and Petkovska-Mircevska stress that the labor force was insufficiently flexible and dynamic because of the Law on Labor Relations, which protected employees, gave excellent trade union rights, directed employers to collective bargaining with unions, set minimum wages

---

17   Blagica Novkovska, "Unemployment in the Republic of Macedonia: Social and Economic Risks", in Unemployment: Risks and Challenges, ed. Jorde Jakimovski (Skopje: Institute for Sociological, Political and Legal Research, 2013), 76.

18   Maja Micevska, Dimitar Eftimovski and Tatjana Petkovska-Micevska, The Failure of the Labour Market in Macedonia: Labour Demand Analysis (Skopje: Institute of South-East Europe, 2004), 4.

19   Sasho Kjosev, "Unemployment in the Republic of Macedonia: Specifics and Possible Solutions", 154.

that employers could hardly afford, etc. All of these factors contributed to the growth of unemployment.[20] Namely, these authors point out that the labor law was defined in terms that the employees had a monopoly over the workplace. Employers were reluctant to hire new employees because it was very difficult to dismiss them later if the need arose. Moreover, although wages were relatively low, employers had to pay high payroll taxes and social security contributions. Also, the budget for active labor market policies was very low: between 1996 and 2002 they accounted for 0.05% of GDP, compared to the 0.7% that was spent by other OECD countries at that time. In the public sector and large private companies, the unions remained powerful players and wages were negotiated through collective agreement.

6   Unemployment Rates in the Republic of North Macedonia

The unemployment rate is the share of unemployed persons aged 15–74 in the total labor force. The labor force consists of the total number of employed and unemployed persons. As can be seen, unemployment in the Republic of North Macedonia is very high but had a decreasing trend in 1997–2000 and in 2006–2010. In 2001–2005, unemployment increased and reached 37.3% in 2005. Since then, it has constantly fallen, so in the first quarter of 2018 it was 20.7%, which is 16.6% less than it was in 2005. The reason for this reduction of unemployment can be seen in the application of active employment measures and in attracting foreign investment (Table 4.2).[21]

Regarding the rate of unemployment based on gender, the rate of female unemployment fell to 38.4% in 2005 and to 32.4% in 2008.[22] From this period until 2013, the female unemployment rate decreased by 3.4%, and in 2013 it was 29% (sustainable).[23] The unemployment rate for women in 2014 was 1% and in 2015 was 1.7%, both of which are lower than the rate for men.[24] Unemployment statistics show that in 1998–2010 there was a trend of increasing unemployment among citizens with higher education. In 1998, 10.8% of

---

20   Maja Micevska, Dimitar Eftimovski and Tatjana Petkovska-Micevska, The Failure of the Labor Market in Macedonia, Labour Demand Analysis (Skopje: Institute of South-East Europe, 2004).
21   Petar Trajkov, The Labour Market in the Republic of Macedonia and in the Countries of the Region (Skopje: Westminster Foundation for Democracy, 2018), 6.
22   Sustainable Development (Skopje: State Statistical Office, 2010), 36.
23   Sustainable Development (Skopje: State Statistical Office, 2014), 40.
24   Sustainable Development (Skopje: State Statistical Office, 2012), 40.

TABLE 4.2 Gender structure of the unemployed in the Republic of North Macedonia

Year	Unemployment rate	Unemployment rate of males	Unemployment rate of females
1997	36.0	33.0	40.8
1998	34.5	32.5	37.6
1999	32.4	31.9	33.3
2000	32.2	30.5	34.9
2001	30.5	29.5	32.0
2002	31.9	31.7	32.3
2003	36.7	37.0	36.3
2004	37.2	36.7	37.8
2005	37.3	36.5	38.4
2006	36.0	35.3	37.2
2007	34.9	34.5	35.5
2008	33.8	33.5	34.2
2009	32.2	31.8	32.8
2010	32.0	31.9	32.2
2011	31.6	/	30.7
2012	31.2	31.5	30.3
2013	29.2	29.0	29.0
2014	28.0	/	/
2015	26.1	26.7	25.1
2016	23.7	/	/
2017	22.4	/	/
2018	20.7	/	/
2019	17.8[a]		

a The data is for the first quarter of 2019 (State Statistical Office).

SOURCE: OWN ELABORATION BASED ON 20 YEARS OF INDEPENDENCE (2011) COMBINED WITH SUSTAINABLE DEVELOPMENT (2010–2016) AND EUROSTAT, UNEMPLOYMENT IN THE EU REGIONS IN 2018, NEWS RELEASE, 75/2019.

unemployed people had completed higher education, while in 2010 this percentage was 17.6%.[25] Increasing unemployment among people with higher education is in line with the increase in the percentage of people with higher

---

25   20 Years of Independence (Skopje: State Statistical Office, 2011), 17.

education in the social structure in the Republic of North Macedonia. In 1998 in the Republic of Macedonia, 4% of the population had completed higher education, while this had risen to 11% in 2010. At the same time, the share of unemployed persons with primary education decreased from 37.3% in 1998 to 29% in 2010.[26] The structure of unemployment in the Republic of North Macedonia is quite unfavorable, especially for young people, for whom it takes a long time to find employment (Table 4.3).[27] This long waiting period reduces the confidence of young people and professionals in the prosperity of the country and in socio-economic institutions; it also puts the country's peace and stability in jeopardy.[28]

TABLE 4.3 Age structure of the unemployed in the Republic of North Macedonia

Age range	Number of unemployed persons in 2015	%
Up to 29 years	28,006	24.4%
30–39 years	23,340	20.2%
40–49 years	24,101	20.9%
Over 50 years	39,632	34.5%
Total	114,979	100%

SOURCE: ANNUAL REPORT OF THE EMPLOYMENT SERVICE AGENCY OF THE REPUBLIC OF NORTH MACEDONIA, (SKOPJE: EMPLOYMENT SERVICE AGENCY OF THE REPUBLIC OF NORTH MACEDONIA, 2016), 18.

The unemployment rate of persons aged 15–24 years rose from 56.1% in 2001 to 65.7% in 2003, and then decreased to 56.4% in 2008; in 2015 it was 47.3%[29] (Table 4.4). In 2015, there was a dramatic 5.8% drop in the youth unemployment rate (age 15–24 years) compared with the previous year.[30]

In 1998–2010, it took most unemployed people more than a year to find employment. With small changes from year to year, the percentage of people

---

26 Ibid.
27 Elizabeta Tosheva, "Effects of the Global Economic Crisis on the Macedonian Economy: Some Macroeconomic Indicators and Future Policy Recommendations", Academicus International Academic Journal MMXVI, no. 13 (2016): 175.
28 Jorde Jakimovski, "Unemployment as a Complex and Serious Personal and Social Issue", 77.
29 Sustainable Development (Skopje: State Statistical Office, 2010), 41.
30 Sustainable Development (Skopje: State Statistical Office, 2016), 40.

TABLE 4.4   Unemployment rate among young people aged 15 to 24 years

Year	Unemployment rate for persons aged 15–24 years
2001	56.1%
2003	65.7%
2008	56.4
2009	55.1%
2010	53.6%
2011	55.3%
2012	53.9%
2013	51.9%
2014	53.3%
2015	47.3%
2016	/
2017	46.7%
2018	45.4%

SOURCE: SUSTAINABLE DEVELOPMENT (2010), 16 COMBINED WITH EUROSTAT, UNEMPLOYMENT IN THE EU REGIONS IN 2018, NEWS RELEASE, 75/2019.

waiting for more than a year for employment in this period basically remained the same. In 1998 it was 82.9%, and in 2010 it was 83.3% (Table 4.5).[31]

The time needed to find a job is correlated with the socio-demographic characteristics of the labor force. Those with a lower level of education wait longer compared to those with a higher level of education. This explains the fact that there is a higher rate of poverty among persons with a lower level of education. It is harder for people who have been unemployed to find employment not only because their skills are possibly out of date, but also because of their low confidence that they will be employed.[32] Analyzing the unemployment situation in the Republic of North Macedonia, the European Commission points out that in 2018 the country achieved its lowest yet unemployment rate of 20.7%. However, it concluded that youth unemployment, long-term unemployment, women's unemployment and regional disparity remain serious challenges to be addressed. Also, the groups which should be focused on are young women, young people living in rural areas and members of small ethnic groups.[33]

---

31   20 Years of Independence (Skopje: State Statistical Office, 2011), 18.
32   Jorde Jakimovski, "Unemployment as a Complex and Serious Personal and Social Issue", 77.
33   Commission Assessment, "The Economic Reform Program of North Macedonia 2019", 14, https://ec.europa.eu/neighbourhood-enlargement/system/files/2019-05/20190529-north-macedonia-report.pdf (accessed November 20, 2018).

TABLE 4.5   Number of job seekers for more than a year

Year	Job seekers for more than a year	%
1998	235,590	82.9
1999	219,195	83.8
2000	218,091	83.3
2001	228,602	86.9
2002	222,689	84.5
2003	268,856	85.1
2004	264,225	85.4
2005	280,988	86.7
2006	277,204	86.3
2007	268,994	84.9
2008	263,556	84.9
2009	244,631	81.9
2010	250,299	83.3
2017	213,564	77.9
2018	198,569	75.6

SOURCE: 20 YEARS OF INDEPENDENCE (2011) AND EUROSTAT, UNEMPLOYMENT IN THE EU REGIONS IN 2018, NEWS RELEASE, 75/2019.

7   Economic Growth and Unemployment

The growth of a country's economy influences both the employment and the unemployment rate, but it is not causally related to them. According to some authors, a 2% fall in the gross product leads to a 1% unemployment increase.[34] Table 4.6 shows the growth rate of the economy in Macedonia between 1999 and 2014. In these years, the economy was growing at relatively high rates of GDP growth. Exceptions are 2001, the year after the military conflict in the country, 2009, one year after the global economic crisis, and 2012. On the other hand, the fastest growth of gross domestic product occurred in the period 2004–2008. This was a period of relatively rapid growth of gross domestic product in the region, but in 2003–2007 the Republic of

---

[34]   Elena Mitreva, Application of Economic and Mathematical Models for Estimation of Youth Unemployment in the Republic of Macedonia, 16.

TABLE 4.6   Economic growth rate with employment and unemployment rate

Year	Economic growth rate	Employment rate	Unemployment rate
1999	4.3	40.2	32.4
2000	4.5	40.3	32.2
2001	-3.1	42.6	30.5
2002	1.5	40.4	31.9
2003	2.2	38.5	36.7
2004	4.7	36.8	37.2
2005	4.7	37.9	37.3
2006	5.1	39.6	36.0
2007	6.5	40.7	34.9
2008	5.5	41.9	33.8
2009	-0.4	43.3	32.2
2010	3.4	43.5	32.0
2011	2.3	43.9	31.6
2012	-0.5	44.0	31.2
2013	2.7	46.0	29.2
2014	/	/	28.0

SOURCE: ELIZABETA DJAMBASKA, ALEKSANDRA LOZANOSKA, "FOREIGN DIRECT INVESTMENT AND UNEMPLOYMENT", INTERNATIONAL JOURNAL OF ECONOMICS, COMMERCE AND MANAGEMENT 3, NO. 12 (2015): 77.

Macedonia had lower GDP growth than Albania, Bosnia and Herzegovina, Croatia, Montenegro and Serbia.[35] Taking into consideration that an important driver of GDP growth is direct foreign investment, the data for 1996–2006 show that the Republic of Macedonia had the lowest level of direct foreign investment per capita in the region. The unemployment rate increased significantly by 4.8% in 2003, and from then until 2005 there was an increasing trend. From 37.3% in 2005, unemployment fell to 29.2% in 2013. There was a similar increasing employment trend from 1999 until 2001; in 2001–2004 the rate fell from 42.6% to 36.8% and then increased from 2004 to 2013. The employment rate increased from 36.8% in2004 to 46.0% in 2013, which is a 9.2% increase (Table 4.6).

---

35   Aleksandar Kostadinov, Labour Market Policies in Republic of Macedonia (Skopje: Centre for Economic Analysis, 2009), 3.

According to some authors, the fall in unemployment is due not to rising employment but to two other factors. Firstly, people who lost their jobs during the period of transition slowly started to retire, and on that basis the number of retirees increased, while the number of unemployed decreased. Secondly, some of the young labor force migrated and do not appear as unemployed in the statistics.[36]

8 The Consequences of Unemployment

Unemployment is a long-term problem for the Republic of North Macedonia and has serious social consequences reflected in increased poverty, social inequality, social exclusion and the living standard of citizens.[37] In 2015, 43% of the unemployed lived in poverty. Unemployment is considered the most important reason for falling into poverty.[38] Also, unemployment has negative consequences for human resources and opportunities for individuals to achieve their professional and social goals.[39] According to unemployed persons, unemployment is a stressful experience that destroys self-confidence, creates financial and family problems, and can lead to depression.[40]

The results of the "Unemployment: Risks and Challenges for Republic of Macedonia" project show that employment is an important factor in building positive self-perception. Thus, a significantly higher percentage of respondents who are employed (94.2%) feel good about themselves in comparison with only 88.5% of the unemployed who have a positive self-image. Compared to (80.3%) of the unemployed, most employees (87.7%) felt they were important members of society. Compared with the unemployed (87.8%), a larger percentage of employees (95.8%) believe that the workplace is related to their abilities and skills. Employment leads individuals to perceive themselves as active individuals who are able to have a decent life.[41]

Young unemployed people exist with the support of their families, i.e., with the solidarity of their parents and close family members. Long-term

---

36 Vanco Uzunova, Niljana Petrevska, "The Unemployment in the Republic of Macedonia", Iustinus Primus Law Review 13, no. 2 (2016):3.
37 Ibid., 2.
38 Jeton Zuka, The High Rate of Unemployment in the Republic of Macedonia, 115.
39 Blagica Novkovska, Measuring Non-Standard and Informal Employment in the Republic of Macedonia, 2.
40 Jeton Zuka, The High Rate of Unemployment In the Republic of Macedonia, 115.
41 Jorde Jakimovski, "Unemployment as Complex and Serious Personal and Social Issue", 77.

unemployment makes them feel frustrated and dissatisfied. Looking from a wider social perspective, they are unable to form their own families and become parents. On the one hand, a longer period of waiting for employment means getting married older, but also the divorce rate is higher for those who marry even though they are not working.[42] Unemployed persons consider that external factors such as the state are responsible for solving their problems. Thus, compared to 81.5% of employees, 93.1% of the unemployed believe that the state has the responsibility to secure them employment. As compared to (31.0%) of the employed, the majority of the unemployed (66.4%) expressed their willingness to emigrate.[43] A 2019 study shows that the high rate of unemployment leads to lower wages and thus indirectly affects poverty, not only for those who are unemployed, but also for those employed in less prestigious jobs. The study, which analyzes the cases of North Macedonia, Montenegro, and Serbia, concludes that this effect of unemployment is the most obvious for North Macedonia.[44]

9 Labor Market Policies

The institution responsible for creating policies in the field of labor is the Ministry of Labor and Social Policy. Employment services are provided by the Employment Service Agency, which has 30 regional offices. Unemployed persons are entitled to benefits if the termination of employment was not at their request. They have the right to benefits for a period of 3 months if they were previously registered as employed for at least 9 months. For persons who have been employed for 20–25 years, the benefit can be paid for 24 months. The amount of the benefit is 50% of the average salary, but not less than 80% of the minimum wage in the sector in which the person worked.[45]

The creation and implementation of labor market policies in the Republic of Macedonia started in 1995 when the Government of the Republic of Macedonia, supported by the World Bank, created the Project for Social Reform and Technical Assistance. The implementation of this project was entrusted

---

42 Ibid.
43 Ibid.
44 Blagica Petreski et al., "Analysis of Youth Unemployment in Republic of North Macedonia, Monte Negro and Serbia", 30.
45 Suzana Saveska and Ron Brown, Unemployment in the Republic of Macedonia: Policy Opinion for Employment Growth, 8.

to the Agency for Transformation of Enterprises with State Capital. Activities under this project were divided into six components:
- employment counseling –within this component until the year 1997, five projects were approved, covering 1,560 unemployed citizens;
- training for unemployed persons – 5,852 persons were covered in 87 projects;
- community work within which a total of 739 persons were temporarily employed for a period of 3 to 6 months and participated in 28 projects;
- counseling centers for start-up projects, which included 19 projects covering 310 unemployed persons, of which 26 started their own businesses;
- incubators for micro and small businesses;
- planning of regional economic development.[46]

These activities were far from sufficient to make much impact on the problem of unemployment. Therefore, in 1998 the Law on Increasing Employment was enacted; it envisages subsidies for employers who employed new workers who had been unemployed for at least one year. Among other things, the law stipulated that employers should be exempted from paying taxes for pension and disability insurance for newly employed persons for a period of one year. The results showed that a total of 26,135 people was employed.[47]

The National Employment Strategy of the Republic of Macedonia 2016–2020 especially focuses on particular groups of unemployed persons, including young people, the long-term unemployed and vulnerable groups such as the elderly, people with disabilities, and single mothers. Also, the Government of the Republic of Macedonia has adopted the National Program for Decent Work 2015–2018, which focuses on internships, allowing various benefits for employers, IT training, integrating women into the labor market, self-employment of young people by giving them grants to start their own business, etc.[48]

Realizing that unemployment is a huge social problem in 2006, the Government of the Republic of Macedonia adopted a National Employment Strategy, and since 2007 Active Labor Market Policies (ALMP) have been implemented. The purpose of these policies was to combat the high unemployment rate. ALMPs are defined within the Annual Operational Plans of the Ministry of Labor and Social Policy. The key objectives of these plans are the following: social inclusion of vulnerable groups on the labor market, reduction of unemployment, more chances for the employment of the long-term unemployed,

---

46   Ibid., 9.
47   Ibid.
48   Vanco Uzunov, Niljana Petrevska, "The Unemployment in the Republic of Macedonia", 9.

strengthening the competitiveness of the economy.[49] These objectives should be achieved through four types of activities:
- Direct job creation, which consists of programs for self-employment and measures for creating jobs by giving support to start-ups and fast-growing companies. Measures within the frames of this group of activities have been designed to help directly reduce unemployment. Also, some of the measures are designed to improve entrepreneurship skills, such as preparing and implementation of a business plan. Some of the measures are aimed at increasing the motivation for self-employment.
- Employment incentives consist of subventions for the employment of young people, members of vulnerable groups and individuals that are difficult to employ. This group of measures consists of financial support for employment and labor force mobility. The purpose of these measures is to increase the demand for labor, to facilitate the transition of young people from school to work, and to increase employability among vulnerable groups such as the long-term unemployed and the handicapped.
- Traineeship, which consists in improving the skills of the labor force members for their current work positions or improving the basic skills of the unemployed. These mostly include courses for learning foreign languages, IT skills and internships.
- Community work consists of part-time employment of the long-term unemployed in local municipality institutions. The main goal of this program is to develop the skills of those who are difficult to employ.[50]

Of all the measures listed above, the most popular were those related to training of the unemployed, which were applied in 52% of all measures related to the Active Labor Market Policies. Next came employment incentives (28%) and job creation measures (15%) (Table 4.7).

Within the framework of unemployment-reduction policies, in 2014 the Government of the Republic of Macedonia started the "Macedonia employs" project, and in 2016 the "Macedonia employs 2" project. Within this project 10,190 companies employed 19,000 people. The "Macedonia employs 2" project exempts employers from the payment of social taxes for each new employee. The scheme of benefits can be seen in Table 4.8.

The "Macedonia employs 2" project lasted one year and, based on the results of the previous "Macedonia employs" project, about 20,000 people are expected to be employed through this project.

---

49   Blagica Petrevski and Despina Tumanovska, Active Labour Market Policies: Challenge for the Macedonian Labor Market, 12.
50   Ibid., 13.

TABLE 4.7 Overview of active labor market policy measures by category for 2007–2015

Category	Number of policy measures	Average per year	Share of policy measures (in terms of number)
Direct job creation	24	2.4	15%
Employment incentives	44	4.4	28%
Training	80	8	52%
Community work	7	1	5%

SOURCE: BLAGICA PETRESKI AND DESPINA TUMANOVSKA, ACTIVE LABOUR MARKET POLICIES: CHALLENGE FOR MACEDONIAN LABOUR MARKET (SKOPJE: FINANCE THINK – ECONOMIC RESEARCH AND POLICY INSTITUTE, 2016), 14.

TABLE 4.8 Benefits for employers foreseen by the project "Macedonia employs 2"

Category of unemployed	Benefits for the employer
Up to 35 years	Exemption from payment of social security taxes and personal income tax for a period of 3 years.
From 35 to 50 years old	Exemption from payment of social insurance for 5 years.
From 50 to 58 years old	Exemption from social security payment for 60 months.
Over 58 years	Exemption from payment of social insurance until retirement conditions are fulfilled. The retirement conditions of unemployed persons are based on old age. Men and women are eligible for retirement at 64 and 62, respectively.
Unemployed persons with 3 or more children, single parents, victims of domestic violence, disabled persons, parents of children with developmental disabilities.	Exemption from payment of social security and personal income tax for a period of 5 years.

SOURCE: MINISTRY OF LABOR AND SOCIAL POLICY, HTTPS://WWW.MTSP.GOV.MK/ (ACCESSED MARCH 8, 2018).

10   What Can Be Done to Increase Employment?

Experience shows that employment in a country depends not only on employment policies, but also on a range of measures in the fields of education, state welfare, regulation of the economy and taxes. Accordingly, the challenge of increasing employment requires a multidimensional approach that should include social assistance as well as active measures in the labor market. Social measures should provide for the subsistence minimum of the unemployed and avoid their social marginalization; however, they should not support and encourage dependence on the welfare state by the unemployed.

Saveska and Brown's recommendations for reducing unemployment concern giving support to micro and small enterprises, improvement of the legal and tax system, and investment support in general and foreign investment in particular to stimulate youth employment because unemployment in this group is higher than in other age groups.[51] Uzunov and Petrevska's recommendations are similar: they highlight the fact that the most important element in the reduction of unemployment is rapid economic development, which should rely on increasing both private and public investment.[52]

Also, they stress the impact of small and medium-sized enterprises that need to absorb a significant part of the unemployed labor force. According to Uzunov and Petrevska, important measures include restructuring agriculture and creating new jobs in this segment of the economy, regulating the informal economy and greater investment in education.

According to Kjosev, policies for increasing employment should consist of the following measures:

- Macroeconomic policies for growth in gross domestic product and employment. Increasing the competitiveness of the economy and achieving 6–8% annual growth of gross domestic product. Increase of both domestic and foreign investments and efficient public administration.
- Regional development by reducing the disparity of development in different regions and creating regional cohesion.
- Social insurance and social protection.
- Reduction of youth unemployment. This includes adjusting the education system and training in accordance with the requirements of the labor market, volunteer practice of students during studies, training for unemployed young people.

---

51   Suzana Saveska and Ron Brown, Unemployment in the Republic of Macedonia, 16.
52   Vanco Uzunov and Niljana Petrevska, "The Unemployment in the Republic of Macedonia", 10.

- Preventing long-term unemployment and encouraging employment of the long-term unemployed.
- Improving the capacities of the Employment Service Agency: increasing the capacity of human resources, closer cooperation and better coordination with employers, analyzing the requirements of the labor market, implementing active measures for employment of unemployed persons, training courses, practical and public work in accordance with the needs of employers.
- Education and training: raising awareness for lifelong learning, improving the quality of education at all levels, improvement of education programs, IT education, raising competitiveness in education through the opening of private secondary schools and universities, improving opportunities for the education of young people in rural areas, encouraging cooperation between domestic and foreign universities.
- Social dialogue: a tripartite social dialogue between employers, trade unions and government; establishing social dialogue at local level.[53]

11 Conclusion

This chapter shows that unemployment in the Republic of North Macedonia is a chronic long-term social problem. Unemployment in the Republic of North Macedonia was very high even before the country gained independence. For example, in 1976 it was 22%, and when the process of state independence and the transition of society began in 1990 it was 23.55%. Unemployment in the Republic of North Macedonia increased dramatically during the transition period and the privatization of capital that had previously been owned by society.[54] Thus, in 1997 the unemployment rate was 36.0%. The reasons for this lie in the unproductiveness of companies from the socialist system that laid off a significant part of the unproductive labor force after privatization, as well as in the wars in the former Yugoslavia, to which many Macedonian products were exported. As a result, many companies could not survive this transition period. Additional reasons for this were the UN sanctions against SR Yugoslavia, due to which it was not possible to co-operate economically with this neighboring

---

53 Sasho Kjosev, "Unemployment in the Republic of Macedonia: Specifics and Possible Solutions", 156.
54 Unlike other communist countries in which capital was owned by the state, in Yugoslavia it was owned by society, more precisely the workers who worked in the enterprises. Namely, in Yugoslavia a model of workers' self-management was developed.

country, as well as Greece's embargo on the export and import of products to the Republic of Macedonia. At one point, no goods could be exchanged with two of the four countries bordering the Republic of Macedonia. From 1997 to 2001 there was a slight reduction in unemployment, but after the military conflict that affected the country in that year there was an economic crisis and the unemployment rose rate until 2005, when it reached a record 37.3%. Since then, there has been a steady decline in unemployment. Data from the State Statistical Office for the first quarter of 2019 show that the unemployment rate is currently 17.8%. This is a very high unemployment rate, but for the Republic of North Macedonia it is the lowest in the last 40 years.

The unemployment rate depends on the way economic policy and labor market policy are pursued; however, it also depends on many external factors such as the political stability of the region and the country. In terms of the structure of unemployment, at the beginning of the transition more women were unemployed than men; however, in 2015, for the first time there was a higher unemployment rate for men than women. Also, unemployment is greatest among young people under 29 years of age and in people over 50 years of age. Most of the unemployed look for work for more than a year. Data from the State Statistical Office show that since 2005 unemployment in the Republic of North Macedonia has been drastically reduced by 19.5%, but it is still very high compared to the European Union and other countries in the region. Hence, the need to continue and intensify policies and measures for reducing unemployment is evident.

Bibliography

Annual Report of the Employment Service Agency of the Republic of North Macedonia. Skopje: Employment Service Agency of the Republic of North Macedonia, 2016.

Aqifi Elsana, and Malaj Visar, "Impact of Economic Growth on Unemployment in the Republic of Macedonia". International Journal of Economics, Commerce and Management 4, no. 1 (2015): 139–146.

Commission Assessment. The Economic Reform Program of North Macedonia. Accessed November 20, 2018. https://ec.europa.eu/neighbourhood-enlargement/system/files/2019-05/20190529-north-macedonia-report.pdf.

Constitution of the Republic of North Macedonia. Skopje: Parliament of the Republic of North Macedonia, 2018.

Djambaska, Elizabeta, and Aleksandra Lozanoska. Foreign Direct Investment and Unemployment. International Journal of Economics, Commerce and Management 3, no. 12 (2015), 77–85.

Eurostat. Unemployment in the EU Regions in 2018. News release, 75/2019.

Gerovska-Mitev, Maja. Report for Poverty and Social Exclusion in the Republic of Macedonia in 2011. Skopje: Macedonian Platform against Poverty, Institute for Human Rights, 2012.

Jakimovski, Jorde. "Unemployment as Complex and Serious Personal and Social Issue". Skola Biznisa, no. 1 (2010): 73–77.

Kjosev, Sasho. "Unemployment it the Republic of Macedonia: Specifics and Possible Solutions". Economic and Organization 4, no. 2 (2007): 153–160.

Kostadinov, Aleksandar. Labour Market Policies in Republic of Macedonia. Skopje: Centre for Economic Analysis, 2009.

Micevska, Maja, Dimitar Eftimovski and Tatjana Petkovska – Mircevska. The Failure of Labour Market in Macedonia: Labour Demand Analysis. Skopje: Institute of South-East Europe, 2004.

Ministry of Labour and Social Policy. Official website, 2017. Accessed March 2, 2018. http://av.gov.mk/nevrabotenost.nspx.

Mitreva, Elena. Application of Economic and Mathematical Models for Estimation of Youth Unemployment in the Republic of Macedonia. Stip: University Goce Delcev, 2015.

Novkovska, Blagica. Measuring Non-Standard and Informal Employment in the Republic of Macedonia. Harvard: Kennedy School of Government, Harvard University, 2008.

Novkovska, Blagica. Unemployment in the Republic of Macedonia: Social and Economic Risks in Unemployment: Risks and Challenges, Jorde Jakimovski. Skopje, Institute for Sociological, Political and Legal Research, 2013.

Petreski, Blagica, and Despina Tumanovska. Active Labour Market Policies: Challenge for Macedonian Labour Market. Skopje: Finance Think – Economic Research and Policy Institute, 2016. Accessed May 9, 2017. https://mpra.ub.uni-muenchen.de/75879/1/MPRA_paper_75879.pdf.

Petreski, Blagica, Jorge Davalos, Ivan Vchkov, Derpina Tumanoska, and Tereza Kochovska, "Analysis of Youth Unemployment in the Republic of North Macedonia, Montenegro and Serbia." Finance Think, Polity Study no. 22 (2019): 6–40.

Saveska, Suzana, and Ron Brown. Unemployment in the Republic of Macedonia: Policy Opinion for Employment Growth. Sofia, Paper Presented at NISPAcee Annual Conference: Improving Relations Between the Academician and the Public, 25–27 March, 1999.

Soylu, Bayram Ozogur, Ismail Cakmak, and Fatih Okur. "Economic Growth and Unemployment Issue: Panel Data Analysis in Eastern European Countries". Journal of International Studies 11, no. 1 (2018): 93–107.

Sustainable Development. Skopje: State Statistical Office, 2010.

Sustainable Development. Skopje: State Statistical Office, 2011.

Sustainable Development. Skopje: State Statistical Office, 2012.

Sustainable Development. Skopje: State Statistical Office, 2013.
Sustainable Development. Skopje: State Statistical Office, 2014.
Sustainable Development. Skopje: State Statistical Office, 2015.
Sustainable Development: Skopje: State Statistical Office, 2016.
Tosheva, Elizabeta. Effects of the Global Economic Crisis on Macedonian Economy: Some Macroeconomic Indicators and Future Policy Recommendations. Academicus: International Academic Journal MMXVI, no. 13 (2016): 171–183.
Trajkov, Petar. Labour Market in the Republic of Macedonia and in the Countries of the Region. Skopje: Westminster Foundation for Democracy, 2018.
Uzunov, Vanco, and Biljana Petrevska. "The Unemployment in the Republic of Macedonia". Iustinianus Primus Law Review 13, no. 2 (2016).
Zuka, Jeton. The High Rate of Unemployment in the Republic of Macedonia (Beograd: Baber Presented at ERAZ Conference, 2015).
20 Years Independence. Skopje: State Statistical Office, 2011.

PART 2

Social Security in the Republic of Montenegro

∴

CHAPTER 5

Pension System and Reforms in Montenegro

Maja Baćović

1   Introduction

The pension system in Montenegro, although multi-pillar by the Law,[1] is largely based on a mandatory, public pay as you go system, operated by the public Pension Fund in Montenegro. The Law on the Pension System defines a three-pillar system, in which the first pillar is the mandatory, public pay-as-you-go system (PAYG), the second pillar is a mandatory capitalized private pension scheme, while the third pillar is a voluntary pension scheme. In practice, the first and third pillars exist, although the first is dominant, while the third is represented by two pension funds, with only 2,500 clients (less than 2% of total number of employees in Montenegro). The pay-as-you go pension system in Montenegro is a mature one, which means that pension insurance contributions are not sufficient to finance the expenditures of the pension system. Also, population is aging, which makes the issue even more important.[2]

The main feature of a PAYG system is financing current expenditures with current revenues from contributions paid by all employees in the country. In its initial phase, when a system is young, the number of contributors and revenues of the Fund are usually larger than expenditures, but as the system matures, imbalances begin to appear, and fund is subsided by the government. Schwarz and Guven point out that:

> When a pension system financed on a pay-as-you-go basis first begins, it only collects revenue. Individuals make contributions, but almost no one has enough contributions in the first years to receive a pension.

---

1 Law on Pension and Disability Insurance, https://www.fondpio.me/zakoni/zakon %20O%20PI O%20pdf.html (accessed 27 May, 2019).
2 Maja Baćović, "Demographic Changes in transition countries: Opportunity or Obstacle for Economic Growth? Case of Montenegro", European Research Studies 11, no. 3–4 (2007): 31–44; Mijanovic Dragica, Mileva Brajuskovic, Dusko Vujacic, and Velibor Spalevic, "Causes and Effects of Aging og Montenegrin Population", Journal of Environmental Protection and Ecology 18, no. 3 (2017): 1249–1259; United Nations, Department of Economic and Social Affairs: World Population Ageing 2017 Highlights (New York: United Nations, 2017), 38.

A few contributors may suffer disability soon after the pension system starts, but this tends to have a small effect. Thus, "immature" systems have few expenditures and generally run surpluses. As the systems mature, contributors begin to reach retirement age, increasing expenditures of the pension system. Finally, when all old-age retirees have spent their entire working lives as contributing members of the pension system a process that may take 50 to 60 years the system is judged to be mature. Expenditures are much higher in mature systems, and whether these systems remain in financial balance or run deficits depends on the relative generosity of the benefit parameters relative to the contribution parameters. The immediate implications of this imbalance between contributors and pensioners are fiscal, with high levels of expenditures in the pension system but moderately low revenues to finance such expenditures.[3]

In most countries with a mature PAYG system, the expenditures of the pension system constitute a significant item in public finances. This is a consequence of demographic changes (aging of the population), but also of the pension insurance system. Each imbalance in the relationship between the number of employees and the contributions they are paying, and the number of pensioners and their monthly pensions, leads to a deficit in the pension system, which is financed from the government's budget. Such a pension system, with the tendency of further population aging, burdens public spending and limits the use of fiscal instruments to achieve long-term stable economic growth.

The problem has been gaining in importance in the last few decades, especially in transition countries, where, along with the aging of the population, in the initial transitional phase unemployment had increased as well as the percentage of employees, who, due to the high level of fiscal burdens, work in the informal economy, avoid the payment of taxes and contributions, thereby reducing the income of the pension system. Although over the last decade, the unemployment rate has fallen in most countries, problems with pension fund deficits and their pressure on public finances still exist. A study by Schwarz and Guven[4] suggests that an attempt by a number of countries to

---

3 Schwarz Anita and Ufuk Guven, "Pensions", in Fiscal Policy and Economic Growth: Lessons for Eastern Europe and Central Asia (Washington, DC: The World Bank, 2007), 217–250.
4 Ibid., 238.

reduce participation in the informal economy by reducing contribution rates yielded partially positive results in the reduction of the informal economy. The rate of pension insurance contributions remains high, however, and while the number of employees has risen, the effect of reducing the rate was stronger, resulting in reduced total revenues. The same research cites the results of Hamermash, which show that a 1% reduction in the contribution rate must be accompanied by an increase in employment by 0.3% in order for the pension system's income to remain unchanged.

The aim of this chapter is to present recent trends in the Montenegrin pension system, reforms implemented since 2003, and to analyze future system sustainability, bearing in mind that population aging will continue in the future, while public debt has increased recently and fiscal burdens remain high, discouraging investment. The pension system in the country is financially insufficient, relying on government transfers, which therefore has strong impact on fiscal policy, but also is strongly determined by demographic changes. Therefore, any analysis of the pension system must incorporate both population changes and the fiscal policy of the country.

For the purpose of this study, we will make population projections until 2091, although similar inputs are available from international sources (UN). Demographic trends are important for the expenditure side of the pension system directly, as an aging population leads to a growing number of pensioners, but also for the revenue side, as this has a direct impact on the labor market, employment and growth, and therefore, fiscal revenues. Population projections were made applying the cohort component method. Forecasting the pension fund's expenditures and revenues was estimated with use of the arithmetic approach.

The chapter is structured in seven sections. The introduction is presented in the first section, while in the second section, we will provide insight into a select analysis of pension systems worldwide. In the third section, we will present a model for analysis of the impact of changes in relevant elements of both the expenditures and revenues sides of the pension system. In the fourth section, we will present an empirical analysis of the pension system in Montenegro since the country achieved independence in 2006 until 2018. In this section, we will provide an overview of the reform measures undertaken since 2003. In the fifth section, we will present key fiscal indicators and trends, followed in the sixth section with the results of population projections. In the seventh section, we will present results of forecasting expenditures and revenues of the pension system. In the final section, we will present our conclusions based on the research results.

2 Selected Examples of Pension Systems Worldwide

Pension systems, aging populations and their impact on fiscal policy have been extensively studied. We will list only a selection of sources. Vogel, Ludwig and Borsch-Supan,[5] studied the three demographically oldest European nations (France, Germany and Italy), and analyzed the impact of the aging population on investing abroad, endogenous human capital formation and increasing the retirement age. They concluded that endogenous human capital formation, in combination with an increase in the retirement age, has strong implications for economic aggregates and welfare, in particular in the open economy. Von Weizsacker[6] researched a politico-economic explanation of actual social security policies in developed countries. Bongaarts[7] researched the impact of the aging population on the costs of pension systems in OECD countries. In their research, Verbic and Spruk,[8] presented a theoretical model of public pension expenditures under endogenous human capital. In a report published by IMF,[9] a study analyzing the aging population and public pension schemes was presented. The study examines the pension-related aging problem primarily from a fiscal perspective. In a study published by the World Bank,[10] public pension systems in Europe and Central Asia were analyzed, mostly from a fiscal and reform instrument perspective.

Population aging, evidenced in most developed countries by the end of the 20th century, attracted the attention of economists, and new research attempted to analyze the impact of the aging population on economic performance in developed countries. Cutler, Poterba, Sheiner, Summers, and Akerlof[11] argued that aging populations have a negative impact on:

---

5   Edgar Vogel, Alexander Ludwig and Axel Borsch-Supan, "Aging and Pension Reform: Extending the Retirement Age and Human Capital Formation", Journal of Pension Economics & Finance 16, no 1 (2017): 81–107.
6   Robert K. Von Weizsacker, "Population Aging and Social Security: A Politico-Economic Model of State Pension Financing", Public Finance 45, no. 3 (1990): 491–509.
7   John Bongaarts, "Population Aging and the Rising Cost of Public Pensions", Population and Development Review 30, no. 1 (2004): 8.
8   Miroslav Verbic and Rok Spruk, "Aging Population and Public Pensions: Theory and Macroeconomic Evidence", Panoeconomicus 61, no. 3 (2014), 295–299.
9   Sheetal Chand and Albert Laeger, Aging Population and Public Pension Schemes (Washington, DC: International Monetary Fund, 1996), 3–7.
10 Anita Schwarz and Guven Ufuk, "Pensions", in Fiscal Policy and Economic Growth: Lessons for Eastern Europe and Central Asia, 218–230.
11 David Cutler, James Poterba, Louise Sheiner, Lawrence Summers, and George Akerlof, "An Aging Society: Opportunity or Challenge?", Brooking Papers on Economic Activity 1 (1990): 53–56.

- saving (as older persons dissave);
- the ratio between productive and unproductive groups, which, if not compensated for by increased productivity, may influence per capita income, fiscal revenues, etc.;
- fiscal policy, through an increase in social security spending.

Other important studies, such as that of Birdsall,[12] projected rising future costs in such areas as education and health care services as a result of population growth whereas other studies analyzed the labor market effects of rapid population growth on such areas as the balance of payments, the food supply and the general availability of material resources.[13]

3 Pay as You Go System: Determinants of Revenues and Expenditures of the Pension System

In the generational solidarity type of the pension system (pay-as-you-go), pensions are financed from contributions of currently employed workers. In case of mandatory, public system, pensions are a legal obligation of the state and pensioners are legally entitled to receive a monthly payment. This payment is determined by the contributions made by pensioners during his (her) working life, not by revenues from current pension contributions. The state pension fund has an obligation to pay pension to all pensioners. If revenues from pension contributions are not sufficient, finance is provided through transfers from the Government's budget.[14]

Basic revenues of the pension funds are equal to:

$$PR_t = f\left(L_t, p_t, W_{avg,t}\right) = L_t \cdot p_t \cdot W_{avg,t} \qquad (1)$$

where PR_t is the revenue of the pension fund in period t, L_t -number of employees paying pension contribution in period t, p_t -pension contribution rate and $W_{avg,t}$ be the average gross wage in period t, which is also the basis for calculating future pension contributions.[15]

---

12 Nancy Birdsall, "Analytical Approaches to the Relationship of Population Growth and Development", Population and Development Review 3, no. 1/2 (1977): 69.
13 Maja Baćović, "Demographic Changes in Transition Countries: Opportunity or Obstacle for Economic Growth? Case of Montenegro", 33.
14 Ibid., 40 – 41.
15 Ibid., 41.

Accordingly, revenues of the pension fund will increase if any or all variables increase, meaning that growth in number of employees, wages and increase of the pension contribution rate will lead to higher revenues, and opposite.

On the other hand, expenditures of the pension fund can be expressed as:

$$PE_t = f(R_t, P_{avg,t}) = R_t \cdot P_{avg,t} \qquad (2)$$

where PE_t is the expenditures of pension fund in period t, R_t -number of pensioners entitled to receive regular monthly pension and $P_{avg,t}$ -average pension in period t. Increase in number of pensioners and/or average monthly pension will lead to higher expenditures, and opposite.

If pension fund revenues and expenditures are nor balancing, or $PE_t > PR_t$, the difference is financed through government transfers.

If we assume that pension fund revenues and expenditures have to be balanced:

$$PR_t = PE_t$$

$$L_t \cdot p_t \cdot W_{avg,t} = R_t \cdot P_{avg,t}$$

If we know that $W_{avg,t}$ and $P_{avg,t}$ are positively correlated, then we may conclude that any change in P_t will be determined by change in the ratio of R_t and L_t.

$$\Delta p_t = \Delta \frac{R_t}{L_t}$$

An increase in the number of pensioners, while (L_t) is constant, will force (p_t) to increase, while an increase in (L_t) if (R_t) is constant, will make it possible to decrease. This leads to the conclusion that, in case of growing number of pensioners and fixed pension contribution rate, either number of employees and/or wages, or both, have to grow by higher rate, otherwise, deficit of the pension fund will increase. There is also an option to change pension contribution rate (to increase it), but investors and policy makers usually see such scenario as non-attractive for investments.[16]

---

16 Ibid.

4 Pension System and Reforms in Montenegro

The pension system of Montenegro is regulated by the Law on Pension and Disability Insurance,[17] according to which pension and disability insurance in Montenegro includes compulsory pension and disability insurance based on current financing; mandatory pension insurance based on individual capitalized savings;[18] and voluntary pension insurance based on individual capitalized savings. The Law regulates compulsory pension and disability insurance on the basis of the current financing.

The rights to pension and disability insurance are as follows: in the case of age, the right to old age pension and early retirement; in case of disability, the right to a disability pension; in case of death: the right to a family pension and the right to compensation for funeral expenses; in case of physical injury caused by work or professional activity, financial compensation for physical damage.

In the current stage of reform of the pension system, the system relies on two pillars: the current financing of pensions (pay-as-you-go system or the system of intergenerational solidarity), organized within the state fund (first pillar) and development of voluntary old-age savings in private pension funds (third pillar). The second pillar has not yet been introduced. The initial pension system reform was implemented in 2003 and redefined again in 2010.

4.1 *Pension System Reform in 2003*

The need to reform the pension system has arisen as a consequence of previous experience, when the system based on the institutional framework of social insurance prioritized the current generation of pensioners instead of the future. This resulted in the growing indebtedness of the state pension fund and financial instability. One of the characteristics of the system prior to 2004 was the minimum age for retirement which did not change despite the prolongation of life expectancy, providing pension rights at the age of 60 (for men), or 55 (for women), and twenty years of employment. The pension system also contained numerous rights that were not based on payment of contributions and which did not depend on the attainment of the retirement age, which further undermined its financial stability.[19]

---

17 Official Gazette of the Republic of Montenegro, no. 54/03, 39/04, 61/04, 79/04, 81/04, 14/07, 47/07, 79/08, 14/10, 78/10, 34/11, 66/12.
18 The second pillar has not yet been introduced.
19 The source of key findings in this section is a document prepared by Government of Montenegro, Council for improvement of the business environment, regulatory and

The Law on Pension and Disability Insurance,[20] in force as of January 1, 2004, introduced several reform measures to the existing pension system of generational solidarity, or the first pillar of the pension system. This law did not change the status of the then pensioners, but the aim was to provide a better and safer financial situation for all pensioners. Basic measures were a gradual increase in the minimum age, a change in the pension formula, an increase in the number of years included in the pension calculation, a SWISS model for the adjustment of pensions, extension of the basis for payment of contributions, and finally, stricter conditions for obtaining disability, family pension and other special rights.

The increasing life expectancy and aging population required an increase in the minimum age. Unlike most countries, Montenegro has opted for the gradual introduction of a higher minimum age. According to the 2004 law, the minimum age rises by six months each year, until it reaches 65 years for men, and 60 for women.

The novelty in relation to the existing pension formula represented a different way of determining the level of pensions. The personal points system was introduced, with the advantages of greater linkage between earnings, paid contributions, age and the resulting pensions, as well as incentives (increasing the importance of paid contributions and the amount of earnings throughout the working period), and simplicity in calculating the amount of pension. The new law in Montenegro introduced the so-called 'points' system for calculating pensions. Every year in which an employee contributes to the current funding system, he or she earns points. A worker who earns one average salary, receives one point, while a worker who earns two average salaries, earns two points; therefore, 'x' salaries lead to 'x' points. The value of the pension is obtained by multiplying the number of personal points (average annual number of points per year multiplied by the numbers of years working) with the value of the point. Until 2004, the pension was calculated on the basis of the best ten consecutive years. In the first year of the reform, in 2004, the best twelve consecutive years were taken into account when calculating the pension. The number of years that are included in the pension calculation will increase every year for two years as long as they reach the entire working life.

The SWISS approach for pension adjustment means that pensions are adjusted in a way that takes into account the change in the cost of living and

---

structural reforms, see Analysis of the Pension system in Montenegro, 2013 (original document is available in Montenegrin language).

20   Official Gazette of the Republic of Montenegro, no. 54/03, 39/04, 61/04, 79/04, 81/04, 14/07, 47/07, 79/08, 14/10, 78/10, 34/11, 66/12.

average gross earnings. The percentage used for alignment is half the sum of the percentage increase (or reduction) of the cost of living and half of the percentage increase (or decrease) of the average gross wage. The percentage of the increase in the cost of living is the annual growth rate of the consumer price index. Nominal earnings are published in the monthly reports of the Statistical Office of Montenegro.

Under the new law, all earnings from paid work are the basis for contributions, regardless of the type of contract, type of earnings or salary compensation, and regardless of whether the income arises from one or more jobs. Stricter conditions for disability, family pensions and others special rights were introduced. Family pensions are awarded only to children and spouses. The high participation of disabled persons in total pensions, assigned for non-medical criteria, without periodic examinations, was a major burden on the pension system. Therefore, the new law proclaimed restrictive disability pensions based on a licensed doctor's certification. A third-year inspection has been introduced. The second pillar, or the mandatory capitalized pension system, is defined by the law, but has not yet been introduced. The idea is to introduce private funds in which each employee will have their own pension account, with contributions defined by law as a percentage of wages, and the size of pensions defined by the value accumulated after contributions were invested by the Fund during the working period. The third pillar, or the voluntarily pension scheme based on individual savings, has been implemented and regulated by the law on voluntarily pension funds.[21] So far, two pension funds operate in Montenegro, with number of contributors at less than 2% of total number of employees.

4.2 Pension System Reform in 2010

In 2010, another major reform of the pension system was implemented. The challenges which the Montenegrin pension system was facing then could be divided into three basic groups: the financial sustainability of the system in the short and long term, low level of activity on the labor market, and negative demographic trends. As presented in Table 5.1, the novelty of the 2010 reform was a redefining of the SWISS formula, giving only 25% of the weight to increase in wages, while 75% of the change is determined by inflation (in the previous model this was 50% for changes in wages and 50% for changes in inflation). The minimum age for receiving an old age pension was changed as well, introducing 67 years for both men and women as the new

---

21   Official Gazette of the Republic of Montenegro, no. 78/06, 14/07, 73/10, 40/11.

TABLE 5.1　Comparison of the basic features from the pension law from 2004 and 2010

	Law of 2004		Law of 2010	
	Men	Women	Men	Women
Minimum age	65	60	67	67
Working period necessary	40	40	40	40
First condition to obtain right for pension	65/15	60/15	67/15	67/15
Second condition to obtain right for pension	55/40	55/35	40 years of work period	40 years of work period
Pension adjustment formula	swiss – 50% of inflation change + 50% of average gross wage change		Modified swiss – 75% of inflation change + 25% of average gross wage change	
Pension adjustments	Two times a year, in January and June		Once a year, in January each year	

SOURCE: GOVERNMENT OF MONTENEGRO, COUNCIL FOR IMPROVEMENT OF THE BUSINESS ENVIRONMENT, REGULATORY AND STRUCTURAL REFORMS, ANALYSIS OF THE PENSION SYSTEM IN MONTENEGRO, 2013, 17.

age defined condition to be entitled to receive a pension. A new element is early retirement, that is, the insured is entitled to early retirement when he or she reaches 62 years of age and has at least 15 years of work, while for each month earlier than the minimum age of 67 the person retires, the pension permanently decreases by 0.35%. In addition, a special provision for women has been introduced, adding six months of work period credit per child born. A second condition for obtaining the right to a pension has been changed, introducing only the criteria of 40 years of work, as an option instead of the minimum age.

4.3　The Pension System in Montenegro, Key Indicators, 2006–2018

The pension system in Montenegro, despite reform measures which produced positive results, has not yet been financially sustainable, requiring transfers from the government, on average at the level of 30% of total expenditures.

After the latest reform measures in 2010, transfers from the government have started to decline, from €180 million in 2009 (47% of total expenditures), to €103 million in 2018 (24.5% of expenditures) (Figure 5.1).

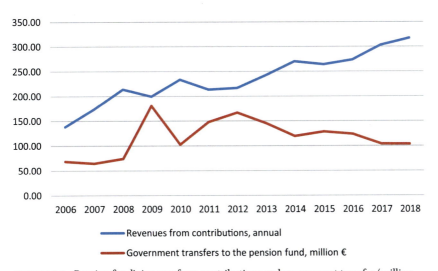

FIGURE 5.1 Pension fund's income from contributions and government transfer (million euro), 2016–2018
SOURCE: CENTRAL BANK OF MONTENEGRO, HTTPS://CBCG.ME/ME/STATISTIKA/STATISTICKI-PODACI/FISKALNI-SEKTOR (ACCESSED JUNE 25, 2019).

Although improved, financial sustainability remains an issue, and burden to the public finances is high. The average expenditures for pensions per GDP from year 2006 to 2018 were 10.4%, while government transfers to the pension fund were on average 3.54% of GDP, though decreasing (Table 5.2). Since 2006, the number of pensioners in Montenegro has increased by 22.5%, from 93,477 in 2006 to 114,676 in 2018, while the number of employees has increased by 28%, from 150,800 to 194,085, respectively. The ratio of the number of employees to the number of pensioners has increased from 1.61 (2006) to 1.69 (2018), although it did decline to 1.54 in 2013 and 2015. Pension expenditures in Montenegro represent on average 10.4% of GDP, although this has declined from 10% (2006) to 9% (2018). Annual revenues from contributions has not been sufficient to finance total expenditures, as expenditures have been higher on average by 51%, although the ratio of expenditures and revenues declined to 1.33 in 2018. Government transfers to the pension fund declined from 3% of GDP (8% of total public expenditures) in 2006, to 3% of GDP (4% of public expenditures) in 2018 (Table 5.2).

TABLE 5.2   The pension system in Montenegro (changes in indicators from 2006 to 2018)

Year	Number of pensioners	Number of employees	Average monthly pension	Expenditures of pension fund, annual	Revenues from contributions, annual
2006	93,477	150,800	142.78	206.80	138.18
2007	92,168	156,408	186.10	238.10	173.52
2008	95,367	166,221	238.83	287.97	213.85
2009	97,088	169,859	252.55	380.10	199.51
2010	99,196	157,679	261.36	335.95	233.50
2011	103,439	162,450	272.75	361.15	213.45
2012	106,477	167,484	278.85	383.24	216.50
2013	108,689	167,173	276.71	387.55	241.95
2014	109,670	171,158	274.76	389.20	270.12
2015	112,362	172,517	269.37	392.33	264.10
2016	108,478	177,473	280.40	397.03	273.55
2017	114,140	177,627	282.90	406.96	303.04
2018	114,676	194,085	284.92	420.48	316.98

SOURCE OF DATA: OWN ELABORATION BASED ON CENTRAL BANK OF MONTENEGRO, HTTPS://CBCG.ME/ME/STATISTIKA/STATISTICKI-PODACI/FISKALNI-SEKTOR (ACCESSED MARCH 08, 2019); PENSION FUND OF MONTENEGRO, HTTPS://WWW.FONDPIO.ME/INDEXS/FINANSIJE.HTML, MONSTAT: STATISTICAL YEARBOOK, 2006–2018.

Ratio of expenditures and revenues	Ratio of number of employees/ number of pensioners	Government transfers to the pension fund, million €	Government transfers to the pension system/ public expenditures	Government transfers to the pension system/GDP	Pensions expenditures per GDP
1.50	1.61	68.62	8.00%	3.00%	10.00%
1.37	1.70	64.58	6.00%	2.00%	9.00%
1.35	1.74	74.12	5.00%	2.00%	9.00%
1.91	1.75	180.59	12.00%	6.00%	13.00%
1.44	1.59	102.45	7.00%	3.00%	11.00%
1.69	1.57	147.70	10.00%	5.00%	11.00%
1.77	1.57	166.74	11.00%	5.00%	12.00%
1.60	1.54	145.60	9.00%	4.00%	12.00%
1.44	1.56	119.08	6.00%	3.00%	11.00%
1.49	1.54	128.23	6.00%	4.00%	11.00%
1.45	1.64	123.48	6.00%	3.00%	10.00%
1.34	1.56	103.92	5.00%	2.00%	9.00%
1.33	1.69	103.50	4.00%	2.00%	9.00%

The average pension over reference period was €254.02, while the average gross wage was €677.07, which points to the rather low standard of living of the older population. Average annual expenditures of the pension fund from year 2006 to 2018 were €352 million or 10.48% of GDP, while revenues from contributions were €235 million. The average annual government transfers to pension fund were €117 million or 2.54% of GDP. The maximum annual value of the government transfers to the pension funds was observed in 2009, amounting €180 million, or 6% of GDP, while the minimum was observed in 2007 (€64 million or 2.24% of GDP) (Table 5.3). This was expected as in 2007, Montenegro's real GDP growth was 6.8%, while in 2009 it was negative (-5.8%), due to the adverse impact of the global financial crisis.

The general pension contribution rate, defined by the Law on Mandatory Social Insurance contribution rates,[22] for pension and disability insurance, is set at 20.5%, but is higher for those employed under the "extended services rule" regime.

In its report, the World Bank stated that:

> there are various routes to early retirement in Montenegro: for those with long work experience, also for workers who lost job due to bankruptcy (in particular aluminum sector, metal-processing industry, or state owned companies), mine workers, for workers in hazardous occupations, those in special retirement rules and also those working in the so called 'armed services', which are treated similarly as those in the extended service, the retirement age is lowered depending on the type of extended services period (12/14, 12/15, 12/16, 12/18 or 12/24). The regular pension contribution rate (20.5%) is increased by supplementary contributions, ranking from 6% to 28%, depending on the extended services rule. The supplementary contribution rate is not sufficient from an actuarial perspective to finance extended service.[23]

---

[22] Official Gazette of the Republic of Montenegro, no. 13/07, 79/08, 86/09, 78/10, 40/11, 14/12, 62/13, 08/15.

[23] World Bank Group, Options for Reforming Early Retirement System for Special and Hazardous Occupations in Montenegro (Washington, DC: World Bank Group, 2017), 4.

TABLE 5.3 The pension system in Montenegro, 2006–2018 (descriptive statistics of indicators)

Sample: 2006–2018, Montenegro

	Number of pensioners	Average pension	Expenditures of pension fund, million €	Revenues from contributions, million €	Government transfers	Expenditures of pension fund per GDP	Transfers to the pension fund per GDP
Mean	104,248.2	254.0215	352.8354	235.2500	117.5854	0.104881	0.035455
Median	106,477.0	272.7500	383.2400	233.5000	119.0800	0.107355	0.032783
Maximum	114,676.0	284.9200	420.4800	316.9800	180.5900	0.126959	0.060320
Minimum	92,168.00	142.7800	206.8000	138.1800	64.58000	0.088542	0.022407
Std. Dev.	7,972.189	42.72680	67.24697	50.52528	36.44447	0.012122	0.011783
Skewness	−0.212276	−1.751387	−1.182999	−0.162689	0.111682	0.268536	0.785223
Kurtosis	1.599976	4.810080	3.029616	2.432039	2.066740	1.930600	2.616122
Jarque-Bera	1.159336	8.420653	3.032696	0.232077	0.498802	0.775702	1.415734
Probability	0.560084	0.014842	0.219512	0.890441	0.779268	0.678514	0.492694
Sum	1355227.	3302.280	4,586.860	3,058.250	1528.610	1.363455	0.460913
Sum Sq. Dev.	7.63E+08	21,906.95	54,265.86	30,633.65	15,938.39	0.001763	0.001666
Observations	13	13	13	13	13	13	13

SOURCE: OWN ELABORATION.

5 Government Spending and Public Debt in Montenegro

Fiscal policy faces major challenges in the 21st century. In Montenegro, as in most countries in transition, government expenditures are high and often financed by growing debt. In combination with high taxes, this limits investment and entrepreneurial activity, but on the other hand, pressures for larger government spending come from the social sphere. From a social perspective, the expectations of financing expenditures for pension insurance, health insurance and social benefits are very high.

Total budget spending in Montenegro, from 41.2% of GDP in 2006, reached its maximum of 59.1% in 2015, while in 2018 it was at the level of 56.3% of GDP. Revenues, in contrast, are falling from 39.7% of GDP (2006) to 37.8% (2018), while annual borrowing is rising, from 1.1% (2006) to a maximum of 24.1% (2018). The total budget balance, from a surplus at the start of independence (a record surplus of 6.6% in 2007), went into deficit later, reaching a maximum value of -8% in 2015. In 2018, it amounted to -3.4% of GDP (Table 5.4).

The public debt of Montenegro, after a decrease in 2007–2008, when the budget surplus was used to repay part of the debt, has risen constantly since 2009, when it was 38.1% of GDP, to 68.3% of GDP in 2018. Foreign debt rose from 23.2% (2006) to 59.8%, while the domestic debt in 2018 was 8.5% of GDP.

5.1 *The Population of Montenegro (1991–2091)*

The most common methods for population projections are mathematical methods[24] and the cohort component method.

> The cohort component method is the most widely used approach to projecting population, and is frequently employed also in preparing population estimates by age and sex. The cohort component method involves calculating the future size of cohorts, taking into accounts the effects of fertility, mortality and migration.[25]

---

[24] Mathematical methods are based on growth rate formulas, as arithmetic, geometric or exponential growth rates; or on a logarithmic curve. Growth rates, whether arithmetic, geometric or exponential growth is assumed to be constant. The problem with such projections is the basic assumption that growth rate will remain constant, which makes long run projections uncertain and less accurate. Also, mathematical methods ignore information on annual birth and death rates and future migrations, assuming that the same overall population growth rate from the past will continue in the future.

[25] Donald Rowland, Demographic Methods and Concepts (USA: Oxford University Press, 2003), 439.

TABLE 5.4 Fiscal indicators in Montenegro, 2006–2018 (%)

Year	2006	2007	2008	2009	2010	2011	2012	2013	2014	2015	2016	2017	2018
Public spending/GDP	41.2	41.4	45.0	49.5	47.0	45.4	46.7	47.7	54.7	59.1	54.5	50.3	56.3
Consolidated spending/GDP	36.3	35.4	41.0	43.5	40.1	40.4	41.9	43.0	42.1	44.3	41.0	42.0	41.3
Primary revenues/GDP	39.7	42.0	41.5	39.3	36.6	34.7	35.4	37.0	39.1	36.3	37.6	36.4	37.8
Annual borrowing/GDP	1.1	0.4	0.3	8.6	7.2	7.2	10.1	9.9	15.5	22.8	16.4	14.3	24.1
Balance/GDP	3.4	6.6	0.6	-4.2	-3.5	-5.7	-6.5	-6.0	-3.0	-8.0	-3.4	-5.5	-3.4
Public debt/GDP	32.3	27.4	28.8	38.1	40.7	45.4	53.4	57.5	56.2	62.3	60.8	61.1	68.3
Foreign debt/GDP	23.2	17.2	15.5	23.4	29.2	32.6	40.7	42.6	45.2	53.5	50.6	51.5	59.8
Domestic debt/GDP	9.1	10.2	13.3	14.7	11.5	12.9	12.7	14.9	11.0	8.8	10.1	9.6	8.5
Capital budget/GDP	0.00	3.07	2.36	3.75	2.02	2.06	2.39	2.30	2.17	6.52	1.64	5.94	5.73

SOURCE: OWN ELABORATION BASED ON DATA FROM CENTRAL BANK OF MONTENEGRO AND MINISTRY OF FINANCE; HTTPS://CBCG.ME/ME/STATISTIKA_STATISTICKI-PODACI/FISKALNI-SEKTOR; HTTPS://MIF.GOV.ME/RUBRIKE/DRZAVNI-DUG/ (ACCESSED JUNE 15, 2019).

The data set which serves as a basis for projections are usually the most recent census. Projections are made for five-year population groups. To make projections of population in five-year periods, it is necessary to estimate three variables in the same time interval: the number of projected survivors, the total number of projected births and net migration.[26]

In order to estimate the number of projected survivors ($L^p_{x+n,x+2n}$), it is necessary to estimate the survival ratios for specific cohorts and multiply the population from previous periods in order to obtain future estimates. If survival ratios ($S_{x,x+n}$) are not available from abridged life tables, several steps have to be followed in order to estimate it. First, we have to estimate annual age-specific death rates ($M_{x,x+n}$) for each age group, defined as

$$M_{x,x+n} = \frac{D_{x,x+n}}{P_{x,x+n}} \cdot 1000$$

n – Number of years in the age interval (in this research n=5)
$D_{x,x+n}$ – Annual average of deaths during the year to persons aged x to $x+n$
$P_{x,x+n}$ – Mid-year population aged x to $x+n$

The next step is to estimate probability of dying between exact ages ($q_{x,x+n}$)

$$q_{x,x+n} = \frac{2 \cdot n \cdot M_{x,x+n}}{2 + n \cdot M_{x,x+n}} \quad [27]$$

The probability of surviving from one exact age to the next (px, x+n) is equal to:

$$p_{x,x+n} = 1 - q_{x,x+n}$$

---

26 Ibid, 285–293.
27 Probability of dying between exact ages is equal to:

$$q_{x,x+n} = \frac{n \cdot D_{x,x+n}}{P_{x,x+n} + 0.5 \cdot n \cdot D_{x,x+n}} = \frac{n \cdot D_{x,x+n}/P_{x,x+n}}{1 + 0.5 \cdot n \cdot D_{x,x+n}/P_{x,x+n}} = \frac{n \cdot M_{x,x+n}}{1 + 0.5 \cdot n \cdot M_{x,x+n}} = \frac{2 \cdot n \cdot M_{x,x+n}}{2 + n \cdot M_{x,x+n}}$$

The probability of dying is equal to the number of deaths divided by initial population. Adding half the deaths to the mid-year population provides an estimate of the size of the initial population.

Now we can estimate following indicators:
number of survivors at exact age x (l_{x+n})

$$l_{x+n} = l_x \cdot p_{x,x+n},$$

or

$$l_{x+n} = l_x - d_{x,\,x+n}$$

number of deaths between ages x and $x+n$ ($d_{x,\,x+n}$)

$$d_{x,x+n} = l_x \cdot q_{x,x+n}$$

or

$$d_{x,\,x+n} = l_x - l_{x+n}$$

Average number living between ages x and x+n ($L_{x,\,x+n}$)

$$L_{x,\,x+n} = \frac{n}{2} \cdot (l_x + l_{x+n})$$

Total population aged x and over (T_x)

$$T_x = \sum_{i-x}^{\infty} L_{i,i+n}$$

The final step is to estimate *survival ratios* ($S_{x,x+n}$), so we can estimate number of projected survivors for the next time period ($t+5$), multiplying specific cohort from period t with survival ratios for each cohort.

$$S_{x,x+n} = \frac{L_{x+n,\,x+2n}}{L_{x,\,x+n}}, \text{ therefore}$$

$$L^p_{x+n,x+2n} = S_{x,x+n} \cdot L_{x,x+n}$$

For an open-ended interval (85+), the survival ratio is equal to

$$S_x = \frac{T_{x+n}}{T_x}$$

Total number of projected births ($N^p_{x+n,x+2n}$) is equal to the sum of number of births to each specific age woman cohort ($B^p_{x+n,x+2n}$).

The number of births to each specific age woman cohort is estimated using *age-specific fertility rate* ($_nf_x$) defined as

$$f_{x,x+n} = \frac{B_{x,x+n}}{F_{x,x+n}} \cdot 1000$$

$B_{x,x+n}$ – Number of births in a year period to women aged x to x+5
$F_{x,x+n}$ – Mid-year population of women in aged x to x+5
The number of projected births to each specific age woman cohort is equal to the age specific fertility rates multiplied with number of specific age females from previous period.

$$B^p_{x+n,x+2n} = \frac{f_{x,x+n} \cdot F_{x,x+n}}{1000}$$

Net migration ($NM_{x,x+n}$) is defined as the difference between number of immigrants and number of emigrants in specific time period (five years).

$$NM_{x,x+n} = I_{x,x+n} + E_{x,x+n}$$

$I_{x,x+n}$ – Number of immigrants aged to x to x+5
$E_{x,x+n}$ – Number of emigrants aged to x to x+5
The projected specific age population group ($_nP^p_{x+n}$) is equal to:

$$P^p_{x+n,x+2n} = N^p_{x+n,x+2n} + L^p_{x+n,x+2n} + N^p_{x,x+n} \text{ if } x = 0, \text{ and}$$
$$P^p_{x+n,x+2n} = L^p_{x+n,x+2n} + N^p_{x,x+n} \text{ if } x > 4$$

The population of Montenegro was estimated up to 2091, applying the cohort components model. The basis for projections were 1991 census data (Table 5.5). The main reason for using 1991 census data instead of 2001[28] or 2011, although

---

28 Census in Montenegro was conducted in 2003, but near a year period provide appropriate insight on accuracy of projections.

TABLE 5.5 Population in Montenegro 1991–2091 (cohort model projections)

Year	Population	Annual growth rate %	Average annual increase	TFR	NRR	Male e0	Female e0	Annual net migration (incl. deaths)	Annual births	Annual deaths	Annual natural increase	CBR	CDR
1991	591,369	0.42	2,501	1.78	0.85	71.64	78.37	(1,200)	7,991	4,290	3,701	13.4	7.2
1996	603,875	0.09	541	1.78	0.85	71.74	78.42	(2,500)	7,990	4,949	3,041	13.2	8.2
2001	606,582	0.24	1,455	1.78	0.85	71.83	78.46	(1,000)	8,021	5,566	2,455	13.1	9.1
2006	613,857	0.22	1,376	1.78	0.85	71.93	78.50	(500)	8,065	6,189	1,876	13.1	10.0
2011	620,737	0.16	1,022	1.78	0.85	72.02	78.54	(200)	7,819	6,596	1,222	12.5	10.6
2016	625,849	0.05	294	1.78	0.85	72.11	78.58	(100)	7,353	6,959	394	11.7	11.1
2021	627,319	-0.06	-393	1.78	0.85	72.20	78.62	(50)	6,972	7,315	-343	11.1	11.7
2026	625,356	-0.14	-881	1.78	0.85	72.28	78.66	0	6,788	7,670	-881	10.9	12.3
2031	620,951	-0.22	-1,383	1.78	0.85	72.37	78.70	0	6,717	8,100	-1,383	10.9	13.1
2036	614,034	-0.30	-1,826	1.78	0.85	72.45	78.74	0	6,601	8,427	-1,826	10.8	13.8
2041	604,901	-0.37	-2,245	1.78	0.85	72.53	78.77	0	6,385	8,630	-2,245	10.7	14.4
2046	593,675	-0.44	-2,599	1.78	0.85	72.61	78.81	0	6,129	8,728	-2,599	10.4	14.9
2051	580,680	-0.50	-2,849	1.78	0.85	72.69	78.84	0	5,912	8,762	-2,849	10.3	15.3
2056	566,434	-0.53	-2,996	1.78	0.85	72.76	78.88	0	5,756	8,752	-2,996	10.3	15.7
2061	551,453	-0.56	-3,043	1.78	0.85	72.84	78.91	0	5,625	8,668	-3,043	10.3	15.9
2066	536,238	-0.57	-3,005	1.78	0.85	72.91	78.94	0	5,478	8,483	-3,005	10.4	16.0
2071	521,215	-0.56	-2,911	1.78	0.85	72.98	78.98	0	5,307	8,218	-2,911	10.3	16.0
2076	506,660	-0.56	-2,806	1.78	0.85	73.05	79.01	0	5,133	7,939	-2,806	10.3	15.9
2081	492,631	-0.57	-2,766	1.78	0.85	73.12	79.04	0	4,975	7,741	-2,766	10.2	15.9
2086	478,802	-0.58	-2,725	1.78	0.85	73.18	79.07	0	4,838	7,563	-2,725	10.2	16.0
2091	465,176												

SOURCE: OWN ELABORATION.

these were available, was to verify the results by comparing projected and actual figures for 2001 and 2011. Fundamental assumptions for projections include:

> specific age fertility rate and specific age death rate were assumed to be constant during [the 21st] century. Absolute specific age net migrations were assumed to be negative and fixed until 2026 (while relative specific age net migration (net migration rate) decreased constantly due to increasing specific age population), and then are equal to zero. Constant absolute specific age net migration, under growing population, provides declining relative specific age net-migration rates.[29]

Negative net migration rates were evidenced in Montenegro in periods of economic and political instability, particularly at the end of the 20th century. It is natural to assume that such migration trends will continue as long as instability exists, with declining trends strongly correlated with increasing stability. Similar experience was evidenced in other transition countries. Korcelli's research has shown that: "(...) since 1989, as a consequence of rapid political and economic change toward democracy and market economy, the level of emigration from Poland has decreased".[30] Zero rates of net migration since 2026 rely on the optimistic scenario of economic and institutional development in Montenegro, despite the fact that demographic components will be more of an obstacle than the source of such trends. If, instead of assuming zero a specific net migration rate starting in 2026, we assume negative rates to continue, the demographic structure of a population will shift so that unproductive groups dominate even more. At the beginning of the 21st century, Montenegro is approaching a post-transition demographic era (Figure 5.2), characterized by almost an equal crude birth rate and crude death rate, both slightly higher than per thousand people. The post-transition period should

---

29 An alternative approach to define the assumptions for net-migration is to assume non-fixed absolute specific net-migration. But as international migration statistics for the last decade in Montenegro are not entirely reliable, there is a possibility that absolute specific net-migrations are higher than reported. If that is so, then the assumption that absolute net-migration will change may disrupt the accuracy of the projections, as the present underreported figures will cause underestimated projected figures. As a more accurate approach, we decided to use fixed absolute specific net-migration rates, which will, under population growth, result in declining specific net-migration rates.

30 Piotr Korcelli, "International Migrations in Europe: Polish Perspectives for the 1990s", The International Migration Review 26, no.2 (1992): 293.

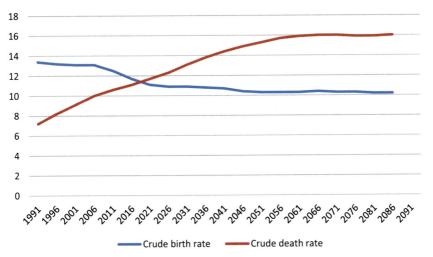

FIGURE 5.2 Demographic transition in Montenegro
SOURCE: MONSTAT (1991–2011); HTTP://MONSTAT.ORG/ENG/PAGE.PHP?ID=52&PAGEID=52 (ACCESSED JUNE 15, 2019). OWN ELABORATION (2021–2091), COHORT MODEL PROJECTIONS.

end in the third decade, when the "future declining" period starts with a constant decline in population, low fertility rates and aging.[31]

5.2   *Age Structure of Population in Montenegro*

The age structure of a Montenegrin population in 1991 (2001) was described as 'mature'; however, the projection for 2091 can be defined as 'old' (Figure 5.3). 'Mature' populations comprise those "transitional between young and old types of profile but still with a relatively high representation of children";[32] whereas, 'old' describes a "rectangular age profile with similar numbers or percentages in each age group up to those where mortality is high. An 'old' population is indicative of low birth and death rates".[33] The demographic transition from 'mature' to 'old' denotes aging population, which results from fertility decline, followed by low death rates of the older population.[34]

---

31   Maja Baćović, Demographic Changes in Transition Countries: Opportunity or Obstacle for Economic Growth? Case of Montenegro, 36–37.
32   Donald Rowland, Demographic Methods and Concepts (USA: Oxford University Press, 2003), 99.
33   Ibid.
34   Maja Baćović, Demographic Changes in Transition Countries: Opportunity or Obstacle for Economic Growth? Case of Montenegro, 36.

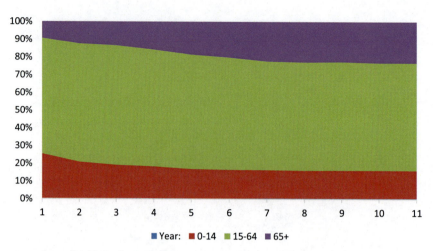

FIGURE 5.3 Population by age groups: 1991–2091
SOURCE: MONSTAT (1991–2011); HTTP://MONSTAT.ORG/ENG/PAGE.PHP?ID=52&PAGEID=52 (ACCESSED JUNE 15, 2019). OWN ELABORATION (2021–2091), COHORT MODEL PROJECTIONS.

As shown in Figure 5.3, the share of the population aged 65 and more years will increase over the projected time period, while the share of the population younger than 14 years and aged 15–64 years will decline, therefore leading to further aging of the Montenegrin population.

5.3 *Dependency Ratio*

As Rowland explains, dependency ratios provide summary measures of age composition, with particular reference to relative number of 'unproductive-dependents' and 'productive-supporters' groups. The ratios are based on a division of the age range into three broad groupings: children (0–14), working age (15–64) and elderly (65 and over). The child dependency ratio represents the number of children per hundred working age persons. The aged dependency ratio is the number of elderly people per hundred working age people. The total dependency ratio represents number of dependents (sum of children and elderly) per hundred working age people.[35]

The total dependency ratio in Montenegro (Table 5.6) is expected to grow from 52.7 (1991) to 62.6 (2051) and then to 64.0 (2091). Growth in the total dependency ratio is mostly influenced by an increase in the old-age dependency ratio,

---

35 Donald Rowland, Demographic Methods and Concepts, 88.

TABLE 5.6   Dependency ratio in Montenegro 1991–2091 (cohort model projections)

Year	1991	2001	2011	2021	2031	2041	2051	2061	2071	2081	2091
Total	52.7	49.5	48.0	51.4	54.5	57.5	62.6	63.1	62.7	64.3	64.0
Child	38.6	30.9	28.0	27.5	25.8	25.7	26.3	25.9	25.9	26.1	25.9
Old	14.2	18.6	19.9	23.9	28.7	31.8	36.3	37.2	36.9	38.2	38.1

SOURCE: OWN ELABORATION.

which is expected to increase from 14.2 (1991) to 38.1 (2091). The child dependency ratio will probably decrease due to the low fertility rate and decrease in births over time.

6   Forecasting Revenues and Expenditures of the Pension Fund in Montenegro from Year 2019 to 2056

6.1   Methodology

Applying the arithmetic approach, using as a basis data from year 2006 to 2018, we estimated expenditures and revenues of the pension fund in Montenegro from year 2019 to 2056.

Expenditures of pension fund are estimated as presented in section 3 (Equation 2.).

The number of pensioners (R_t) is estimated as:

$$R_t = P_{60+,t} \cdot average\left(\frac{R_{t,\,2006-2018}}{P_{60+,\,2006-2018}}\right),$$

where $P_{60+,t}$ is the population aged 60+ in year t (t=2019–2056), value estimated by applying population projections cohort method (Annex: Table 9 and 10), and $average\left(\frac{R_{t,\,2006-2018}}{P_{60+,\,2006-2018}}\right)$ is the average value of the ratio of the number of pensioners and the population aged 60+ on an annual level, from 2006 to 2018.

The average pension in year t ($P_{avg,t}$) is estimated as:

$$P_{avg,t} = P_{avg,t-1} \cdot \delta,$$

where $P_{avg,t-1}$ is the average pension in year t-1, while δ is the annual average pension growth rate, value set exogenously.

Revenues of the pension fund are estimated as:

$$PR_t = L_t \cdot p_t \cdot W_{avg,t} \cdot \epsilon$$

where PR_t is the revenue of the pension fund in period t, L_t – the number of employees paying pension contributions in period t, p_t – the pension contribution rate, $W_{avg,t}$ the average gross wage in period t, which is also the basis for calculating future pension contributions, and ϵ is the percentage of the contribution actually paid, set as 0.7, as empirically evidenced based on empirical data from 2006–2018.

The number of employees (L_t) is estimated as:

$$L_t = P_{15+,t} \cdot e \cdot \mu,$$

where $P_{15+,t}$ is the population aged 15+ in year t (t=2019–2056), value estimated applying population projections cohort method (Appendix Table 5.9 and Table 5.10), e is the number of employees per population aged 15–64, and μ is annual growth rate in the number of employees, set exogenously.

The average gross wage in year t ($W_{avg,t}$) is estimated as:

$$W_{avg,t} = W_{avg,t-1} \cdot \rho,$$

where $W_{avg,t-1}$ is the average pension in year t-1, while ρ is the annual average gross wage growth rate, value set exogenously.

As values of δ, μ, ρ were set exogenously, and p_t is assumed to be constant over the entire period (20.5%), the impact of population aging will be clearly visible. Also, an important assumption is a zero inflation rate in the period from 2019 to 2056, so growth in gross wages and pensions is assumed in real terms, assuming positive real growth rates of the economy.

6.2 Estimation Results

Changing the assumptions for δ, μ, ρ, we estimated two scenarios. Population data in both scenarios are identical, as extracted from cohort model population projections. Data on yearly levels were estimates applying absolute changes in population per year, estimated as an average annual value in five years intervals, as follows:

$$P_t = P_{t-1} \frac{P_{t+5} - P_t}{5}$$

In scenario 1, we assumed that $\delta = 0.125\%$,[36] $\mu = 0.5\%$ and $\rho = 0.5\%$. Using data on population from population projections, and applying a constant pension contribution rate of 20.5%, we may see that expenditures of the pension fund will be higher than revenues over the entire period, despite positive employment and wage real growth rates, as presented in Table 5.7.

As shown in Figure 5.4, the ratio of expenditures to revenues will decline slightly over the years, but the pension fund will not be sustainable and will need transfers from the budget.

The ratio of the number of employees to the number of pensioners is growing from year 2019 to 2056, as the annual growth rate of the number of employees is higher than the growth rate of the number of pensioners (Figure 5.5).

In scenario 2, we assumed that $\delta = 0.075\%$,[37] $\mu = 0.3\%$ and $\rho = 0.3\%$. Data on population and the pension contribution rate of 20.5% have equal value as in scenario 1. Results are presented in Table 5.8. and Figures 5.6. and 5.7.

The ratio of the number of employees per number of pensioners in scenario 2 even declines until 2040, as employment growth rate is lower than the pension growth rate (Figure 5.7), while, as presented in Figure 5.6, the ratio of expenditures to revenues will decline over time but will be higher than the one calculated in scenario 1.

From these two different forecasting scenarios, we may see that the financial balance of the pension fund is sensitive to both employment and the growth rate of the number of pensioners, but also to the average gross wage growth rate. This leads to the conclusion that, unless employment/wages growth is higher than the growth in the number of pensioners, imbalances in the pension fund may even increase in the future.

---

[36] 25% of real wages growth.
[37] 25% of real wages growth.

TABLE 5.7 Forecasting revenues and expenditures of the pension system in Montenegro, 2019–2056 (scenario 1)

Year	Population 15+	Number of employees/ population 15+	Number of employees	Average monthly gross wage	Contributions for pension fund-contribution rate – 20.5% – annual, million €	Number of pensioners
	1	2*	3=1*2/100	4*	5= 3*4*12*0.205*0.7*	6=7*8
2006	497.357	0.30	150,800	433.00	120.47	93,477
2016	508.779	0.35	177,473	751.00	245.91	108,478
2026	516.708	0.42	217,069	797.18	319.26	129,876
2036	513.479	0.47	241,386	837.95	373.19	139,085
2046	496.902	0.52	258,438	880.80	419.98	147,672
2056	475.910	0.57	271,316	925.85	463.46	145,013

Notes: 2*– growth rate of 0.5% per year, 4* – growth rate of 0.5% per year, 5* – actual collection rate is 0.7; 9* – growth rate of 0.125% per year.
SOURCE: OWN ELABORATION (SEE DATA IN ANNEX – TABLE 5.9).

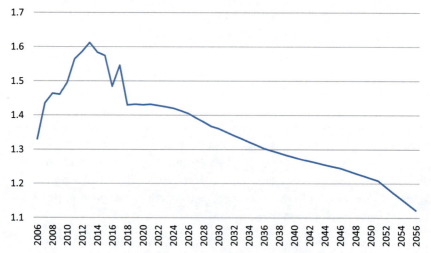

FIGURE 5.4 Ratio of expenditures and revenues of the pension fund (scenario 1)
SOURCE: CENTRAL BANK OF MONTENEGRO (2006–2018), HTTPS://WWW.CBCG.ME/EN/STATISTICS/STATISTICAL/FISCAL-DEVELOPMENTS (ACCESSED JUNE 25, 2019). OWN ELABORATION (2019–2056), SCENARIO 1.

Population 60+	Number of pensioners/ population 60+	Average monthly pension	Pension fund expenditures, million €	Expenditures/ revenues ratio	Number of employees/ number of pensioners ratio
7	8	9*	10= 6*9*12	11= 10/5	12=3/6
107,049	0.87	142.78	160.16	1.329	1.613
125,858	0.86	280.40	365.01	1.484	1.636
145,888	0.89	287.78	448.51	1.405	1.671
156,446	0.89	291.40	486.35	1.303	1.736
166,180	0.89	295.06	522.87	1.245	1.750
163,202	0.89	298.77	519.91	1.122	1.871

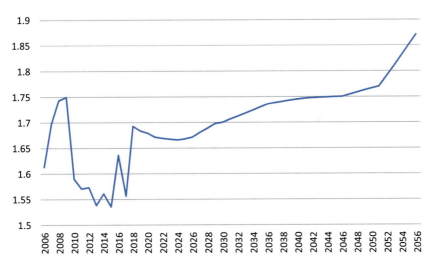

FIGURE 5.5 Number of employees per number of pensioners (scenario 1)
SOURCE: CENTRAL BANK OF MONTENEGRO (2006–2018), HTTPS://WWW.CBCG.ME/EN/STATISTICS/STATISTICAL/FISCAL-DEVELOPMENTS (ACCESSED JUNE 25, 2019). OWN ELABORATION (2019–2056), SCENARIO 1.

TABLE 5.8 Forecasting revenues and expenditures of the pension system in Montenegro, 2019–2056 (scenario 2)

Year	Population 15+	Number of employees/ population 15+	Number of employees	Average monthly gross wage	Contributions for pension fund- contribution rate – 20.5% – annual, million €	Number of pensioners
	1	2*	3=1*2/100	4*	5= 3*4*12*0.205*0.7*	6=7*8
2006	497,357	0.30	150,800	433.00	120.47	93,477
2016	508,779	0.35	177,473	751.00	245.91	108,478
2026	516,708	0.40	208,801	784.58	302.25	129,876
2036	513,479	0.43	222,901	808.44	332.47	139,085
2046	496,902	0.46	230,612	833.02	354.43	147,672
2056	475,910	0.49	235,147	858.35	372.39	145,013

Notes: 2*– growth rate of 0.3% per year, 4* – growth rate of 0.3% per year, 5* – actual collection rate is 0.7; 9* – growth rate of 0.075% per year.
SOURCE: OWN ELABORATION.

FIGURE 5.6 Ratio of expenditures and revenues of the pension fund (scenario 2)
SOURCE: CENTRAL BANK OF MONTENEGRO (2006–2018); HTTPS://WWW .CBCG.ME/EN/STATISTICS/STATISTICAL/FISCAL-DEVELOPMENTS (ACCESSED JUNE 25, 2019). OWN ELABORATION (2019–2056), SCENARIO 2.

Population 60+	Number of pensioners/ population 60+	Average monthly pension	Pension fund expenditures, million €	Expenditures/ revenues ratio	Number of employees/ number of pensioners ratio
7	8	9*	10=6*9*12	11=10/5	12=3/6
107,049	0.87	142.78	160.16	1.329	1.613
125,858	0.86	280.40	365.01	1.484	1.636
145,888	0.89	286.63	446.72	1.478	1.608
156,446	0.89	288.79	482.00	1.450	1.603
166,180	0.89	290.96	515.61	1.455	1.562
163,202	0.89	293.15	510.13	1.370	1.622

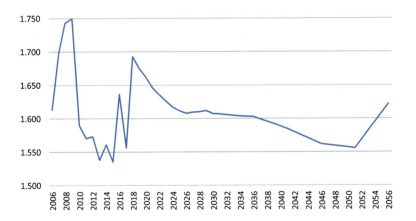

FIGURE 5.7 Number of employees per number of pensioners (scenario 2)
SOURCE: OWN ELABORATION (2019–2056), SCENARIO 2 BASED ON CENTRAL BANK OF MONTENEGRO (2006–2018), HTTPS.//WWW.CBCG.ME/EN/STATISTICS/STATISTICAL/FISCAL-DEVELOPMENTS (ACCESSED JUNE 25, 2019).

7 Conclusion

The pension system in Montenegro has been mainly organized in the form of a mandatory pay-as-you-go system. Although the institutional opportunity is in place for a privately funded, capitalized system, less than 2% of currently employed persons use it as a means of savings. A mandatory capitalized system, although defined by law, has not yet been introduced. The pay-as-you go pension system in Montenegro is a mature one, meaning that pension insurance contributions are not sufficient to finance the expenditures of the pension system. Therefore, key characteristics of the pension system in Montenegro are an unsatisfactory ratio between the number of employees and the number of pensioners, as well as insufficient funding from paid contributions for mandatory pension and disability insurance, which leads to government transfers, although these have been declining. There is also an aging population, making the issue even more important, as the population aged 60+ will gradually increase in the coming decades, as well as the working age population, although by slower rate, leading to growth in the old-age dependency ratio, which estimated to reach 38.1 in 2091 (14.2 in 1991).

Although two comprehensive reform packages were implemented in Montenegro, in 2003 and 2010, mostly directed at change in the minimum retirement age, the pension adjustment formula and early retirement criteria, and despite significant improvements of the pension system in terms of its financial sustainability, further work should be done in the future. All reform measures aimed to provide the possibility of faster growth in pension fund revenues than expenditures, which would make the pension fund more financially sustainable and eventually provide the opportunity to further reduce the pension contribution rate, encouraging investment and further productivity and income growth.

In their policy notes for 2017, the World Bank's team recommended following measures: introduction of the wage valorization of points and CPI indexation of pensions; tightening early retirement policy to prolong labor market, narrowing the eligibility to extended service pensions to those working in workplaces that include conditions with long-lasting impact on health; abstaining from ad-hoc interventions in the pension system.[38]

In its report on the early retirement system, the World Bank recommended the following measures: limiting early retirement for long service and revision of other early retirement routes, revision of the list of occupations covered by

---

[38] The World Bank, Montenegro Policy Notes 2017 (Washington, DC, 2017).

early retirement schemes, transparent financing of early retirement, individual prevention measures applied to workers in special and hazardous jobs, and to develop public information activities.[39]

Other than direct instruments that can be applied to reform the pension system, such as those suggested by the World Bank, other economic policy instruments may have positive indirect effects on the pension system, especially those applied in order to encourage growth in employment, productivity and wages. These will further lead to growth in pension fund revenues and a more financially sustainable pension system, but also to growth of the amount of average pensions, which will improve the standard of living of the elderly population.

---

[39] World Bank Group, "Options for Reforming Early Retirement System for Special and Hazardous Occupations in Montenegro", 2017, https://documents1.worldbank.org/curated/en/983131503425997272/pdf/117099-REVISED132p-Montenegro-report-revision-ENG-26-06-17-FINAL-CLEAN-All-authors-v-6.pdf (accessed June 25, 2019).

8 Appendix

TABLE 5.9 Forecasting revenues and expenditures of the pension system in Montenegro, 2019–2056 (scenario 1)

Year	Population 15+	Number of employees/ population 15+	Number of employees	Average monthly gross wage	Contributions for pension fund- contribution rate – 20.5% – annual, million €	Number of pensioners
	1	2*	3=1*2/100	4*	5=3*4*12*0.205*0.7*	6=7*8
2006	497357	0.30	150800	433.00	120.47	93477
2007	498515	0.31	156408	497.00	143.42	92168
2008	499673	0.33	166221	609.00	186.77	95367
2009	500831	0.34	169859	643.00	201.51	97088
2010	501989	0.31	157679	715.00	208.01	99196
2011	503148	0.32	162450	722.00	216.40	103439
2012	504274	0.33	167484	727.00	224.65	106477
2013	505400	0.33	167173	726.00	223.92	108689
2014	506526	0.34	171158	723.00	228.31	109670
2015	507652	0.34	172517	725.00	230.76	112362
2016	508779	0.35	177473	751.00	245.91	108478
2017	509698	0.35	177627	765.00	250.71	114140
2018	510617	0.38	194085	766.00	274.29	114676
2019	511536	0.39	196992	769.83	279.79	117020
2020	512455	0.39	199908	773.68	285.36	119062
2021	513375	0.40	202834	777.55	290.98	121379
2022	514041	0.40	205667	781.44	296.52	123233
2023	514707	0.41	208507	785.34	302.12	125082
2024	515373	0.41	211354	789.27	307.77	126887
2025	516039	0.42	214207	793.22	313.49	128438
2026	516708	0.42	217069	797.18	319.26	129876
2027	516826	0.43	219702	801.17	324.75	130741
2028	516944	0.43	222337	805.17	330.29	131676
2029	517062	0.44	224973	809.20	335.88	132526
2030	517180	0.44	227611	813.25	341.52	133891
2031	517302	0.45	230250	817.31	347.20	134940
2032	516538	0.45	232493	821.40	352.34	135811
2033	515774	0.46	234728	825.50	357.50	136651

Population 60+	Number of pensioners/ population 60+	Average monthly pension	Pension fund expenditures, million €	Expenditures/ revenues ratio	Number of employees/ number of pensioners ratio
7	8	9*	10=6*9*12	11=10/5	12=3/6
107049	0.87	142.78	160.16	1.329	1.613
108666	0.85	186.10	205.83	1.435	1.697
110283	0.86	238.83	273.32	1.463	1.743
111900	0.87	252.55	294.23	1.460	1.750
113517	0.87	261.36	311.11	1.496	1.590
115136	0.90	272.75	338.56	1.565	1.570
117280	0.91	278.85	356.29	1.586	1.573
119424	0.91	276.71	360.90	1.612	1.538
121568	0.90	274.76	361.60	1.584	1.561
123712	0.91	269.37	363.20	1.574	1.535
125858	0.86	280.40	365.01	1.484	1.636
128045	0.89	282.90	387.48	1.546	1.556
130232	0.88	284.92	392.08	1.429	1.692
132419	0.88	285.28	400.60	1.432	1.683
134606	0.88	285.63	408.10	1.430	1.679
136793	0.89	285.99	416.56	1.432	1.671
138612	0.89	286.35	423.45	1.428	1.669
140431	0.89	286.71	430.34	1.424	1.667
142250	0.89	287.06	437.09	1.420	1.666
144069	0.89	287.42	442.99	1.413	1.668
145888	0.89	287.78	448.51	1.405	1.671
147112	0.89	288.14	452.06	1.392	1.680
148336	0.89	288.50	455.86	1.380	1.689
149560	0.89	288.86	459.38	1.368	1.698
150784	0.89	289.22	464.69	1.361	1.700
152012	0.89	289.58	468.92	1.351	1.706
152898	0.89	289.95	472.54	1.341	1.712
153784	0.89	290.31	476.05	1.332	1.718

TABLE 5.9 Forecasting revenues and expenditures of the pension system in Montenegro, 2019–2056 (scenario 1) *(cont.)*

Year	Population 15+	Number of employees/ population 15+	Number of employees	Average monthly gross wage	Contributions for pension fund- contribution rate – 20.5% – annual, million €	Number of pensioners
	1	2*	3=1*2/100	4*	5=3*4*12*0.205*0.7*	6=7*8
2034	515010	0.46	236955	829.63	362.70	137487
2035	514246	0.47	239175	833.78	367.93	138294
2036	513479	0.47	241386	837.95	373.19	139085
2037	512015	0.48	243258	842.14	377.96	139966
2038	510551	0.48	245115	846.35	382.75	140828
2039	509087	0.49	246958	850.58	387.56	141694
2040	507623	0.49	248785	854.83	392.38	142571
2041	506157	0.50	250598	859.11	397.21	143469
2042	504307	0.50	252204	863.40	401.76	144305
2043	502457	0.51	253791	867.72	406.31	145162
2044	500607	0.51	255359	872.06	410.86	145997
2045	498757	0.52	256909	876.42	415.42	146837
2046	496902	0.52	258438	880.80	419.98	147672
2047	494879	0.53	259861	885.21	424.41	148125
2048	492856	0.53	261263	889.63	428.83	148575
2049	490833	0.54	262644	894.08	433.25	149023
2050	488810	0.54	264006	898.55	437.68	149470
2051	486784	0.55	265345	903.04	442.10	149922
2052	484610	0.55	266583	907.56	446.38	148938
2053	482436	0.56	267800	912.10	450.66	147956
2054	480262	0.56	268994	916.66	454.93	146975
2055	478088	0.57	270167	921.24	459.20	145996
2056	475910	0.57	271316	925.85	463.46	145013

Notes: 2*– growth rate of 0.5% per year, 4* – growth rate of 0.5% per year, 5* – actual collection rate is 0.7; 9* – growth rate of 0.125% per year.
SOURCE: OWN ELABORATION.

Population 60+	Number of pensioners/ population 60+	Average monthly pension	Pension fund expenditures, million €	Expenditures/ revenues ratio	Number of employees/ number of pensioners ratio
7	8	9*	10=6*9*12	11=10/5	12=3/6
154670	0.89	290.67	479.56	1.322	1.723
155556	0.89	291.04	482.98	1.313	1.729
156446	0.89	291.40	486.35	1.303	1.736
157459	0.89	291.76	490.04	1.297	1.738
158472	0.89	292.13	493.68	1.290	1.741
159485	0.89	292.49	497.33	1.283	1.743
160498	0.89	292.86	501.04	1.277	1.745
161514	0.89	293.23	504.82	1.271	1.747
162447	0.89	293.59	508.40	1.265	1.748
163380	0.89	293.96	512.06	1.260	1.748
164313	0.89	294.33	515.65	1.255	1.749
165246	0.89	294.69	519.26	1.250	1.750
166180	0.89	295.06	522.87	1.245	1.750
166690	0.89	295.43	525.13	1.237	1.754
167200	0.89	295.80	527.38	1.230	1.758
167710	0.89	296.17	529.63	1.222	1.762
168220	0.89	296.54	531.89	1.215	1.766
168735	0.89	296.91	534.16	1.208	1.770
167629	0.89	297.28	531.32	1.190	1.790
166523	0.89	297.65	528.47	1.173	1.810
165417	0.89	298.03	525.63	1.155	1.830
164311	0.89	298.40	522.78	1.138	1.851
163202	0.89	298.77	519.91	1.122	1.871

TABLE 5.10 Forecasting revenues and expenditures of the pension system in Montenegro, 2019–2056 (scenario 2)

Year	Population 15+	Number of employees/ population 15+	Number of employees	Average monthly gross wage	Contributions for pension fund- contribution rate – 20.5% – annual, million €	Number of pensioners
	1	2*	3=1*2/100	4*	5= 3*4*12*0.205*0.7*	6=7*8
2006	497357	0.30	150800	433.00	120.47	93477
2007	498515	0.31	156408	497.00	143.42	92168
2008	499673	0.33	166221	609.00	186.77	95367
2009	500831	0.34	169859	643.00	201.51	97088
2010	501989	0.31	157679	715.00	208.01	99196
2011	503148	0.32	162450	722.00	216.40	103439
2012	504274	0.33	167484	727.00	224.65	106477
2013	505400	0.33	167173	726.00	223.92	108689
2014	506526	0.34	171158	723.00	228.31	109670
2015	507652	0.34	172517	725.00	230.76	112362
2016	508779	0.35	177473	751.00	245.91	108478
2017	509698	0.35	177627	765.00	250.71	114140
2018	510617	0.38	194085	766.00	274.29	114676
2019	511536	0.38	195969	768.30	277.79	117020
2020	512455	0.39	197858	770.60	281.31	119062
2021	513375	0.39	199754	772.91	284.85	121379
2022	514041	0.39	201555	775.23	288.29	123233
2023	514707	0.40	203360	777.56	291.74	125082
2024	515373	0.40	205169	779.89	295.22	126887
2025	516039	0.40	206983	782.23	298.72	128438
2026	516708	0.40	208801	784.58	302.25	129876
2027	516826	0.41	210400	786.93	305.48	130741
2028	516944	0.41	211998	789.29	308.72	131676
2029	517062	0.41	213598	791.66	311.98	132526
2030	517180	0.42	215198	794.04	315.26	133891
2031	517302	0.42	216801	796.42	318.56	134940
2032	516538	0.42	218030	798.81	321.33	135811
2033	515774	0.43	219255	801.20	324.11	136651
2034	515010	0.43	220475	803.61	326.89	137487

Population 60+	Number of pensioners/ population 60+	Average monthly pension	Pension fund expenditures, million €	Expenditures/ revenues ratio	Number of employees/ number of pensioners ratio
7	8	9*	10=6*9*12	11=10/5	12=3/6
107049	0.87	142.78	160.16	1.329	1.613
108666	0.85	186.10	205.83	1.435	1.697
110283	0.86	238.83	273.32	1.463	1.743
111900	0.87	252.55	294.23	1.460	1.750
113517	0.87	261.36	311.11	1.496	1.590
115136	0.90	272.75	338.56	1.565	1.570
117280	0.91	278.85	356.29	1.586	1.573
119424	0.91	276.71	360.90	1.612	1.538
121568	0.90	274.76	361.60	1.584	1.561
123712	0.91	269.37	363.20	1.574	1.535
125858	0.86	280.40	365.01	1.484	1.636
128045	0.89	282.90	387.48	1.546	1.556
130232	0.88	284.92	392.08	1.429	1.692
132419	0.88	285.13	400.40	1.441	1.675
134606	0.88	285.35	407.69	1.449	1.662
136793	0.89	285.56	415.93	1.460	1.646
138612	0.89	285.78	422.61	1.466	1.636
140431	0.89	285.99	429.27	1.471	1.626
142250	0.89	286.20	435.79	1.476	1.617
144069	0.89	286.42	441.45	1.478	1.612
145888	0.89	286.63	446.72	1.478	1.608
147112	0.89	286.85	450.04	1.473	1.609
148336	0.89	287.06	453.59	1.469	1.610
149560	0.89	287.28	456.86	1.464	1.612
150784	0.89	287.49	461.92	1.465	1.607
152012	0.89	287.71	465.89	1.462	1.607
152898	0.89	287.93	469.24	1.460	1.605
153784	0.89	288.14	472.50	1.458	1.604
154670	0.89	288.36	475.75	1.455	1.604

TABLE 5.10 Forecasting revenues and expenditures of the pension system in Montenegro, 2019–2056 (scenario 2) (cont.)

Year	Population 15+	Number of employees/ population 15+	Number of employees	Average monthly gross wage	Contributions for pension fund-contribution rate – 20.5% – annual, million €	Number of pensioners
	1	2*	3=1*2/100	4*	5= 3*4*12*0.205*0.7*	6=7*8
2035	514246	0.43	221691	806.02	329.68	138294
2036	513479	0.43	222901	808.44	332.47	139085
2037	512015	0.44	223801	810.86	334.82	139966
2038	510551	0.44	224693	813.29	337.16	140828
2039	509087	0.44	225576	815.73	339.50	141694
2040	507623	0.45	226450	818.18	341.84	142571
2041	506157	0.45	227315	820.64	344.17	143469
2042	504307	0.45	227997	823.10	346.24	144305
2043	502457	0.46	228668	825.57	348.30	145162
2044	500607	0.46	229328	828.04	350.35	145997
2045	498757	0.46	229977	830.53	352.40	146837
2046	496902	0.46	230612	833.02	354.43	147672
2047	494879	0.47	231158	835.52	356.34	148125
2048	492856	0.47	231691	838.02	358.23	148575
2049	490833	0.47	232213	840.54	360.11	149023
2050	488810	0.48	232722	843.06	361.99	149470
2051	486784	0.48	233218	845.59	363.85	149922
2052	484610	0.48	233630	848.13	365.58	148938
2053	482436	0.49	234029	850.67	367.31	147956
2054	480262	0.49	234415	853.22	369.02	146975
2055	478088	0.49	234789	855.78	370.71	145996
2056	475910	0.49	235147	858.35	372.39	145013

Notes: 2*– growth rate of 0.3% per year, 4* – growth rate of 0.3% per year, 5* – actual collection rate is 0.7; 9* – growth rate of 0.075% per year.
SOURCE: OWN ELABORATION.

Population 60+	Number of pensioners/ population 60+	Average monthly pension	Pension fund expenditures, million €	Expenditures/ revenues ratio	Number of employees/ number of pensioners ratio
7	8	9*	10=6*9*12	11=10/5	12=3/6
155556	0.89	288.57	478.90	1.453	1.603
156446	0.89	288.79	482.00	1.450	1.603
157459	0.89	289.01	485.41	1.450	1.599
158472	0.89	289.22	488.77	1.450	1.596
159485	0.89	289.44	492.14	1.450	1.592
160498	0.89	289.66	495.56	1.450	1.588
161514	0.89	289.88	499.06	1.450	1.584
162447	0.89	290.09	502.34	1.451	1.580
163380	0.89	290.31	505.70	1.452	1.575
164313	0.89	290.53	509.00	1.453	1.571
165246	0.89	290.75	512.31	1.454	1.566
166180	0.89	290.96	515.61	1.455	1.562
166690	0.89	291.18	517.58	1.452	1.561
167200	0.89	291.40	519.54	1.450	1.559
167710	0.89	291.62	521.49	1.448	1.558
168220	0.89	291.84	523.45	1.446	1.557
168735	0.89	292.06	525.43	1.444	1.556
167629	0.89	292.28	522.37	1.429	1.569
166523	0.89	292.50	519.32	1.414	1.582
165417	0.89	292.71	516.26	1.399	1.595
164311	0.89	292.93	513.21	1.384	1.608
163202	0.89	293.15	510.13	1.370	1.622

Bibliography

Baćović, Maja. "Demographic Changes in Transition Countries: Opportunity or Obstacle for Economic Growth? Case of Montenegro". European Research Studies 11, no. 3–4 (2007): 31–44.

Baletic-Wertheimer, Alica. Stanovnistvo i razvoj. Zagreb: MATE, 1999.

Becker, Gary, Kevin Murphy, and Robert Tamura. "Human Capital, Fertility, and Economic Growth". The Journal of Political Economy 98, no. 5/2 (1990): 12–37.

Birdsall, Nancy. "Analytical Approaches to the Relationship of Population Growth and Development". Population and Development Review 3, no. 1/2 (1977): 63–102.

Bongaarts, John. "Population Aging and the Rising Cost of Public Pensions". Population and Development Review 30, no. 1 (2004): 1–23.

Chand, Sheetal, and Albert Laeger. Aging Population and Public Pension Schemes. Washington. DC: International Monetary Fund, 1996.

Cutler, David, James Poterba, Louise Sheiner, Lawrence Summers, and George Akerlof. 1990. "An Aging Society: Opportunity or Challenge". Brooking Papers on Economic Activity, no. 1 (1990): 1–73.

Korcelli, Piotr. "International Migrations in Europe: Polish Perspectives for the 1990s". The International Migration Review 26, no. 2 (1992): 292–304.

Mijanovic, Dragica, Mileva Brajuskovic, Dusko Vujacic, and Velibor Spalevic. "Causes and Effects of Aging of Montenegrin Population". Journal of Environmental Protection and Ecology 18, no. 3 (2017): 1249–1259.

Official Gazette of the Republic of Montenegro, no. 54/03, 39/04, 61/04, 79/04, 81/04, 78/06, 13/07, 14/07, 47/07, 79/08, 86/09, 14/10, 73/10, 78/10, 34/11, 40/11, 14/12, 66/12, 62/13, 08/15.

Rowland, Donald. Demographic Methods and Concepts. Oxford, Oxford University Press, 2003.

Schwarz, Anita, and Ufuk Guven. "Pensions". In Fiscal Policy and Economic Growth: Lessons for Eastern Europe and Central Asia. Washington, DC: The World Bank, 2007.

The World Bank. Montenegro Policy Notes. Washington, DC: 2017. p: 217–250.

United Nations. Department of Economic and Social Affairs. World Population Ageing 2017 Highlights. New York: United Nations, 2017.

Verbic, Miroslav, and Rok Spruk. "Aging Population and Public Pensions: Theory and Macroeconomic Evidence". Panoeconomicus 61, no. 3 (2014): 289–316.

Vlada Crne Gore. Savjet za unapredjenje poslovnog ambijenta, regulatornih i strukturnih reformi. Analiza penzijskog sistema. Podgorica: 2013.

Vogel, Edgar, Alexander Ludwig, and Axel Borsch-Supan. "Aging and Pension Reform: Extending the Retirement Age and Human Capital Formation". Journal of Pension Economics & Finance 16, no. 1 (2017): 81–107.

Von Weizsacker, Robert K. "Population Aging and Social Security: A Politico-Economic Model of State Pension Financing". Public Finance, 45(3) 1990: 491–509.

World Bank Group. Options for Reforming Early Retirement System for Special and Hazardous Occupations in Montenegro. Washington, DC: World Bank Group, 2017.

CHAPTER 6

The Public Health Care Sector in Post-transition Montenegro

Natalija Perišić

1   Introduction

Until the dissolution of the Socialist Federal Republic of Yugoslavia (SFRY) in 1992, as one of its constituent parts, Montenegro shared Yugoslav doctrines and practices of socialist self-management in general and also in the health care system. The federal organization of Yugoslavia introduced the guiding principles and rules for social policy and social security systems that the Republics were to follow, with the latter in charge of their subsequent development and adaptations. Therefore, the regulations in the health care sector were under the auspices of the Republics, resulting in certain differences among them. The differences were most frequently a mere reflection of their economic development, with Montenegro being one of least developed areas in the SFRY. Therefore, its progress towards the health care provision for the population was modest compared to other Republics of SFRY. However, in contrast to the underdeveloped health care sector in the period before the end of the Second World War,[1] the socialist Montenegro saw massive improvement in terms of health care indicators, the health care infrastructure and facilities, etc.[2] The characteristic of the health care system that was the most prominent and in common with other Republics of ex-Yugoslavia was the dominant position of public health care sector.[3]

---

1   Jovan Kujačić, Prilozi istoriji zdravstvene kulture Crne Gore do kraja 1918 godine (Beograd: Srpska akademija nauka, 1950), Petar - Niko - Miloš Miljanići, Crnogorski medicinski velikani (Podgorica: Društvo ljekara Crne Gore, 2003).
2   Jelena Džankić, "Political Transformations: Welfare States in Transition: A Long Drive Down a Tough Road", in Marija Stambolieva and Stefan Dehnert eds., Welfare States in Transition – 20 Years after the Yugoslav Welfare Model, (Sofia: Friedrich Ebert Foundation, 2011) 202–22.
3   Interestingly, in the Rule Book on Private Medical Practice (Pravilnik o privatnoj ljekarskoj praksi) of 1946 medical doctors were authorized to be engaged in private practice. Those employed with the public health care sector were authorized to that too, in which case private practice was considered their overtime work. Soon this was abolished, resulting in the exclusive existence of the public health care system.

Towards the end of the 1980s and the multiple crises of the Yugoslav socialist project, and then especially at the beginning of the 1990s, the public health care system grew increasingly ineffective. The socialist achievements in terms of improving the health status of the population and providing health care services that were universal and free of charge in the public sector started to fade.

Therefore, unsurprisingly, the post-socialist transition was accompanied by the population's aspirations and expectations of having more choices, i.e., multiple sources of higher quality health care provision. But the diversification remained rather modest and even more worrisome. It came with high expenses for the population with falling incomes, thus jeopardizing their living conditions.

The focus of this chapter is on the public health care sector, which is the dominant, albeit not the sole source of health care provision in post-socialist Montenegro. Its aim is to describe and analyze the reforms of the health care system in the last three decades, i.e., from 1989 to 2019.

The main research questions are structured around the following concerns: the access of the population to health care, the quality of public health care services and the financial sustainability of the public system along with its relationship to the private health care sector. The research methodology deployed is that of qualitative analysis of the regulations (laws and strategies that were guiding the reforms) and data (first of all statistical) relevant to the research questions.

The introductory section is followed by the theoretical framework, which scrutinizes the alternative roles states can take in regard to health care. The main part of the chapter presents and assesses the normative framework of the reforms and the consequences of its implementation. The conclusion points to the main challenges and dilemmas for the reforms of the public health care sector in the future.

2 Theoretical Framework – Roles of the State in the Field of Health Care

It is commonly accepted that "health is a strategic public good".[4] Therefore, the health care sector, its programs and measures, are subjected to economic

---

[4] André J. Van Rensburg and Piet Bracke, "Politics and Power: The Case of the Global Opioid Epidemic", in Hertie School of Governance, The Governance Report 2019 – Health Governance, Inequalities, Health Security, Patient-centred Care, Health Politics, Global Health (Oxford: Oxford University Press, 2019), 103.

rationality to a lesser extent than other forms of welfare state consumption[5] as well as governmental austerity plans and spending cuts. Encouraged and supported since 1948 by the World Health Organization,[6] among other stakeholders, state involvement in health care provision has been high on governments' agendas worldwide, with a view to providing comprehensive access to health care for their populations. This is not to say that there are no drawbacks. Namely, global inequalities have been on the rise, with high proportions of populations without any form of health security. This is a consequence of numerous factors, some in connection with the withdrawal of state from the health care sector and inadequate regulation of private provision.

The classic reasons in favor of state provision of the welfare to citizens are well known and elaborated in theory.[7] The arguments for state involvement in the provision of health care closely correspond to general ones for state services. As summarized by Martin Potuček, public provision is more effective than private in the following areas: "policy management, administrative regulation, rapidly mobilizing and using resources, ensuring the continuity and stability of services, preventing exploitation and discrimination, ensuring public safety, ensuring equity, maintaining social cohesion".[8] All of this is highly relevant for the provision of health care. The argument of economies of scale is frequently added:

> where there are social objectives to be met, and there are substantial economies of scale or effort in meeting them through a unified system, rather than through fragmented services (for example, the considerable economies achieved by national health services).[9]

Once again, there is a list of arguments against state provision, but this is beyond the scope of this article, given its focus on the activities states perform in the health care sector and not evaluation of them.

---

5 Pierre Pestieau, The Welfare State in the European Union – Economic and Social Perspectives (Oxford Oxford University Press, 2006), 116.
6 Meri Koivusalo and Eva Olila, "Globalna zdravstvena politika", in Nikola Jejts ed., Globalna socijalna politika (Beograd: Fakultet političkih nauka, 2017), 185.
7 Pol Spiker, Socijalna politika – teorija i praksa, Fakultet političkih nauka, (Beograd: Fakultet političkih nauka, 2013), 231–232.
8 Martin Potuček, "Policy Coordination: Government, Markets, and the Civic Sector", in Martin Potůček, Lance T. LeLoup, György Jenei, and László Váradi eds., Public Policy in Central and Eastern Europe: Theories, Methods, Practices, (Bratislava: NISPAcee, 2003), 84.
9 Pol Spiker, Socijalna politika – teorija i praksa, 231–232.

In his Social Policy: A Comparative Analysis of 1996, Michael Hill identified three roles states can play and currently do play in health care, that of
- regulator;
- funder/purchaser;
- provider/ planner.[10]

The regulating activities of the state reflect its capacity of creating a normative framework for health care. However, the state does not act solely or at least not independently from other stakeholders in the society in the performance of its role of regulator. Here, Hill explains that the regulatory role of the state in relation to the practice of medicine specifically dates back very early in history for the following reasons:

> if you kill someone when treating a disease, or if someone dies because you refrain from offering treatment or care that might save them, you may be deemed to be guilty of a crime, even perhaps a murder. Therefore, if individuals are offering services that purport to provide help for the sick they need some assurance that their honest mistakes will not normally bring retribution upon them. Conversely, the sick need help in distinguishing which of the practitioners offering services are likely to have something positive, or at least relatively safe, to offer.[11]

On the other hand, at least equally important, there were strong demands from the medical practitioners for protection of the profession by allowing them to govern the profession itself. And while in the past this 'withdrawal' of the state was motivated by its inexperience, today the illustration of the impact of professionals upon state action is again the profession of medical doctors (the so-called medical power).

However, the co-production of policies and regulations has been clearly on the agenda since the 1990s. Its impact on the role of the state as regulator has arguably resulted in more diversified approaches to the regulation of health care, allowing different voices to be heard, namely those of patients (users of services) and their organizations, medical professionals, etc.

The funding or purchasing activities of state cannot be explained without referring to the diverse funding schemes that exist in practice: comprehensive tax-funded schemes; tax-funded schemes involving elements of earmarked

---

10   The description of the roles that follows is that based on Hill's analysis. Not all authors have the same understandings of the roles mentioned.
11   Michael Hill, Social Policy: A Comparative Analysis (London: Prentice Hall 1996), 33–34.

taxation, often called health insurance; comprehensive insurance schemes; partial schemes involving public and private insurance plus elements of tax funding; and residual systems with some injections of tax funds and state-controlled insurance into broadly privately funded systems.[12]

In tax-funding schemes, states have the most straightforward funder/purchaser role. However, due to aspirations to offer universal health care coverage to citizens, states have assumed this role even where there is a scheme of public health insurance contributions. Consequently, public spending on health care is "the second most extensive branch of social spending"[13] globally. The existence of private health care arrangements does not preclude state funding, directly or indirectly. An example of the former is the policy design allowing private insurance companies to receive support from national health insurance funds. The latter type of cross-subsidy exists in the following situation: "if doctors are trained in public hospitals but can then practice in private ones the latter will secure the benefit of their expensive training".[14]

Finally, the providing and/or planning activities of state are related to its funding or purchasing activities, but in various ways. The state can be a funder and provider, neither a funder nor a provider, a funder but not a provider, and finally a provider but not a funder.[15] Thus, the state can provide health care either directly or indirectly. The main providers of health care services in societies are those from the public and private (either profit or non-profit) sectors.[16] Increasingly complex forms of health care provision have led governments to include the mechanisms for the control, monitoring and planning of health care. Planning of health care has come to the forefront of the political agenda, due to numerous uncertainties regarding health risks, jeopardized equity and increasing inequalities along with requirements for cost savings. The main threat to its planning activities is interference from political and economic demands, while the impact of user perspectives cannot be over-stated.

---

12   Ibid, 100–101.
13   Hanna Schwander, "Healthcare as Social Investment", in Hertie School of Governance, The Governance Report 2019 – Health Governance, Inequalities, Health Security, Patient-centred Care, Health Politics, Global Health (Oxford: Oxford University Press, 2019), 121.
14   Michael Hill, Social Policy: A Comparative Analysis (London: Prentice Hall, 1996), 102.
15   Ibid, 105–106.
16   Theodore Marmor, Claus Wendt, "Conceptual Frameworks for Comparing Healthcare Politics and Policy". Health Policy 107 (2012): 15.

3 Health Care Reforms in Post-Socialist Montenegro

As mentioned in the introduction, the pre-transition, socialist health care system in Montenegro was structured around public regulation, provision and planning of health care. The funding mechanisms were health care contributions in compliance with the Bismarckian principles of social insurance, complemented in 1981 with copayments of very modest amount to be paid under certain circumstances prescribed by the regulations.

Health care reforms in the transition period that are of relevance for this article were enacted and implemented based on five key laws. These are briefly presented and contextualized below.

"The Law on Health Care and Health Insurance", already enacted in 1990, unsurprisingly largely represented continuity with the socialist period, but also introduced certain changes. It provided for the establishment of health care facilities in public, social, mixed and private forms, with the public forms to be constituted on state, social and private property (Article 6). Health care facilities were to be established in the following forms: health centers, pharmacies, general hospitals, special hospitals, clinical hospitals, institutes for health care, medical institutes, and institutes and natural health resorts (Articles 66–75). Private health care facilities were allowed to be organized in any of the forms mentioned, with the addition of ambulances (general and special), laboratories, X-ray offices, ambulance-polyclinics and hospital health care facilities (Article 87). The organization of private and mixed health care facilities was prohibited in the forms of health care facilities for blood transfusion, human organ transplantation, emergency units and health care institutes (Article 87). The purported purpose of detailed regulations on the types of health care facilities in the public, private and mixed forms was to provide and maintain the public interest regarding the health of the population. Health care professionals employed in the public sector were prohibited from engagement in the private sector (Article 88).

Health contributions were retained as the main source of health care funding (via the Republic Fund for Health), along with co–payments and budgetary funds.

The health care package consisted of the rights to health care at the primary, polyclinic-specialist and stationary levels of health care, sick leave and compensation of travel costs incurred in connection with the exercise of the right to health care.[17]

---

17 Zakon o zdravstvenoj zaštiti i zdravstvenom osiguranju, Službeni list Crne Gore, 39/90.

The amendments to the law enacted in 1994 and 1995 introduced changes with a view to expanding the private provision of health care services. The regulations of 1994 on the establishment of healthcare facilities in any of the property forms resulted in rapid development of health care services provided at market prices, outside of the public health care system. The absence of regulations that would continue to prohibit health care professionals employed in the public sector from working in the private sector meant that virtually all health care professionals could be engaged in the private sector, without any barriers.[18] This was followed by allowing health care professionals employed in the public sector to take on an additional engagement in the private sector per regulations of 1995. The health care package was slightly redesigned in terms of tightened eligibility criteria.[19]

The two laws that followed in 2004 represented a more prominent shift compared to the previous period. They were prepared in consultation with experts from the World Bank and within the scope of the then governing global agenda of the World Health Organization. The reflections were strong, among other things, regarding the regulation of the organization of the public health care sector, with a view to delineating clearly the divisions between the levels of care and the introduction of changed funding mechanisms.

"The Law on Health Care" of 2004 detailed the organization and provision of services at the levels of primary, secondary and tertiary health care. It clearly positioned the primary health care as the gatekeeper by prescribing that the secondary and tertiary levels of health care complement and support the primary level (Article 35). It also changed the operation of primary health care in terms of introducing the concept of chosen doctors. The complementary process of the introduction of capitation at the level of primary health care started already in 2005, to be completed in 2008. The types of health care facilities regulated by the law were slightly and not substantially changed compared to the previous regulation. The law enabled both public and private sectors to establish health care facilities and again listed exceptions for the private ones. The restrictions on private health care facilities remained almost the same as they had been, with the addition of a ban on engagement of the private sector in public health activities and founding clinics (Article 51). For the first time, the law enabled public health care facilities to rent their premises and equipment to another provider, based on an agreement of the Ministry of Health

---

18   Zakon o izmjenama Zakona o zdravstvenoj zaštiti i zdravstvenom osiguranju, Službeni list Crne Gore, 06/94.
19   Zakon o izmjeni Zakona o zdravstvenoj zaštiti i zdravstvenom osiguranju, Službeni list Crne Gore, 20/95.

(Article 75). It was also provided that a network of health care facilities would be established (within one year after the enactment of the law) to supersede the network defined in 1991 (Article 142). Finally, it envisaged the determination of a program of public-private integration over a period of one year.[20]

The "Law on Health Insurance" of 2004 kept already existing mandatory public health insurance and introduced the voluntary health insurance (Articles 3 and 4). The latter was decided to be the one to allow its beneficiaries to obtain special benefits and services within the regulated standards as well as those outside of the scope of the mandatory insurance (Article 79). The Health Insurance Fund (HIF) (previously the Republic Health Fund) was appointed to be in charge of the provision and implementation of both types of insurance. Other stakeholders were also allowed to organize voluntary insurance (Articles 81–86). Copayments were retained, however in a different form than in the preceding period. The Ministry of Health was in charge of setting the amount of copayments, based on the calculations of the Fund. Copayments were dependent on a range of criteria (type of disease; costs of diagnostic procedures, treatment and rehabilitation; and the level of health care involved). Exemptions included children, pregnant women, the elderly, social welfare beneficiaries and those with certain listed diseases (Articles 59 and 60). Budgetary transfers were prescribed for those who could not provide health care for themselves.[21]

The intention of the decision makers was to retain public health insurance, but also to make the options more versatile. However, there were no developments regarding voluntary health insurance, and this was finally abolished in 2016. Independent experts declared the lack of political will on the part of the government as an obstacle to its implementation. Inadequate capacities for its implementation on the part of the HIF are an additional reason, which can be interpreted as a consequence of the lack of political will.

Currently in force, the "Law on Healthcare" of 2016 details the Health Care Network which comprises

> the type, number and distribution of all health care facilities founded by the state and certain health care facilities or part thereof founded by other legal and/or physical entity [...] based on a contract concluded with the Health Insurance Fund [...] In case the health care cannot be provided within the Health Care Network, health care can be provided by

---

20   Zakon o zdravstvenoj zaštiti, Službeni list Crne Gore, 39/04.
21   Zakon o zdravstvenom osiguranju, Službeni list Crne Gore, 39/04.

health care facilities out of the Network, based on a contract concluded with the Health Insurance Fund.[22]

A new type of health care facility has been added to those already in existence: nursing facilities that can provide long-term, palliative and end-of-life care (Article 32). The prohibitions on private sector activities remained the same with an explicit ban on them organizing health care activities at the tertiary level (Article 58). The law contains a reference to public–private partnership. It also entitles public health care facilities to offer the public, within the framework of prescribed standards, special conditions for their health care, regarding the health care personnel, accommodation, nursing and time, as per the rules of the Ministry of Health. The costs for these extra services are to be paid by patients (Article 67). Again, it enables public health care facilities to rent out their premises and equipment to another provider, based on an agreement with the Ministry of Health (Article 84).[23]

Currently also in force, the "Law on Health Insurance" of 2016 introduces the supplementary health insurance along with the mandatory public insurance (Article 2). This supplementary insurance is to relate only to those who have the mandatory health insurance. It is envisaged that it can be provided either by the HIF or by insurance companies, based on a contract (Articles 68 and 69). The amount of the premium for supplementary health insurance is to be determined by the Fund.[24] This type of insurance was not implemented within the HIF, despite the deadline of the beginning of 2017, provided by the law. The reasons for this stem from the absence of necessary preconditions for its implementation – the lack of an integrated health information system that would include all health care facilities throughout the country, the lack of cashiers in them, and the lack of technical and administrative personnel in the Fund and all its branches.[25] Moreover, the Ministry of Health declared its intention to produce a feasibility study, i.e. a cost–benefit analysis of supplementary health insurance, mentioning that "significant number of countries which introduced this type of insurance have been increasingly involved in such analyses and initiated its abolition, having in mind the costs incurred to the insured population".[26]

---

22 Zakon o zdravstvenoj zaštiti, Službeni list Crne Gore, 03/16, Article 31.
23 Zakon o zdravstvenoj zaštiti, Službeni list Crne Gore, 03/16.
24 Zakon o zdravstvenom osiguranju, Službeni list Crne Gore, 06/16.
25 Vlada Crne Gore, Predlog Zakona o izmjenama zakona o zdravstvenom osiguranju, https://zakoni.skupstina.me/zakoni/web/dokumenta/zakoni-i-drugi-akti/340/1627-10214-28-2-17-4.pdf (accessed December 7, 2018), 3.
26 Ibid., 4.

4 Assessment of Health Care Reforms

4.1 *Access to Health Care*

In compliance with the law, all public health care facilities established in Montenegro are included in the Health Care Network. These are 18 health centers, seven general hospitals, three special hospitals, the Clinical Center of Montenegro, the Institute for Public Health, the Institute for Emergency Health Care, and the Montefarm Institute for Blood Transfusion and Pharmacies of Montenegro.[27] The legal provisions give them the position of the dominant, but not exclusive, provider of health care. Private health care facilities are also included in the Health Care Network, but the majority of them are outside of it. Currently, three private hospitals are a part of it and about 50 health care facilities have contracts with the HIF but are not part of the Network. More than half of those 50 private health care facilities are in Podgorica, the capital. Furthermore, the HIF has contracts with health care facilities operating outside of Montenegro – 29 providing health care to its citizens in Serbia and one in Turkey.

The Health Care Network covers all three levels of health care. Primary health care is provided through health centers, while the secondary and tertiary levels are provided through general and special hospitals, and the Clinical Center.[28] The regulations prescribe detailed criteria based on which the Health Care Network is established for the purpose of providing accessible, quality and sustainable health care.

"All citizens, regardless their ethnicity, race, sex, gender identity, sexual orientation, age, disability, language, religion, education, social origin, material funds and other personal characteristics"[29] are granted equal access to health care by law. Foreigners in general, but also asylum seekers, and persons provided with additional and temporary protection in Montenegro[30] are entitled to health care.[31] In its Montenegro 2019 Report, the European Commission

---

[27] Ministarstvo zdravlja, Master plan razvoja zdravstva Crne Gore 2015–2020 (Podgorica: 2015), 14.
[28] Ibid, 33.
[29] Zakon o zdravstvenoj zaštiti, Službeni list Crne Gore, 03/16, Article 5.
[30] Montenegro was not heavily affected by migration from the region of Middle East and North Africa, in contrast to the period of the 1990s when huge numbers of refugees from former Yugoslav Republics fled there (predominantly from Bosnia and Herzegovina, but also Croatia). Based on data reported by the Health Insurance Fund, in 2008 refugees accounted for 3% of those covered with mandatory health insurance. Health Insurance Fund, Health Insurance for You and with You (Podgorica: HIF), 31.
[31] Zakon o zdravstvenoj zaštiti, Službeni list Crne Gore, 03/16, Articles 12 and 13.

acknowledged the contribution of the "Master Plan for the Health Care Development for the period from 2015 to 2020" to increased health care access and reduced health care inequalities.[32]

In its representative survey, the Center for Monitoring and Research (CeMI) reported the percentage of population with access to health care was as high as 92% in 2017, with notable differences based on age. 99.3% of the elderly, i.e., those over 65 years of age and 81.3% of those aged 18 to 24 reported they had access to health care.[33] The World Bank, the United Nations Development Program and the European Commission reported that 80% of the Roma and Egyptian population had access to health care in the same year.[34]

Still, certain groups, denoted as vulnerable by stakeholders, such as persons with disabilities, persons affected by HIV/AIDS, drug addicts, prisoners, sex workers, the LGBT population, internally displaced persons, and Roma, are targeted in numerous governmental and non-governmental documents as in need of improved access to health care.

In 2017, only 68.6% of respondents in the survey conducted by CeMI reported that they can obtain health care service when in need for it. Still, the percentage was higher than in 2016, when 65.6% of respondents claimed the same. The majority of respondents complain of long waiting lists, 66.8%, while 44.5% were of the opinion that they have to wait too long once they come to see a doctor. Finally, on average 22.9% of respondents waited for a check-up or other health care service longer than one month, with notable regional differences. For example, 40.1%, 21.5% and 27.1% of respondents waited for less than a week in the southern, central and northern parts of the country respectively.[35]

Another indicator of health care access, the ratio of medical doctors per 1,000 inhabitants was increased in 2017 compared to the past and stood at 2.6 to 1,000, much lower than in the member states of the EU.[36]

---

32   Izvještaj Evropske komisije o Crnoj Gori 2019, https://www.eu.me/mn/pregovori-o-pristupanju/dokumenti-pregovori/category/57-izvjestaji-o-napretku (accessed February 13, 2020), 99.
33   Marko Savić, Stevo Muk, Bojana Knežević and Ivan Šćekić, Sistem zdravstvene zaštite i prava pacijenata u Crnoj Gori – osvajanje povjerenja građana (Podgorica: CeMI, 2017), 23.
34   Izvještaj Evropske komisije o Crnoj Gori 2019, https://www.eu.me/mn/pregovori-o-pristupanju/dokumenti-pregovori/category/57-izvjestaji-o-napretku (accesed February 13, 2020), 101.
35   Marko Savić, Stevo Muk, Bojana Knežević and Ivan Šćekić, Sistem zdravstvene zaštite i prava pacijenata u Crnoj Gori – osvajanje povjerenja građana, 21.
36   Institut za javno zdravlje Crne Gore, Situaciona analiza zdravstvene zaštite u Crnoj Gori za 2017 godinu, (Podgorica 2018), 10.

4.2 Quality of Health Care

In the legislation, the quality of health care is in the focus from the point of view of

> conditions and funds for health care provision, personnel, their knowledge and expertise and implementation thereof, health care situation, satisfaction of patients, prevention and reduction of harmful effects of risky behaviors and environmental factors, as well as the quality of life.[37]

With a view to monitoring and evaluating the quality of health care as defined per Articles 149 and 156, the Commission for Health Care Quality Control under the auspices of the Ministry of Health is established and voluntary accreditation of health care facilities has started. The recently adopted "Strategy for the Improvement of Health Care Quality and Patients' Safety for the period from 2019 to 2023" strives to significantly improve this area because of the fact "that not all stakeholders in the health care system were interested in and motivated for the establishment of the quality and safety program"[38] despite the pre-defined legislative and strategic framework. Data on the progress in this area seem to be largely absent. Some comparatively relevant indicators regarding the quality of health care services, such as average years of life and infant mortality, have been improving, but they do not position Montenegro high on the list. In 2017, life expectancy at birth was 79.4 and 74.1 years of life for women and men respectively.[39] In 2016, the infant mortality rate[40] was 3.4.[41] The self-assessment of the health situation of Montenegro's residents in 2012 shows that less than half of adults and young people consider their health worse and moderate respectively, with more women estimating their health as worse and fair.[42]

---

37 Zakon o zdravstvenoj zaštiti, Službeni list Crne Gore, 03/16, Article 114.
38 Ministarstvo zdravlja, Strategija za poboljšanje kvaliteta zdravstvene zaštite i bezbjednosti pacijenata za period 2019–2023. godine sa Akcionim planom za 2019–2020. godine, (Podgorica 2019), 9.
39 Zavod za statistiku Crne Gore, Žene i muškarci u Crnoj Gori, (Podgorica 2018), 35.
40 The infant mortality rate shows considerable variations in Montenegro, but these seem to be a result of the phenomena of small numbers – "small variations in infant mortality significantly change the value of the indicator". Ministarstvo održivog razvoja i turizma, III Godišnji izveštaj o sprovođenju Milenijumskih ciljeva razvoja u Crnoj Gori, Pogorica: MORT, 2014), 16.
41 Institut za javno zdravlje Crne Gore, Situaciona analiza zdravstvene zaštite u Crnoj Gori za 2017. godinu (Podgorica 2018), 6.
42 Tatijana Đurišić, Ljiljana Golubović and Boban Mugoša. Istraživanje o kvalitetu života, životnim stilovima i zdravstvenim rizicima stanovnika Crne Gore: Nacionalni izvještaj istraživanja (Podgorica: Institut za javno zdravlje Crne Gore i MONSTAT, 2017), 16.

In its 2017 survey, CeMI reported the perceptions of respondents about the quality of health care, with 43.7% of them considering it unchanged compared to two years prior to the survey, compared to 29.3% and 27.1% considering it lower and higher respectively. A decreasing percentage of respondents, 68.2% and 58.3% of them, considered that medical doctors and nurses respectively treat them with dignity and respect. An increasing percentage of respondents, 50.8% believed that medical personnel keep private information confidential, while 35.6% of them reported that unknown persons entered the premises in which they were receiving a medical check-up, without any information regarding their presence.[43]

The focus groups which CeMI organized in eight cities in Montenegro included service users, i.e. patients, who gave important observations regarding health care quality. Interestingly, the first suggestion of patients with a view to improving the quality of health care was to improve access by increasing the number of medical doctors employed, especially specialists. The findings also addressed overburden of medical personnel, the poor conditions in which they work, the excess of administrative work, etc. In-depth interviews conducted with twenty service providers, i.e. medical personnel, showed that the majority of them "evaluate the health care quality as moderate, highlighting that the system has disadvantages and that it is not ideal, but within the possibilities of the society".[44] One fourth of respondents reported that health care service is of high quality, but that there are differences depending on the level of health care and the region in which the health care facilities are located.[45]

A series of training and educational activities have been targeted towards medical personnel with a view to improving their knowledge and skills and introducing a life–long learning approach. Preventive measures have been on the agenda, among other things, due to the need to reduce health care costs. Still, progress seems limited.

There have been important steps regarding eHealth, in terms of its incorporation into documents, and also in the field. This mainly relates to the introduction of information technologies in the Health Insurance Fund, but also in health care facilities at the primary, secondary and tertiary levels of care, albeit with some exceptions, as well as reporting. In addition, all patients have electronic health care documentation. However, eHealth is still underdeveloped.

---

43   CeMI, Sistem zdravstvene zaštite i prava pacijenata u Crnoj Gori – osvajanje povjerenja građana, (Podgorica: CeMI, 2017), 18–19, 31–38.

44   Marko Savić, Stevo Muk, Bojana Knežević and Ivan Šćekić, Sistem zdravstvene zaštite i prava pacijenata u Crnoj Gori – osvajanje povjerenja građana, 18.

45   Ibid.

In the "Strategy of the Development of Information Society of Montenegro up to 2020" of 2016, six indicators were defined and targets thereof for 2018 and 2020, among them the percentage of registered users of electronic services in health care and of e-receipts, as well as of e-referrals.[46] Still, there are no patients recorded for any of six indicators under scrutiny.

4.3 Sustainability of Health Care

The European Commission reports that the absence of the fiscal sustainability has adverse effects on the work of public health care facilities, programs and actions, despite the funds devoted to it.[47]

The law stipulates mandatory health insurance contributions of 12.8% of gross income, of which 4.3% are paid by the employer and 8.5% by the employee. The health contribution of 12.8% of gross income is also paid by the self-employed (including farmers), in contrast to the 1% of gross income paid by pensioners.[48] The share of the Health Insurance Fund expenditures in GDP from 2009 to 2017 was declining from 5.32% to 4.00%. Its total incomes amounted to nearly 167 million euro per year. Incomes from health contributions accounted from 75% to 82% in the period observed. The remaining part was covered from the budget. Funds collected based on copayments constituted a negligible amount.[49] Payments from private households for health care (out of pocket payments) as a proportion of total costs for health care accounted for 26.66% in 2012, according to WHO data.[50] Based on the estimate of the WHO, total health care costs per capita in 2014 amounted to 888 Intl$, while total expenditure on health accounted for 6.4% of GDP.[51]

The Health Insurance Fund did not take any steps with a view to implementing the supplementary health care insurance, in contrast to certain private companies, including Uniqa, Grawe, Lovćen, Sava and Wiener Städtische. Contributions paid for health insurance to all insurance companies that have

---

46 In 2016 there were no patients recorded for any of six indicators under scrutiny.
47 Izvještaj Evropske komisije o Crnoj Gori 2019, https://www.eu.me/mn/pregovori-o-pristupanju/dokumenti-pregovori/category/57-izvjestaji-o-napretku (accessed February 13, 2020), 101.
48 Zakon o doprinosima za obavezno socijalno osiguranje, Službeni list Crne Gore, 14/2012, Articles 6 and 17.
49 Natalija Perišić, "Montenegro" in Health Politics in Europe: A Handbook, ed. Ellen M. Immergut, Karen M. Anderson, Camilla Devitt and Tamara Popić (Oxford: Oxford University Press 2021).
50 Ministarstvo zdravlja, Master plan razvoja zdravstva Crne Gore 2015–2020, (Podgorica 2015), 22.
51 WHO, Data – Montenegro, https://www.who.int/countries/mne/en/ (accessed February 15, 2020).

been active amounted to as low as 2.3% of the total of paid fees for all types of insurance in 2017.[52]

In-patient care is financed based on hospitalization rates and average length of treatment. In parallel, the DRG approach is being piloted. The Health Insurance Fund has been in charge of defining, introducing and implementing the DRG approach (Diagnosis Related Groups) for the payment of an acute hospital care – Australian version 6.0. The activities are in the final phase, and 2018 was planned to be the test year, with a view to improving the model and eliminating any mistakes.[53]

Reform of the funding of the out-patient care resulted in the introduction of a combined approach of capitation and provided services,[54] motivated by the need to strengthen the good sides of both models and minimize the negative ones.[55]

Co-payments by patients, prescribed both for in-patient and out-patient care, represent insignificant revenues for the Health Insurance Fund[56] and do not contribute to the purpose. The reasons are the low co-payment amounts and the large number of groups exempted.

Assessments of the savings brought by the reforms of the primary, but also by ongoing reforms of the secondary and tertiary levels of care are mainly qualitative and not quantitative. The reforms implemented are summarized by the Ministry of Health as satisfactory, but insufficient in terms of the still vast amount of spending on health care. The reforms yet to be fully implemented are to be assessed, as requested by the Health Insurance Fund. Cost containment measures by the Fund have been primarily in the area of more strict controls of contracted work in health care facilities and the consumption of medicines, as demonstrated in its annual reports.[57] In addition, for the

---

52 Insurance Supervision Agency, Izvještaj o stanju na tržištu osiguranja u Crnoj Gori za 2017. godinu, https://zakoni.skupstina.me/zakoni/web/dokumenta/zakoni-i-drugi-akti/487/1777-10840-00-72-18-40.pdf (accessed December 3, 2018).

53 Ministarstvo zdravlja, Izvještaj Ministarstva zdravlja za 2017. godinu o radu i stanju u upravnim oblastima sa izvještajem Fonda za zdravstveno osiguranje za 2017. godinu (Podgorica 2018), 40–41.

54 Ministarstvo zdravlja, Master plan razvoja zdravstva Crne Gore 2015–2020 (Podgorica 2015), 31.

55 WHO, UNDP, MZ, Ocjena integriteta zdravstvenog sistema u Crnoj Gori (Podgorica 2011), 13.

56 Ministarstvo zdravlja, Master plan razvoja zdravstva Crne Gore 2015–2020 (Podgorica 2015), 20.

57 Fond za zdravstveno osiguranje, Izvještaj o radu Fonda za zdravstveno osiguranje Crne Gora za 2017 (Podgorica 2018),12–14.

purpose of cost containment, the Fund has been arguing in favour of non–referrals of patients to private health care facilities and to those abroad.[58]

The CeMI survey showed that an increasing number of respondents, currently 22.2%, reported that they had been referred by a doctor in public health care facilities to a specific private clinic for a health care service they could have received free of charge in the public facility, and for which they had to pay in the private sector. Also, one fourth reported that they often or always paid for a medication or medical device that is on the list of free medicines or those that are refunded, but that they had never been reimbursed. A plurality of respondents considered that there is corruption in the sector, 42%, contrary to only 12.3% claiming that it is absent.[59]

5 Conclusion

In Montenegro, thirty years after the transition, the public sector has retained a dominant, though not an exclusive position in the provision of health care. However, the lack of longitudinal data hampers effective assessment of health care reforms from the past and makes possible qualitative evaluations of only certain aspects.

The state is the regulator, funder/purchaser and provider/planner in the health care as per description of the roles in the theoretical framework, with limited roles and activities of the private sector and consequently, a rather under-developed public-private mix.

Its role as regulator has been largely complemented by consultations with professionals and their associations, advising in compliance with evidence-based practice. However, the process of designing reform laws, strategies and institutions seems to be highly influenced by the impact and expert opinion of stakeholders outside of the country. The most influential of these was the World Bank, which offered its expertise in the design of the system (division of responsibilities among the primary, secondary and tertiary levels of care and their funding mechanisms, the operation of the Health Insurance Fund, etc.). Unsurprisingly, the decisive shift aimed at the introduction of private funding and private provision was enacted based on legal changes in 2004, when the World Bank assumed a rather active role. Another influential external

---

58 Fond za zdravstveno osiguranje, Institut za javno zdravlje, Program zdravstvene zaštite u Crnoj Gori za 2016. godinu (Podgorica 2016), 53.

59 CeMI, Sistem zdravstvene zaštite i prava pacijenata u Crnoj Gori – osvajanje povjerenja građana (Podgorica 2017), 8.

stakeholder has been the European Union, which has been producing its reports, containing a section on the effectiveness of the national health care system. The EU's soft power has been strong, but apart from the evaluation of the compliance of the Montenegrin legislation in this area with the *acquis communautaire,* there have been no other remarks. The largely acknowledged compliance of the Montenegrin health care regulations with EU regulations is rather compromised when it comes to implementation. The elements of the Open Method of Coordination (access, quality, and financial sustainability) in the area of health care could prove to be of increasing importance for Montenegro in the future. It can be seen here that there are many obstacles to accessible and quality health care services, despite the rather broad legal proclamations. However, the EU's concern over corruption could be also of importance for health care reform in Montenegro. The main concern here could be the referrals from public hospitals to the private facilities in which patients have to pay for the services they could legally obtain in the public sector, but in fact cannot do so in practice.

Its funder/purchaser role seems to be jeopardized in the future. Mandatory health care contributions are not sufficient for the provision of health care as prescribed by law. However, the efforts aimed at the introduction of alternatives have been failing continuously for manifold reasons. Even though it might be supposed that good regulation and implementation of some of the forms of private health care insurance could be beneficial for contributors, it would probably not result in better health care for the vulnerable. In general, health care reforms were motivated by savings and therefore it is not surprising that the funder/purchaser role of the state has been shrinking. The sustainability of health care system has been aiming from the aspects of changed formula for cost containment, the gate-keeping role of primary health care, reducing public dental protection and so on.

Finally, its provider/planner role is somewhat unusual in Montenegro, since the Health Care Network is comprised of public and private health care facilities. The provision of services by private health care facilities is motivated by savings: they are engaged in those situations in which there is no available public provision. Therefore, the state has been setting the arena in which it gives the private sector those responsibilities that it cannot provide.

Bibliography

CeMI. Sistem zdravstvene zaštite i prava pacijenata u Crnoj Gori – osvajanje povjerenja građana. Podgorica 2017.

Đurišić, Tatijana, Ljiljana Golubović, and Boban, Mugoša, Istraživanje o kvalitetu života, životnim stilovima i zdravstvenim rizicima stanovnika Crne Gore: Nacionalni izvještaj istraživanja. Podgorica: Institut za javno zdravlje Crne Gore i MONSTAT, 2017.

Džankić, Jelena. "Political Transformations: Welfare States in Transition: A Long Drive Down a Tough Road". In Welfare States in Transition – 20 Years after the Yugoslav Welfare Model, edited by Marija Stambolieva and Stefan Dehnert, 202–227. Sofia: Friedrich Ebert Foundation, 2011.

Fond za zdravstveno osiguranje, Institut za javno zdravlje. Program zdravstvene zaštite u Crnoj Gori za 2016. godinu. Podgorica 2016.

Fond za zdravstveno osiguranje, Izvještaj o radu Fonda za zdravstveno osiguranje Crne Gora za 2017. Podgorica 2018.

Hill, Michael. Social Policy: A Comparative Analysis. London: Prentice Hall, 1996.

Institut za javno zdravlje Crne Gore. Situaciona analiza zdravstvene zaštite u Crnoj Gori za 2017. godinu. Podgorica 2018.

Insurance Supervision Agency, Izvještaj o stanju na tržištu osiguranja u Crnoj Gori za 2017. godinu. Accessed December 3 2018. http://zakoni.skupstina.me/zakoni/web/dokumenta/zakoni-i-drugi-akti/487/1777-10840-00-72-18-40.pdf.

Izvještaj Evropske komisije o Crnoj Gori 2019. Accessed February 13, 2020. https://www.eu.me/mn/pregovori-o-pristupanju/dokumenti-pregovori/category/57-izvjestaji-o-napretku.

Koivusalo, Meri, and Eva Olila. "Globalna zdravstvena politika". In Globalna socijalna politika, edited by Nikola Jejts, 179–207. Beograd: Fakultet političkih nauka, 2017.

Kujačić, Jovan, Prilozi istoriji zdravstvene kulture Crne Gore do kraja 1918. godinu. Beograd: Srpska akademija nauka, 1950.

Marmor, Theodore, and Claus Wendt. "Conceptual Frameworks for Comparing Healthcare Politics and Policy ". Health Policy 107 (2012): 11–20.

Miljanići, Petar - Niko - Miloš. Crnogorski medicinski velikani. Podgorica: Društvo ljekara Crne Gore, 2003.

Ministarstvo održivog razvoja i turizma. III Godišnji izveštaj o sprovođenju Milenijumskih ciljeva razvoja u Crnoj Gori. Pogorica 2014.

Ministarstvo zdravlja. Izvještaj Ministarstva zdravlja za 2017. godinu o radu i stanju u upravnim oblastima sa izvještajem Fonda za zdravstveno osiguranje za 2017. godine. Podgorica 2018.

Ministarstvo zdravlja. Master plan razvoja zdravstva Crne Gore 2015–2020. Podgorica 2015.

Ministarstvo zdravlja. Strategija za poboljšanje kvaliteta zdravstvene zaštite i bezbjednosti pacijenata za period 2019–2023. godine sa Akcionim planom za 2019–2020. godine. Podgorica 2019.

Perišić, Natalija. "Montenegro". In Health Politics in Europe: A Handbook, edited by Ellen M. Immergut, Karen M. Anderson, Camilla Devitt and Tamara Popić. Oxford: Oxford University Press 2021.

Pestieau, Pierre. The Welfare State in the European Union – Economic and Social Perspectives. Oxford: Oxford University Press 2006.

Potůček, Martin. "Policy Coordination: Government, Markets, and the Civic Sector". In Public Policy in Central and Eastern Europe: Theories, Methods, Practices, edited by Martin Potůček, Lance T. LeLoup, György Jenei, and László Váradi, 77–102. Bratislava: NISPAcee, 2003.

Savić Marko, Stevo Muk, Bojana Knežević and Ivan Šćekić, Sistem zdravstvene zaštite i prava pacijenata u Crnoj Gori – osvajanje povjerenja građana. Podgorica: CeMI, 2017.

Schwander, Hanna. "Healthcare as Social Investment". In Hertie School of Governance, The Governance Report 2019 – Health Governance, Inequalities, Health Security, Patient-centred Care, Health Politics, Global Health, 121–134. Oxford: Oxford University Press, 2019.

Spiker, Pol. Socijalna politika – teorija i praksa. Beograd: Fakultet političkih nauka, 2013.

Van Rensburg, André J., and Piet Bracke. "Politics and Power: The Case of the Global Opioid Epidemic". In Hertie School of Governance, The Governance Report 2019 – Health Governance, Inequalities, Health Security, Patient-centred Care, Health Politics, Global Health, 103–120. Oxford: Oxford University Press, 2019.

Vlada Crne Gore, Predlog Zakona o izmjenama zakona o zdravstvenom osiguranju. Accessed December 7, 2018. https://zakoni.skupstina.me/zakoni/web/dokumenta/zakoni-i-drugi-akti/340/1627-10214-28-2-17-4.pdf.

WHO, Data – Montenegro. Accessed February 15, 2020. https://www.who.int/countries/mne/en/.

WHO, UNDP, MZ. Ocjena integriteta zdravstvenog sistema u Crnoj Gori. Podgorica 2011.

Zakon o doprinosima za obavezno socijalno osiguranje. Službeni list Crne Gore, 14/2012.

Zakon o izmjenama Zakona o zdravstvenoj zaštiti i zdravstvenom osiguranju. Službeni list Crne Gore, 06/94.

Zakon o izmjeni Zakona o zdravstvenoj zaštiti i zdravstvenom osiguranju, Službeni list Crne Gore, 20/95.

Zakon o zdravstvenoj zaštiti i zdravstvenom osiguranju. Službeni list Crne Gore, 39/90.

Zakon o zdravstvenoj zaštiti. Službeni list Crne Gore, 39/04.

Zakon o zdravstvenoj zaštiti. Službeni list Crne Gore, 03/16.

Zakon o zdravstvenom osiguranju. Službeni list Crne Gore, 06/16.

Zakon o zdravstvenom osiguranju. Službeni list Crne Gore, 39/04.

Zavod za statistiku Crne Gore. Žene i muškarci u Crnoj Gori. Podgorica 2018.

CHAPTER 7

Social Protection System in Montenegro

Marzena Żakowska and Tomasz Ferfecki

1   Introduction

After the breakup of the Socialist Federal Republic of Yugoslavia (SFRY), Montenegro was a part of the Federal Republic of Yugoslavia (FRY),[1] and then a part of the State Union of Serbia and Montenegro.[2] In the FRY, the system of social welfare was a combination of contributory and non-contributory cash benefits with additional benefits in kind, generally granted on a universal basis, with some provided by employers to their staff.[3] From the beginning of the 1990s, the costs of such a widespread social welfare system could no longer be sustained. Undertaken general reforms relocated funding from local self-management communities of interest to the national republican welfare funds. Yugoslavia's successor states have also inherited this republic-based welfare system.[4] In June 2006, Montenegro became an independent country[5] and one year later it signed an Agreement on Stabilization and Association with the EU. In December 2008, Montenegro applied for EU membership and its candidate status was granted in December 2010. This obliged the government in Podgorica to start a reform process adjusting the political, economic and social policy to the EU requirements by taking the necessary measures to

---

1   Bruno Coppieters, Michael Emerson, Michel Huysseune, Tamara Kovziridze, Gergana Noutcheva, Nathalie Tocci, and Marius Vahl, Europeanization and Conflict Resolution. Case Studies from European Peripheries (Gent: Academia Press, 2004), 115–119.
2   Przemysław Żukiewicz, Pozycja ustrojowa rządu w państwach postjugosłowiańskich. Analiza prawno-porównawcza (Wrocław: Instytut Politologii Uniwersytetu Wrocławskiego, 2017), 67–68.
3   William Bartlett and Merita Xhumari, "Social Security Policy and Pension Reforms in the Western Balkans", European Journal of Social Security, no. 9 (2007): 7.
4   Ibid., 7–8.
5   Anna Krukowska, "Nietypowy federalizm serbsko-czarnogórski", Wschodnioznawstwo 1(2007): 69–70.

improve the socio-economic status of its citizens, especially those in need of services and support in the social protection area.[6]

The aim of this chapter is to examine the social protection system in Montenegro by analysis of the legal framework, organization of institutions, financing mechanisms, benefits and allowances systems. This seeks to provide an answer to the following question: what measures are needed to be taken to improve the social protection system in Montenegro? The study was based on secondary research using data from legal documents, the Statisitcal Office of Montenegro (MONSTAT), the Ministry of Labor and Social Welfare of Montenegro and the European Commission (EC). It was conducted over the period 2016–2019.

The starting point for this research is a broad understanding of security, social security and social protection. Paul D. Williams states that security is not only the possession of arms, but human dignity (including the well-being of children), prevention of diseases, reduction of ethnic tensions, open engagement of decision-makers for the benefit of society, and the respect for human rights.[7] Karina P. Marczuk argues that social security encompasses societal security, securing a dignified human existence, preventing economic threats in various life situations, to a range of civil rights and liberties and the subjectivity of human beings in relationships with other people and institutions.[8] In this way, the human needs are the main subject of state and social security and is analyzed on the level of functioning of state institutions, local governments, NGOs, the local and family environments. Drèze and Sen[9] as well as

---

[6] Drenka Vuković and Natalija Perišić, Opportunities and Challenges of Social Security Transition in Montenegro, in Welfare States in Transition, ed. Marija Stambolieva and Stefan Dehnert (Sofia: Friedrich Ebert Foundation, 2011), 165–188.

[7] Paul D. Williams, "Security Studies. An Introduction", in Security Studies. An Introduction, ed. Paul D. Williams (New York: Routledge 2008), 6–7.

[8] Karina Paulina Marczuk, "Bezpieczeństwo społeczne: potrzeba szerokiego ujęcia. Implikacje dla Polski", in Bezpieczeństwo społeczne. Pojęcia, uwarunkowania, wyzwania, ed. Aleksandra Skrabacz, Stanisław Sulkowski (Warszawa: Elipsa, 2012), 35–37. See also: International Labour Organization, World Social Protection Report 2017–2019. Universal Social Protection to Achieve the Sustainable Development Goals (Geneva: International Labour Office, 2017), 1, 27. Human Security Unit, Human Security in Theory and Practice (New York: Office for the Coordination of Humanitarian Affairs, United Nation, 2009), 6; Janusz Gierszewski, "Bezpieczeństwo społeczne jako dziedzina bezpieczeństwa narodowego", Historia i Polityka nr 23 (30) 2018: 21–38.

[9] Jean Drèze and Amartya Sen, "Public Action for Social Security: Foundation and Strategy", in Social Security in Developing Countries, ed. Ehtisham Ahmad, Jean Drèze, John Hills and Amartya Sen (New York: Oxford University Press, 1991), 3–26.

Burgess and Stern[10] emphasize two characteristics of social security which are particularly important, defining them as the use of social means to prevent deprivation (promote living standards) and vulnerability to deprivation (protect against falling living standards, poverty).

In the case of social protection Devereux and Sabates-Wheeler define it as "the set of all initiatives, both formal and informal, that provide: social assistance to extremely poor individuals and households; social services to groups who need special care or would otherwise be denied access to basic services; social insurance to protect people against the risks and consequences of livelihood shocks; and social equity to protect people against social risks such as discrimination or abuse".[11] Also pointing out that the main aim is alleviating the needs of the poor and deprived (vulnerable and marginalized groups), which is achieved by the transfer of resources from governmental and non-governmental sources thus reducing exposure to socio-economic risks. The functions of social protection are described as follows:
- protective - providing relief from deprivation (e.g., social assistance, state pensions);
- preventative - averting deprivation (e.g., social insurance, savings clubs);
- promotive - enhancing incomes and capabilities (e.g., microcredit);
- transformative - social equity and inclusion, empowerment, and rights (e.g., labor laws).[12]

William Bartlett and Merita Xhumari emphasize that social protection covers the cost of all social transfers such as pensions and health care funding and social security benefits with public expenditure on health care. Social security includes the following financial benefits: pensions, paid sick leave, family and child allowances, unemployment benefits and income support and health benefits.[13] From the viewpoint of the UN Department of Economic and Social Affairs, social protection is characterized as a set of nationally-owned policies and programs, delivered by using state assets amassed by either voluntary payments or taxes. In the case of states with less-developed economies and hence

---

10   Robin Burgess and Nicholas Stern, Social Security in Developing Countries: What, Why, Who, and How? in Social Security in Developing Countries ed. Ehtisham Ahmad, Jean Drèze, John Hills and Amartya Sen (New York: Oxford University Press, 1991), 3–6.
11   Stephen Devereux and Rachel Sabates-Wheeler, Transformative Social Protection, Institute of Development Studies Working Paper 232, Brighton, 2004, 9.
12   Ibid., 9–10.
13   William Bartlett, Merita Xhumari, "Social Security Policy and Pension Reforms in the Western Balkans", 10.

insufficient revenue streams the deficiency can be made up from gifts or loans from richer nations or institutions.[14] The delivery of social protection is dependent on adequate funding to counteract the effects of nature or conflict on the environment and economy. Social protection must ensure that those who are disconnected from sufficient means by disability, education, gender, or birth are not left without the means to support the minimum.

2   Legal Framework

The Constitution of the Republic of Montenegro[15] is the primary legal regulation that contains a number of basic principles regarding social security and social protection. These provisions of law proclaim that Montenegro is a state of social justice (Article 1) and promotes, among all human rights, the right to social insurance (Article 67). According to Article 62, every single person is also guaranteed the right to work, while enjoying freedom of choice regarding the occupation and place of employment and is entitled to proper protection and fair and humane work conditions. The Constitution also stipulates the obligation of the state to ensure those who are not able to work and cannot provide material security for themselves (Article 67). Individuals with disabilities are guaranteed special protection (Article 68). For certain categories of individuals, the law stipulates the right to health protection financed from public revenues, unless they are entitled to that right on other grounds. Article 69 specifies children, pregnant women, elderly persons, and persons with disabilities. The Constitution contains the assurance of special protected status for mothers and children (Article 73). Children are also entitled to rights and freedoms appropriate to their age and level of maturity. In particular protection is guaranteed to children from exploitation or abuse of any kind, specifically mental, physical, or economic (Article 74). The system of social security in Montenegro is mostly insurance based, with the exception of social protection (assistance) and child welfare schemes which are assistance based and means-tested.[16]

---

14   UN Department of Economic and Social Affairs (DESA), Promoting Inclusion through Social Protection, UN: New York 2018, 5–6.
15   Constitution of Montenegro 2007, https://www.wipo.int/edocs/lexdocs/laws/en/me/me004en.pdf (accessed April 16, 2019).
16   Constitution of Montenegro, Article 1, 62, 67–69, 72–74.

In addition to the Consitution several new laws and amendments have been implemented. Thus, the following laws are relevent in this area:
- the Law on Social and Child Protection[17] establishes the basic principles of state-based and state-related social and child/infant protection (e.g., protection from abuse, right and obligations to education, minimum food supply/ access to school food schemes) in terms of minimum social and health guarantees and human needs to be respected, here defined as activity in the public interest of the Republic of Montenegro;
- the Law on Health Insurance[18] creates conditions for the provision of compulsory health insurance and stable financing of health care to ensure a readily accessible health service and additionally the possibility of voluntary health insurance contributions;
- the Law on Health Care[19] establishes citizens' rights and obligations in the execution of their entitlement to healthcare protection, providing accessible healthcare protection under equal conditions and preventing any discrimination in the process of providing medical services;
- the Law on Contributions for Compulsory Social Insurance[20] regulates "contributions for compulsory social insurance, contribution obligors, contribution bases and rates, obligors for calculation and payment of contribution, deadlines for payment and other matters related to payment of contributions for compulsory social insurance";[21]
- the Labor Law[22] specifies employee rights and obligations resulting from employment, advertising employment and facilitating labor market flexibility, collective agreement and contract of employment;
- the Law on Pension and Disability Insurance[23] governs mandatory pension and disability insurance based on inter-generational solidarity.

A number of measures have been approved and implemented highlighting matters of social protection, eg., the Strategy for the Development of the Social Protection System for the Elderly 2013–2017; Strategy of Social and Child

---

[17] Official Gazette of the Republic of Montenegro, no. 27/13.
[18] Official Gazette of the Republic of Montenegro, no. 39/04, 14/12.
[19] Official Gazette of the Republic of Montenegro, no. 39/04, 3/16, 39/16, 2/17.
[20] Official Gazette of the Republic of Montenegro, no. 13/07, 79/08, 86/09, 78/10, 40/11, 14/12, 62/13, 08/15, 22/17, 42/19.
[21] Ibid.
[22] Official Gazette of the Republic of Montenegro, no. 49/08, 26/09, 59/11, 66/12.
[23] Official Gazette of the Republic of Montenegro, no. 54/03, 78/10, 34/11, 40/11, 66/12, 38/13, 61/13, 6/14, 60/14, 10/15, 44/15, 42/16, 55/16.

Protection System Development 2013-2017; the Strategy for the Prevention and Protection of Children from Violence 2017–2021. It should be noted that the Ministry of Labor and Social Welfare has set in place relevant provisions detailing conditions of how services are to be used and provided and establishing minimum standards and norms for them.[24]

3 Structure of Social Protection

The Ministry of Labor and Social Welfare (MLSW) was the main institution overseeing social protection in Montenegro and responsible for social security in the area of pension, disability and health insurance issues.[25] Within the Ministry, the Directorate for Social Welfare and Child Protection was the main entity responsible for social services which are provided through the following departments:
- Department for Social and Child Protection and Control;
- Department for the Protection of Groups at Risk;
- Department for the Development of Services.[26]

---

24 Rulebook on Detailed Conditions for the Provision and Use, Norms and the Minimum Standards of Accommodation Service for Adults and the Elderly, Official Gazette of Montenegro, no. 58/14; Detailed Conditions for the Provision and Use, Norms and the Minimum Standards of Accommodation Services for Children and Young Persons in an Institution and a Small Home Community, Official Gazette of Montenegro, no. 43/14; Rulebook on Detailed Conditions for the Provision and Use of Services of Family Placement - Foster Care and Family Placement, Official Gazette of Montenegro, no. 19/14; Rulebook on Detailed Conditions for the Provision and Use, Norms and the Minimum Standards of Services for the Community Living Support, Official Gazette of Montenegro, no. 30/15; Rulebook on Detailed Conditions for the Provision and Use, Norms and the Minimum Standards of Advisory-Therapeutic and Socio-Educational Services, Official Gazette of Montenegro, no. 32/15.

25 From December 2020 the main institution overseeing social protection in Montenegro is the Ministry of Finance and Social Welfare, established by the merger of the Ministry of Finance and the Ministry of Labour and Social Welfare, https://www.gov.me/en/mif (accessed January 6, 2021). However, the Ministry of Labor and Social Welfare had been organized in the following way: Welfare Directorate of Labour, Directorate for Labour Market and Employment, Directorate for Pension and Disability Insurance and Veterans' and Disability Protection, Directorate for Social Welfare and Child Protection, Directorate for Informatics and Analytical Statistical Affairs, Directorate for European Integration, Programming and Implementation of EU Funds, Internal Audit Department.

26 Civil Society Organizations in the Process of Standardization of Social Services in Montenegro (Podgorica: SOS Hotline for Women and Children Victims of Violence Podgorica,

At municipality level the Centers for Social Work – CSW (Centri Za Socijalni Rad) are the bodies in charge of implementing activities in the social and child areas. CSWs make decisions regarding the rights to social and child protection, on the basis of the law. These can be established over the area of one or more municipalities. CSWs also assess the status and needs, the strengths and risks of beneficiaries and other people who they are responsible for. They appraise the eligibility of potential caregivers, foster and adoptive parents, and develop and monitor individual plans for service provision. They are the initial adjudicators of rights to social and child protection. Their legal obligations include taking measures, initiating and participating in hearings in court as well other legal proceedings, maintaining records, and preserving documentation about individual cases.[27] There are thirteen CSWs, responsible for the 25 Montenegrin municipal areas. Eight of them cover neighboring municipalities through the work of the Services for Social Work (SSW).[28] There is either a CSW or an SSW located in each principal municipal town. SSWs remain associated with their closest CSW, as they are generally situated in smaller urban areas.[29] The shared connection of CSWs and SSWs is that the former have the legal authority of first instance decision-making on:
- provision of benefits in cash;
- account management;
- forwarding information regarding benefits to the MLSW;
- provision of services in support of the process of receiving a caregiver's allowance;
- forwarding the funds for a single instance of aid and care in facilities not in the Republic of Montenegro;

2018), 23–25, https://www.academia.edu/42920922/Civil_Society_Organizations_in_the_process_of_standardization_of_social_services_in_Montenegro (accessed June 15, 2019).

27 JU Centri za socijalni rad, https://www.csrcg.me/index.php/mapa/795-ju-centri-za-socijalni-rad-na-teritoriji-crne-gore (accessed April 20, 2019).

28 Ibid. The CSWs are located in the following locations: the capital Podgorica also covering the municipalities of Golubovci and Tuzi; and CSWs for the municipalities or groups of municipalities - Herceg Novi; Danilovgrad; Bar and Ulcinj; Berane, Andrijevica and Petnjica; Bijelo Polje; Mojkovac and Kolašin; Kotor, Tivat and Budva; Rožaje; Plav and Gusinje; Pljevlja and Žabljak; Nikšić, Plužine i Šavnik; and Cetinje.

29 According to the Law on Social and Child Protection, professional workers in CSWs are social workers, psychologists, educators, special pedagogues, dialectologists, lawyers.

– facilitating the financial requirements of the SSWs and CSWs, including the disbursement of benefits in cash.[30]

An SSW is entitled to ask CSW staff to visit a recipient of social benefits. A number of CSWs have staff rotating weekly between the CSW and SSWs providing the SSWs with assistance. Others possess selected SSW personnel who are also members of the boards that make the initial benefit decisions. In some cases, the relationship is only by occasional official correspondence. This form of CSWs organization allows for municipalities to access the provision of cash benefits and social services.[31]

Aside from the MLSW, CSWs and SSWs, the social protection system of Montenegro also has extra-budgetary funds responsible for the provision of insurance-based social protection: the Pension and Disability Insurance Fund (PIO Fund), the Health Insurance Fund (HIF), and the Employment Agency of Montenegro (EAM).[32] Despite these being separate institutions, they remain under the supervision of the MLSW. They have been a part of the treasury system of the Ministry of Finance since 2008. Furthermore, there are also residential institutions which provide social care services.[33] These institutions support youngsters with disabilities, foster care, and facilities for the elderly. Six of them were established by the MLSW, which is also responsible for their staff costs, while the remaining three, in charge of children and youth education, were founded and are financed by the Ministry of Education.

4   Social Protection, Financial Benefits and Allowances

The social protection system is mainly defined by the Law on Social and Child Protection (adopted in 2013 and amended in 2015, 2016 and 2017) and consists of two main parts, namely a contributory part, which is based on the social insurance system (pensions and disability, health and unemployment insurance) and a non-contributory part, which draws its funding from tax

---

30   Statistical Office of Montenegro, Assessment of Feasibility of Data and Data Collection in Montenegro, Montenegro 2011, 13.
31   Ibid.; Boryana Gotcheva and Aylin Isik-Dikmelik. Activation and Smart Safety Nets in Montenegro: Constraints in Beneficiary Profile, Benefit Design, and Institutional Capacity (Washington DC: World Bank, 2013), 45–46.
32   European Commission, Social Protection and Social Inclusion in Montenegro - Executive Summary (Brussels: EC, 2008), 6.
33   Ibid.

revenues flowing into the central budget (the first being social services that are defined by law – prevention, counselling, therapy and advice, care in and outside of institutions, and social welfare benefits). The data provided in Table 7.1 presents a broad range of both contributory and non-contributory financial benefits delivered to citizens in Montenegro.

TABLE 7.1   Overview of social assistance benefits

Program	Type of benefit	Eligibility	Funding	Implementing agency
Family material support (Materijalno Obezbjedjenje Porodice, MOP)	€63.5 to €120.7 per month in benefits for family, depending on family size	Tests of assets and income (an income limit is set by the MOP for a specified family size)	Central budget	Ministry of Labor and Social Welfare, Centers for Social Work
Personal disability benefit	Monthly benefit €178.19	Individuals disabled prior to attaining age 18	Central budget	Ministry of Labor and Social Welfare
Carer's allowance	Monthly benefit €65.35	MOP beneficiaries, in need of constant nursing care because of chronic illness, who receive personal disability benefits	Central budget	Ministry of Labor and Social Welfare
Residential institutional care	Covers the cost of accommodation in special institutions	Children who are either orphans or developmentally delayed; adults with disabilities	Central budget or users if they sign contract with institution	Ministry of Labor and Social Welfare
Accommodation in foster family	Covers accommodation expenses plus compensation for the foster family	Children who are either orphans or developmentally delayed; adults with disabilities	Central budget	Ministry of Labor and Social Welfare

TABLE 7.1 Overview of social assistance benefits *(cont.)*

Program	Type of benefit	Eligibility	Funding	Implementing agency
Assistance for professional rehabilitation and job training	Covers expenses for accommodation in a residential institution and transportation expenses	Children and youth with special needs	Central budget	Ministry of Labor and Social Welfare
Health care	Health insurance paid for	MOP recipients, recipients of personal disability benefits and individuals in residential or foster family accommodations	Central budget	Ministry of Labor and Social Welfare
Funeral costs	€315 in funeral costs covered	MOP recipients, recipients of personal disability benefits and individuals in residential or foster family accommodations	Central budget	Ministry of Labor and Social Welfare
One-time cash assistance	Available for the family of persons who are in extreme social need	Family or individual in extreme need due to accommodation-related problems, material or health needs	Central budget	Ministry of Health; Ministry of Labor and Social Welfare
Birth allowance	Benefit in the amount of €109.07 to €130.8 for every newborn	Universal benefit for all parents for each newborn	Central budget	Ministry of Labor and Social Welfare

TABLE 7.1 Overview of social assistance benefits (*cont.*)

Program	Type of benefit	Eligibility	Funding	Implementing agency
Child allowance	Monthly benefit amounting from €23.68 to €39.57	For the first three children in an MOP beneficiary family, for children with severe disabilities who cannot live independently, and children who are orphans	Central budget	Ministry of Labor and Social Welfare
Compensation for unemployed mothers and full-time students	Monthly benefit paid for one calendar year	Mothers who are enrolled as full-time students or who are unemployed	Central budget	Ministry of Labor and Social Welfare
Compensation of salary for part-time work	Parent benefit; employers pay parents full-time wages and may request reimbursement by the Ministry	Parents who need to provide care for a sick child	Central budget	Ministry of Labor and Social Welfare
Holiday and recreation for children	Covers expenses for holidays and recreation for children	Children of MOP recipients and children in foster families	Central budget	Ministry of Labor and Social Welfare

SOURCE: LAW ON SOCIAL AND CHILD PROTECTION, OFFICIAL GAZETTE OF THE REPUBLIC OF MONTENEGRO, NO. 27/13, 01/15, 42/15, 47/15, 56/16, 66/16, 001/17, 31/17, 42/17, 50/17; STATISTICAL OFFICE OF MONTENEGRO, ASSESSMENT OF FEASIBILITY OF DATA AND DATA COLLECTION IN MONTENEGRO, MONTENEGRO 2011, 18–20.

The cash benefits can be broadly grouped into the following categories:
- guaranteed minimum income for those who lack minimum resources;
- benefits for children and families with children;
- disability benefits;
- benefits for war veterans and their families.[34]

Out of this set, benefits for children and families with children include those that also cover the working population. From the set of child protection benefits, working parents are eligible to include the birth grant. The birth grant or benefit for a newborn child is a universal benefit for each newborn child and amounts from €109.07 to €130.88 for parents who received material family support.[35] Moreover, workers with an employer and the self-employed are eligible for wage compensation for maternity or parental leave. The amount of wage compensation depends on the current salary of the beneficiary and the length of their work record and is capped at two average wages for the country in the preceding year. For example, if the employment "has lasted for twelve months or more, the employer is reimbursed with an average income of the employee over the twelve months preceding the month when the right to maternity or parental leave was acquired. In addition, reimbursement of salary for half-time work is also provided."[36]

The next instrument intended for individuals is unemployment benefit. To be eligible for this assistance individuals must have been insured without interruption for twelve months, or for any twelve months of the past eighteen months. Furthermore, within 30 days of termination of employment, they must submit a claim stating whether they were at fault for said termination or whether it was voluntary. An exception to this rule is young people with disabilities, who can receive this benefit while seeking a job, provided they were disabled prior to reaching the age of 18 and have completed specialized vocational education. The period of eligibility for benefits depends on the period in which the person was insured. The benefit is granted due to the following rules:
- for an insurance period of one to five years: three months;
- for an insurance period of five to ten years: four months;
- for an insurance period of ten to fifteen years: six months;
- for an insurance period of fifteen to 20 years: eight months;
- for an insurance period of twenty to 25 years: ten months;

---

34 Jadranka Kaludjerović and Vojin Golubović, European Social Policy Network (ESPN) Thematic Report on In-work Poverty in Montenegro (Brussels: European Commission Directorate-General for Employment, Social Affairs and Inclusion, 2019), 11–12.

35 Law on Social and Child Protection, Article 41, Official Gazette of the Republic of Montenegro, no. 27/13, 01/15, 42/15, 47/15, 56/16, 66/16, 001/17, 31/17, 42/17, 50/17.

36 Jadranka Kaludjerović and Vojin Golubović, European Social Policy Network (ESPN) Thematic Report on In-work Poverty in Montenegro, 12.

- for an insurance period of more than 25 years: twelve months;
- for a period of insurance contributions of more than 35 years: until re-employment, or if there is the occurrence of one of the grounds for termination of rights to receive monetary benefits under this law;
- an unemployed person with more than 25 years of insurance contributions, who is the parent of a child eligible by law for a personal disability allowance, is entitled to unemployment benefits until again employed or until the occurrence of any of the grounds for termination of rights to unemployment benefit according to this law.[37]

Additionally, provided that an individual has acquired a working experience of over 30 years, they are entitled to unemployment benefits until again employed or eligible for retirement. Only young mothers, who have recently given birth, are excluded from this rule - they are entitled to this benefit for twelve months. The unemployment benefit equals 65% of the national basic minimum wage with additional social security contributions and is fairly low compared to the average wage and consequently cannot be seen as an income actually providing support for the unemployed. Usually, the benefit in Montenegro lasts around twelve months. Taking into account only those currently obtaining the benefit, this increases to 48 months. What contributes to this phenomenon is that open-ended beneficiaries are the largest group among recipients. The majority of this group are mainly older former employees of bankrupt public companies. If not provided for otherwise, every unemployed person along with their family members is eligible for health insurance.[38]

Maternity leave is another important allowance. Insured mothers with at least six continuous months of insurance before their terms' start are entitled to it. The administration of this benefit is the responsibility of the Ministry of Labor and Social Affairs and individuals are provided with one full-year's salary as compensation. 45 days before the expected delivery date, a woman is entitled to optional pregnancy leave, which becomes mandatory 28 days before delivery. As a general practice, the employer applies to the Ministry for refund of the payment to the mother after it has been made. In accordance with the law, fathers with insurance are eligible to paternity leave.[39]

---

[37] Law on Employment and Exercising Rights from Unemployment Insurance, Article 51, Official Gazette of the Republic of Montenegro, no. 14/10, 40/11, 45/12, 61/13, 20/15.

[38] For more information see Labour Law in Montenegro, https://cms.law/en/int/expert-guides/cms-expert-guide-to-labour-law-in-central-eastern-europe/montenegro, (accessed June 15, 2019); Law on Employment and Exercising Rights from Unemployment Insurance.

[39] Iftikhar Ahmad and Ayesha Ahmed, Montenegro Decent Work Check 2020 (Amsterdam: WageIndicator Foundation, 2020), 20–21. For detailed information see Labor Law, Article 126; regarding the beneficiary of reimbursement of salary compensation for maternity or parental leave see Law on Social and Child Protection, Article 50–53.

In the case of illness or injury, employees are entitled to sickness benefits, and are eligible for salary compensation. If the leave is shorter than 60 days, the employer is responsible for the payment. However, after 60 days, the Health Insurance Fund takes over this responsibility. If the leave period exceeds ten months, before approving further leave, the employees have to be assessed by the medical commission of the Health Insurance Fund and Pension Insurance Fund on their ability to return to work or to evaluate their eligibility for retirement due to disability (Law on Compulsory Health Insurance, Article 38–44).

Benefits for social assistance are both categorized and means-tested. They can be broadly divided into family/individual social assistance benefits and child protection benefits. The number of people who have benefited from this type of support in 2015–2019 is presented in Table 7.2.

TABLE 7.2 Social welfare beneficiaries

Material support of family	2015	2016	2017	2018	2019
Number of families	11,463	8,961	7,987	9,319	8,777
Number of members	36,986	26,873	24,586	31,066	29,470
Personal disability allowance	2,033	2,222	2,343	2,500	2,608
Care and support allowance	11,439	14,856	14,539	15,298	17,573
Children's allowance beneficiaries	8,992	6,728	6,200	7,622	7,358

SOURCE: STATISTICAL OFFICE OF MONTENEGRO, STATISTICAL YEARBOOK 2018 (PODGORICA: MONSTAT 2018), 204–205; STATISTICAL OFFICE OF MONTENEGRO, STATISTICAL YEARBOOK 2020 (PODGORICA: MONSTAT 2020), 210–211.

The purpose of family/individual social assistance benefits is to provide assistance for individuals and families to reduce their vulnerability. These include:
– financial support (family material support);
– carer's allowance;
– personal disability benefit, parent/guardian's allowance;
– health protection;
– funeral costs and single payments.[40]

Family material support (Materijalno Obezbjedjenje Porodice, MOP) is one of the basic forms of social assistance. It is intended for families and family members

---

40   Law on Social and Child Protection, Article 20.

unable to work. It also applies to individuals capable of maintaining work provided they are according to Article 21 of the Law on Social and Child Protection:
- pregnant;
- single parent;
- a parent providing for a dependent child or a disabled child unable to work (who was already disabled prior to reaching the age of 18);
- a child who is an orphan until employed, or a child with special needs who has completed special vocational training.

Adjustments to the amount of the benefits are made on the basis of the financial condition of the central budget in accordance with the legislation.[41] The set amount of MOP benefit is:
- an individual €63.50;
- family with one member €65.86;
- two-member family €76.20;
- three-member family €91.50;
- four-member family €108.00;
- five- or more member family €120.70;
- a person who is a child without parental care €120.70 monthly.[42]

The MOP benefits include also the personal disability benefits introduced by the Law on Social and Child Protection and intended for a person who has been declared unable to live an independent life before the age of 18. Since 2017, the amount of this benefit has been €178.19 per month.[43] In 2019 the personal disability benefit was provided for 2,608 individuals which is an increase compared to 2,343 in 2017.[44] Another benefit is the caregiver allowance granted to those entitled to material family support and who need permanent care and individual assistance due to their physical or mental disorders and at the same time benefit from personal disability benefit. Individuals suffering from physical, mental, intellectual, sensory disorders or changes in their health condition and who require care and support are entitled to the care and support allowance. Moreover, individuals may claim the right to care and support allowance if they are not already exercising this right due to other laws and that they are not a beneficiary of personal disability

---

41 According to the law hitherto in force, the amount of family material support has adjusted to a change in the average national net wage in the previous quarter.
42 Law on Social and Child Protection, Article 31.
43 Ibid., Article 32.
44 Statistical Office of Montenegro, Statistical Yearbook 2018 (Podgorica: MONSTAT, 2018), 204, http://monstat.org/eng/novosti.php?id=2696 (accessed June 15, 2019); Statistical Office of Montenegro, Statistical Yearbook 2020 (Podgorica: MONSTAT, 2020), 210, http://www.monstat.org/eng/novosti.php?id=3218 (accessed December 27, 2020).

allowance. The care and support allowance amounts to €65.35 per month. In 2019, the caregiver allowance benefit was provided for 17,573 individuals,[45] which was more than in 2017, when 14,539 individuals[46] received this benefit.

Health protection is also an important benefit given to MOP beneficiaries, those who receive personal disability benefits and individuals who are placed either in foster families or in residential institutions. In addition, single payments are offered as a benefit to families or persons with social requirements due to unusual conditions connected to accommodation, health, and material status. However, in the event of death, funeral costs are covered for the following beneficiaries:

- MOP recipients;
- recipients of personal disability benefits;
- persons placed either in foster families or residential institutions.[47]

Child protection benefits are given to children with disabilities and/or from poor families to reduce poverty and vulnerability risks. Social protection systems, especially social protection floors, make a significant contribution to lifting children out of poverty as well as improvements to their health and overall well-being. They lower child mortality and increase access to essential things such as a nutritious diet, education, health, and other care services. What is more, these help reduce child labor, therefore ensuring that youngsters have the chance to reach their full potential and stopping the process of falling into poverty and becoming vulnerable. Furthermore, social protection contributes to recognizing children's rights to social security and a suitable standard of living. The basic level of child protection benefits includes according to Article 40 of the Law on Social and Child Protection:

- grants on the birth of a child;
- allowances for children;
- benefits for women who give birth to a child and are either employed or unemployed and suffer a loss or drop of income;
- assistance for up-bringing and education of children and young people with special educational needs.

---

45 Statistical Office of Montenegro, Statistical Yearbook 2020 (Podgorica: MONSTAT, 2020), 210, http://www.monstat.org/eng/novosti.php?id=3218 (accessed December 27, 2020).
46 Statistical Office of Montenegro, Statistical Yearbook 2018, 204, (Podgorica: MONSTAT, 2018) http://monstat.org/eng/novosti.php?id=2696 (accessed June 15, 2019).
47 Law on Social and Child Protection, Article 35–36.

The birth grant entitles parents who are eligible to receive €130.88[48] for every newborn child. In 2019 there were 7,358 beneficiaries of this benefit in Montenegro.[49] There are two benefits payable to women giving birth to a child whether they are employed or unemployed - compensation for salary during the period of maternity/paternity leave, and compensation for mothers who are either enrolled as full-time students or are unemployed mothers. Only individuals entitled to the benefit for a full one-year are eligible to the monthly amount of €79.03.[50] It should be noted that parents, who are temporarily out of work to take care of a child with an illness are entitled to compensation for loss of earnings. Consequently, it remains the responsibility of the employer to pay the full salary and then submit a request to be reimbursed by the MLSW.

Children from MOP beneficiary families as well as children who have physical, mental or sensory disorders and are able to take up ordinary life and work, through education and training; those with such disorders and cannot do so, as well as children who are orphans are entitled to child allowance. However, each family can only claim this benefit for the first three children. According to Article 44 of the Law on Social and Child Protection, the monthly value of the benefit is:

- €23.68 for MOP beneficiaries and children whose caregiver obtained employment on the ground of the individual activation plan;
- € 31.87 for beneficiaries of a care and support allowance;
- €39.57 for beneficiaries of personal disability allowance;
- €39.57 for children who are orphans.

5 Financing Social Protection

Guaranteeing long-term financial stability is one of the main principles of financing social security systems. A complete system can only be maintained on the basis of a constant income, but health and pension spending make this difficult. National social protection funds (SPFS) should generally

---

48 Ibid., Article 41.
49 Statistical Office of Montenegro, Statistical Yearbook 2020 (Podgorica: MONSTAT 2020), 211, http://www.monstat.org/eng/novosti.php?id=3218 (accessed December 27, 2020).
50 Law on Social and Child Protection, Article 54.

be covered by national resources. Yet, transitional international assistance is an additional means for the members whose financial and economic capabilities are insufficient to provide the whole range of assurances. To ensure the stability of national SPFs the state government should consider the contributory capabilities of various groups within society for instance the effective enforcement of tax and contribution obligations either individually or in combination, reprioritizing expenditure or a broader and sufficiently progressive revenue base.[51]

As Gotcheva and Isik-Dikmelik claim "the welfare system in Montenegro is centralized in terms of its design and financing, while implementation is delegated to the local level. The system of social and child protection is centralized, with the MLSW responsible for policymaking, provision of finance, and supervision of CSWs as institutions that implement social and child protection at the municipal level."[52] There are two main funding sources for the system of social protection – subsidies from the central government budget and contributions by insured persons. The central budget is responsible for supporting the social assistance part of expenditure for child and parent protection. Insurance-based funding contributes to its respective areas. If any deficit occurs the central budget covers it. Public spending in 2018 was assessed at €2.085 billion, which equals 45.3% of GDP. This was less than in 2017, although this was agreed on during the budget revision adopted in July 2018 and as a percentage of GDP. The need for the revision of expenditure, relative to the former plans, was a result of the following:

– there was a need for an increased aggregate gross wage bill resulting from the need to strengthen the HR of institutions involved in the execution of matters particularly significant for the quality of the public services provided, primarily in education, health and social protection, as well as the necessity of bolstering the ability to meet the requirements of EU integration;
– health-related contingent expenses resulting in part from arrears of the previous period and in part from additional costs incurred in the current year for ongoing treatment and the purchase of drugs and medical supplies;

---

51   Jean-Michel Servais, "International Standards on Social Security, Lessons from the Past for a Better Implementation" (Manila: ILO, 2014), 10, https://islssl.org/wp-content/uploads/2014/12/Servais_2014_Asian_Conf.pdf (accessed August 10, 2019).
52   Boryana Gotcheva and Aylin Isik-Dikmelik. Activation and Smart Safety Nets in Montenegro: Constraints in Beneficiary Profile, Benefit Design, and Institutional Capacity (Washington DC: World Bank, 2013), 44.

- changes to the handling of expenses for the purchase of securities, to harmonize these with internationally accepted methodology. This category constitutes an integral part of the financing of transactions.[53]

The public finance deficit in 2018 was projected at €122.1 million (2.7% of GDP) and in contrast to the planned level, this is €24.1 million (24.5%) higher. The chief cause of this is a lower level of public revenue generation. The primary public finances deficit was estimated at 0.6 percent of GDP or €29.3 million.[54] A notable change can be observed in social protection spending since 2000, both when looking at the general amount and its structure. 2018 shows a tendency to spend more funds on the benefits themselves, while reducing the operational costs of the institutions. This may be a sign of the application of a better management mechanism, as well as exercising the will to distribute funds instead of spending them on the system itself.

6 Strategic Reforms in the Social Protection

The purpose of social protection for the Government of Montenegro is to boost the quality of life and to empower Montenegrin citizens for independent and productive lives. In order to create equivalent conditions for inclusion in all spheres of life, the Montenegrin establishment has adopted various strategic documents, according to EU requirements and standards:

- The Strategy of Social and Child Protection System Development 2013–2017[55] is focused on harmonisation with international social protection norms and standards, decentralization to increase participation in decision-making by recipients, reduction of support delivery costs and provision of better quality services.
- The Strategy for the Integration of Persons with Disabilities in Montenegro 2016–2020[56] is a continuation of work on improving the

---

53 Government of Montenegro, Montenegro Economic Reform Programme 2019–2021 (Podgorica: The Ministry of Finance, 2019), 28, https://www.gov.me/en/documents/008d13bb-ec19-451d-9084-d05011b6b3d8 (accessed May 20, 2019).
54 Ibid., 28.
55 Strategy of Social and Child Protection System Development 2013-2017, https://www.gov.me/en/documents/bb1359a8-fb50-4829-a52f-cad54f1b5b02 (accessed May 20, 2019).
56 Strategy for Integration of Persons with Disabilities in Montenegro for the period 2016–2020, https://www.gov.me/en/documents/08615fc8-872f-4473-8677-1967e3c23d74 (accessed May 20, 2019).

position of persons with disabilities. At the end of 2007, the Government of Montenegro adopted the first Strategy for the Integration of Persons with Disabilities in Montenegro for the period 2008–2016 with a whole series of measures and recommendations to improve the position of this group in the population.

- The Strategy for the Prevention and Protection of Children from Violence 2017–2021.[57] The goal of this strategy is to strengthen the national framework in preventing violence against children, including improving legislation and the judicial system by 2021. Additionally, it includes administrative care and services for child victims or those at risk of violence.
- The Strategy for the Development of the Social and Child Protection System for the period from 2018 to 2022[58] was adopted in September 2017. Taken as a whole, the objective of this strategy is to improve the quality of life of social and child welfare beneficiaries. The specific objectives are to improve the normative framework and quality of the system as well as enhanced social and childcare services and prerequisites for continued deinstitutionalization.
- The Strategy for the Development of the Social Protection System for the Elderly 2013–2017.[59] The overall objective of this strategy is to improve the social protection of the elderly, with integrated services and support to preserve and improve their quality of life. The specific objectives are to improve social responsibility and an integrative approach that promotes social inclusion, enhances the quality of life, and uses older people's capacities to live independently. Moreover, the aim of the strategy is to enhance social care services for the elderly and the quality of service of this group of society.
- The Strategy for Exercising the Rights of the Child 2019–2023[60] is a national, comprehensive and interdepartmental document that deals with the

---

57 Strategy for the Prevention and Protection of Children from Violence 2017–2021 (Strategija za prevenciju i zaštitu djece od nasilja sa AP 2017–2021, April 2017), https://www.gov.me/en/documents/4f98be5b-58e7-4df7-822a-34a9d4fdcf65 (accessed May 20, 2019).
58 Strategy for the Development of the Social and Child Protection System for the period from 2018 to 2022, https://www.social-protection.org/gimi/RessourcePDF.action?id=55821 (accessed May 20, 2019).
59 Strategy for the Development of the Social Protection System for the Elderly 2013-2017 (Strategija Razvoja sistema socijalne zaštite starih lica 2013–2017), https://www.zsdzcg.me/images/Biblioteka/STRATEGIJA%20RAZVOJA%20SISTEMA%20SOCIJALNE%20ZAŠTITE%20STARIH%20LICA%202013-2017.pdf (accessed May 20, 2019).
60 Strategy for Exercising the Rights of the Child 2019–2023, https://www.unicef.org/montenegro/en/reports/strategy-exercising-rights-child-2019–2023 (accessed May 20, 2019).

improvement of conditions for the realization of the rights of the child in all areas covered by the United Nations (UN) Convention on the Rights of the Child and its Optional Protocols. This document refers to a five-year strategic period, and its implementation begins in the jubilee thirtieth year since the adoption of the UN Convention on the Rights of the Child.

In parallel with the above listed strategies, implementation Action Plans (AP) have been prepared and adopted by the Government of Montenegro. Annually, on the basis of the indicators included in APs implementation, evaluation progress of all strategies is carried out.

7 Conclusion

On its road to become a member of the European Union, Montenegro faces challenges adopting European social policy principles in its social protection system according to EU standards, requirements and best practices. Montenegro has adopted, conducted, and still is implementing documents, a wide range of reforms and projects focused on social inclusion and protection. However, in order to meet requirements resulting from EU regulation to close negotiations on Chapter 19 – Social Policy and Employment and bring EU accession forward, the Government of Montenegro ought to introduce active labor market measures for women negatively affected by the repeal of the social benefits and increase the collaboration with the social partners and other NGO actors operating in the sector. Additionally, to support the transition from institutional service provision to community-based care for children with special needs, persons with disabilities and the elderly, strengthening the CSW's is necessary. Furthermore, the introduction of a better employment quality measures aimed at young people, women, minorities and other job seekers are strongly recommended to continue the fight with the grey economy. Establishing the conditions for evidence-based policymaking, the Government should also implement sufficient monitoring assets to available mechanisms and reports. To ensure the provision of continuous, social services at local level, as well as assisting in the implementation of local social inclusion plans adequate financial resources must be secured. Moreover, to strengthen functioning of the Institute for Social and Child Protection its budget needs to be reinforced.

Much important work on alignment and preparation for the implementation of the acquis has taken place in most areas since Chapter 19 was opened on December 13, 2016. However, it is considered that the country has not yet reached a good enough level of preparation in areas such as social policy and employment to assume its full membership obligations. Consequently, strengthening the administrative capacity for ensuring the application of the EU requirements remains a significant challenge.

In summary, the Government of Montenegro should now circumspectly prepare and conduct a review of the social security system to get a clear picture of this area and prepare to offer a wide range of social support and assistance to those in need, including increased protection of vulnerable groups such as the elderly and creating a better child protection system. This is a vital and great challenge which requires an efficient and synchronized effort at all administrative levels.

Bibliography

Ahmad Iftikhar, and Ayesha Ahmad. Montenegro Decent Work Check 2020. Amsterdam: WageIndicator Foundation, 2020.

Bartlett, William. Europe's Troubled Region: Economic Development, Institutional Reform and Social Welfare in the Western Balkans. New York: Routledge, 2008.

Bartlett, William, and Merita Xhumari. "Social Security Policy and Pension Reforms in the Western Balkans". European Journal of Social Security no. 9 (2007): 297–322.

Burgess, Robin, and Nicolas Stern. "Social Security in Developing Countries: What, Why, Who, and How?". In Social Security in Developing Countries edited by Ahmad Ehtisham, Jean Drèze, John Hills and Amartya Sen, 41–80. New York: Oxford University Press, 1991.

Centar Za Socijalni Rad Podgorica. PI Center for Social Work for the Capital Podgorica, the Municipality within the Capital Golubovci and the Municipality of Tuzi". Accessed April 20, 2019. https://www.csrcg.me/index.php/podgorica/o-nama.

Civil Society Organizations in the Proces of Standarization of Social Services in Montenegro. Podgorica: SOS Hotline for Women and Children Victims of Violence Podgorica, 2018. Accessed June 15, 2019. https://www.academia.edu/36601093/SOS_CSOs_in_process_of_standardisation_of_social_services_in_Montenegro_ENG_pdf.

Constitution of Montenegro 2007. Accessed April 16, 2019, https://www.wipo.int/edocs/lexdocs/laws/en/me/me004en.pdf.

Coppieters, Bruno, Michael Emerson, Michel Huysseune, Tamara Kovziridze, Gergana Noutcheva, Nathalie Tocci, and Marius Vahl. Europeanization and Conflict Resolution. Case Studies from European Peripheries. Gent: Academia Press, 2004.

Devereux, Stephen and Rachel Sabates-Wheeler. Transformative Social Protection, Institute of Development Studies Working Paper 232. Brighton, 2004.

Drèze, Jean, and Amartya Sen. "Public Action for Social Security: Foundation and Strategy." In Social Security in Developing Countries, edited by Ahmad Ehtisham, Jean Drèze, John Hills and Amartya Sen. New York: Oxford University Press, 1991.

European Commission. Economic Reform Program of Montenegro 2018–2021. Brussels, 2017.

European Commission. Montenegro 2019 Report. Brussels, 2019.

European Commission. Social Protection and Social Inclusion in Montenegro. Brussels, 2008.

European System of Integrated Social Protection Statistics. ESSPROS Manual. Luxembourg: Eurostat, 1996.

Gierszewski, Janusz. Bezpieczeństwo społeczne jako dziedzina bezpieczeństwa narodowego", Historia i Polityka nr 23 (30) 2018: 21–38.

Gotcheva, Boryana, and Aylin Isik-Dikmelik. Activation and Smart Safety Nets in Montenegro: Constraints in Beneficiary Profile, Benefit Design and Institutional Capacity. Washington D.C: World Bank, 2013.

Government of Montenegro. EU Accession Negotiation. Analysis of Benchmarks for Montenegro through Comparison with Croatia and Serbia. The Ministry of European Affairs of Montenegro, 2018.

Government of Montenegro. Montenegro Development Directions 2018–2021. Podgorica: The Ministry of Finance, 2017.

Government of Montenegro. Montenegro Economic Reform Programme 2019–2021. Podgorica: The Ministry of Finance, 2019. Accessed May 20, 2019. https://www.gov.me/en/documents/008d13bb-ec19-451d-9084-d05011b6b3d8.

Human Security Unit. Human Security in Theory and Practice. New York: Office for the Coordination of Humanitarian Affairs, United Nation, 2009.

International Labor Office. Social Security and the Rule of Law. Report III (Part 1B). Geneva: ILO, 2011.

International Labour Organization. World Social Protection Report 2017–2019: Universal Social Protection to Achieve the Sustainable Development Goals International Labor Office. Geneva: International Labour Office 2017.

JU Centri za socijalni rad. Accessed April 20, 2019. https://www.csrcg.me/index.php/mapa/795-ju-centri-za-socijalni-rad-na-teritoriji-crne-gore.

Kaludjerović, Jadranka. European Social Policy Network (ESPN) Flash Report 2020/57. Brussels: European Commission, European Social Policy Network, 2020.

Kaludjerović, Jadranka, and Golubović Vojin. European Social Policy Network (ESPN) Thematic Report on In-work Poverty – Montenegro. Brussels: European Commission, Directorate General for Employment, Social Affairs and Inclusion, 2019.

Krukowska, Anna. "Nietypowy federalizm serbsko-czarnogórski". Wschodnioznawstwo 1, (2007): 55–77.

Law on Compulsory Health Insurance, Official Gazette of the Republic of Montenegro, no. 6/16, 2/17, 22/17, 13/18, 67/19.

Law on Employment and Exercising Rights from Unemployment Insurance, Official Gazette of the Republic of Montenegro, no. 14/10, 40/11, 45/12, 61/13, 20/15.

Law on Social and Child Protection, Official Gazette of the Republic of Montenegro, no. 27/13, 01/15, 42/15, 47/15, 56/16, 66/16, 001/17, 31/17, 42/17, 50/17.

Marczuk, Karina Paulina. „Bezpieczeństwo społeczne: potrzeba szerokiego ujęcia. Implikacje dla Polski". In Bezpieczeństwo społeczne. Pojęcia, uwarunkowania, wyzwania, edited by Aleksandra Skrabacz, Stanisław Sulowski, 26–52. Warsaw: Elipsa, 2012.

Matković, Gorgana. The Welfare State in Western Balkan Countries – Challenges and Opinion. Belgrade: Centre for Social Policy, 2017.

Official Gazette of the Republic of Montenegro no. 13/07, 79/08, 86/09, 78/10, 40/11, 14/12, 62/13, 08/15, 22/17, 42/19.

Official Gazette of the Republic of Montenegro no. 54/03, 78/10, 34/11, 40/11, 66/12, 38/13, 61/13, 6/14, 60/14, 10/15, 44/15, 42/16, 55/16.

Official Gazette of the Republic of Montenegro, no. 49/08, 26/09, 59/11, 66/12.

Official Gazette of the Republic of Montenegro, no. 39/04, 3/16, 39/16, 2/17.

Official Gazette of the Republic of Montenegro, no. 39/04, 14/12.

Radović, Dragana. Mapping of Social Protection Services in Montenegro. Podgorica: Institute Alternative, 2013.

Rosandić, Andreja. Social Economy in Eastern Neighborhood and in the Western Balkans. Country Report Montenegro. Brussels: Directorate-General for Neighborhood and Enlargement Negotiations, 2018.

Rulebook on Detailed Conditions for the Provision and Use, Norms and the Minimum Standards of Accommodation Service for Adults and the Elderly, Official Gazette of Montenegro, no. 58/14.

Rulebook on Detailed Conditions for the Provision and Use, Norms and the Minimum Standards of Accommodation Services for Children and Young Persons in an Institution and a Small Home Community, Official Gazette of Montenegro, no. 43/14.

Rulebook on Detailed Conditions for the Provision and Use of Services of Family Placement-Foster Care and Family Placement, Official Gazette of Montenegro, no. 19/14.

Rulebook on Detailed Conditions for the Provision and Use, Norms and the Minimum Standards of Services for the Community Living Support, Official Gazette of Montenegro, no. 30/15.

Servais, Jean-Michel. International Standards on Social Security, Lessons from the past for a better implementation. Manila 2014. Accessed August 10, 2019, https://islssl.org/wp-content/uploads/2014/12/Servais_2014_Asian_Conf.pdf.

Statistical Office of Montenegro. Assessment of Feasibility of Data and Data Collection in Montenegro. Montenegro, 2011. Accessed April 10, 2019. http://transmonee.org/wp-content/uploads/2016/03/Montenegro_CAR_2011.pdf.

Statistical Office of Statistical Office of Montenegro. Statistical Yearbook 2018. Podgorica: MONSTAT, 2018. Accessed June 15 2019. http://monstat.org/eng/novosti.php?id=2696.

Statistical Office of Montenegro. Statistical Yearbook 2020. Podgorica: MONSTAT, 2020. Accessed December 27, 2020. http://monstat.org/eng/publikacije_page.php?id=1674&pageid=1

Strategy of Social and Child Protection System Development 2013–2017. Accessed May 20, 2019. https://www.gov.me/en/documents/bb1359a8-fb50-4829-a52f-cad54f1b5b02.

Strategy for the Development of the Social and Child Protection System for the period from 2018 to 2022. Accessed May 20, 2019, https://www.social-protection.org/gimi/RessourcePDF.action?id=55821.

Strategy for the Development of the Social Protection System for the Elderly 2013–2017 (Strategija Razvoja sistema socijalne zaštite starih lica 2013–2017). Accessed May 20, 2019. https://www.zsdzcg.me/images/Biblioteka/STRATEGIJA%20RAZVOJA%20SISTEMA%20SOCIJALNE%20ZAŠTITE%20STARIH%20LICA%202013-2017.pdf.

Strategy for Exercising the Rights of the Child 2019-2023. Accessed May 20,2019. https://www.unicef.org/montenegro/en/reports/strategy-exercising-rights-child-2019-2023.

Strategy for Integration of Persons with Disabilities in Montenegro for the period 2016–2020. Accessed May 20, 2019. https://www.gov.me/en/documents/08615fc8-872f-4473-8677-1967e3c23d74.

Strategy for the Prevention and Protection of Children Against Violence 2017–2021 (Strategija za prevenciju i zaštitu djece od nasilja sa AP 2017-2021, April 2017). Accessed May 20, 2019 https://www.gov.me/en/documents/4f98be5b-58e7-4df7-822a-34a9d4fdcf65.

UN Department of Economic and Social Affairs (DESA). Promoting Inclusion Through Social Protection. UN: New York 2018.

Vuković Drenka, and Natalija Perišić. Opportunities and Challenges of Social Security Transition in Montenegro. In Welfare States in Transition, edited by Marija Stambolieva and Stefan Dehnert, 165-199. Sofia: Friedrich Ebert Foundation, 2011.

Williams, Paul. D. "Security Studies. An Introduction". In Security Studies. An Introduction, edited by Paul D. Williams, 1–12. New York: Routledge, 2008.

Żukiewicz, Przemysław. Pozycja ustrojowa rządu w państwach postjugosłowiańskich. Analiza prawno-porównawcza. Wrocław: Instytut Politologii Uniwersytetu Wrocławskiego, 2017.

CHAPTER 8

Unemployment and Emigration as a (Main) Challenge for the Social Security System and Stability of a Multiethnic State: The Case of Montenegro

Agata Domachowska

1 Introduction

Montenegro is a small Balkan state, which recently (in 2006) declared its independence. From the end of World War II until 1992, the state was a part of the Socialist Federal Republic of Yugoslavia. Next, together with Serbia, it formed the Federal Republic of Yugoslavia (1992–2003), and for the subsequent three years the State Union of Serbia and Montenegro. After declaring its independence, it soon became a member of the United Nations (UN), the Council of Europe, and the Organization for Security and Co-operation in Europe (OSCE). In 2007, Montenegro joined the World Bank and the International Monetary Fund, and four years later (2011), the World Trade Organization as its 154th member.[1]

After joining NATO in 2018, the current priority of Montenegro's foreign policy remains its accession to the European Union. In 2012, Montenegro initiated negotiations with the EU and to date, it has managed to open 32 out of 33 accession chapters, three of which (25 Science and research, 26 Education and culture, 30 External relations) have been provisionally closed.[2]

When analyzing the phenomena of unemployment and emigration, it is important to take into account the territorial and regional division of the country. One of the characteristics of Montenegro's unemployment is differences between regions. Currently, Montenegro is divided into 24 municipalities (in recent years, three new ones have been established: Tuzi (2018), Gusinje (2014) and Petnjica (2013)), and three regions:

---

[1] WTO, Montenegro, 2019, https://www.wto.org/english/thewto_e/acc_e/a1_montenegro_e.htm (accessed November 15, 2019).
[2] Ministry of Foreign Affairs and European Integration of Montenegro, 2019, https://www.eu.me/wp-content/uploads/2021/02/Tabela_poglavlja_MNE verzija EU4ME.png (accessed November 15, 2019).

- Central Region, consists of the municipalities of Cetinje, Danilovgrad, Nikšić, Podgorica and Tuzi;
- Coastal Region – located on the Adriatic Sea, consists of the municipalities of Bar, Budva, Herceg Novi, Kotor, Tivat and Ulcinj;
- Northern Region, the largest by area, but with a much smaller population than the Central Region. It comprises the following municipalities: Andrijevica, Berane, Bijelo Polje, Gusinje, Kolašin, Mojkovac, Petnjica, Plav, Plužine, Pijevlja, Rožaje, Šavnik and Žabljak.[3]

The aim of this chapter is to present two key challenges to the social security of a state, unemployment and emigration, through the analysis of the case of Montenegro. One of the greatest threats to the security of each country remains the relatively high unemployment rate, which at the same time can effect an increase in emigration. In fact, the employment issues facing many young people in Montenegro foster a desire to find work somewhere abroad.[4] In turn, emigration can bring not only short and long-term benefits, but also problems for the country. Social security is a public good and as such requires specific state activity. The main task for every government is to ensure improvement in the quality of life of every citizen. However, today every state faces huge challenges in the sphere of social security. This is particularly visible in states threatened by economic crisis, high unemployment and poverty rates, high levels of external migration, aging of the society or a decline in fertility. Certainly, security is always closely related to what is happening in the economy. The stronger the economy, the lower the unemployment, and the richer the society.

The analytical basis of this study is a review of economic, sociological and security-related literature, including a secondary data analysis of public policy documents, statistics (published by the Statistical Office of Montenegro and the World Bank) and also media reports. Considering the subject of this study, qualitative research seemed necessary while the research topic formulated justifies the application of the content analysis and the desk research in order to analyze the secondary data sources. The case study method has been selected as well.[5]

---

3 See more Will Bartlett "International Aid, Policy, Transfer and Local Economic Development in North Montenegro", in Transformation and European Integration (London: Palgrave Macmillan 2006), 142–157.
4 Idris Iffat and Anna Strachan, "Economic Drivers of Conflict in the Western Balkans", K4D Helpdesk Report, (Brighton: Institute of Development Studies, 2017): 13, https://gsdrc.org/publications/economic-drivers-of-conflict-in-the-western-balkans/ (accessed November 9, 2019).
5 The study was carried out in 2019.

The analysis opens with information on the current state of Montenegro's economy, including the economic changes that have occurred there over the last thirty years. Moreover, it presents predictions about economic development of Montenegro. Next, it discusses the issue of unemployment with particular focus on differences in its scale between individual regions of Montenegro. The last part of the analysis presents the phenomenon of emigration. The economic situation and the level of unemployment also has an impact on a scale of emigration.[6] Unemployment (permanent or temporary), and the unfavorable situation on the labor market are push factors for emigration.[7] The chapter offers an overview of current challenges for the Montenegrin social security system such as unemployment and emigration and represents a summary of current knowledge about these phenomena.

2   Montenegro's Economy – General Overview

Since the 1990s, Montenegro's economy has undergone the processes of urbanization and industrialization. The service sector has also started to develop and the society itself has experienced significant changes, influenced by the turn in Montenegro's politics which took place in the second half of the 1990s.[8] At that time, the newly elected president of Montenegro, Milo Djukanović, decided to reorient the country's policy towards the West and at the same time tried to distance Montenegro from Serbia, then ruled by Slobodan Milošević.[9] As Ivan Vuković explained:

---

6   See more Lorena Škuflić and Valentina Vučković, "The Effect of Emigration on Unemployment Rates: The Case of EU Emigrant Countries", Economic Research-Ekonomska Istraživanja 31, no. 1 (2018): 1826–1836, DOI: 10.1080/1331677X. 2018.1516154.

7   Tomasz Homoncik, Klaudia Pujer and Iwona Wolańska, Ekonomiczno-społeczne aspekty migracji. Wybrane problemy (Wrocław: Exante, 2017), 9.

8   Dragan Đurić, "The Economic Development of Montenegro", in Montenegro in Transition: Problems of Identity and Statehood, ed. Florian Bieber (Baden-Baden: Nomos Verlagsgesellschaft, 2003); Dragan Đurić, "Montenegro's Prospects for European Integration: on a Twin Track", SEER-South-East Europe Review for Labour and Social Affairs, no. 4 (2004), 82–83; Maja Drakic, Frederic Sautet and Kyle McKenzie, "Montenegro: The Challenges of a Newborn State", *Mercatus Policy Series Country Brief*, no. 2 (Arlington: Mercatus Center at George Mason University, 2007): 1–3, 9–10.

9   Florian Bieber, "Montenegrin Politics since the Disintegration of Yugoslavia", in Montenegro in Transition: Problems of Identity and Statehood, ed. Florian Bieber (Baden-Baden: Nomos Verlagsgesellschaft, 2003), 27–28; what is more "Because of its independent political stance, the Djukanović government secured substantial economic and political support from the international community, which viewed the republic as a bastion of anti-Milosevic' sentiment and was willing to support political and economic liberalization with

> [t]he alliance of its incumbent party with Slobodan Milošević thus resulted in international economic and political isolation of Montenegro. What is more, given the absolute political domination of the DPS, it was clear that as long as the party was loyal to the regime in Belgrade the country itself would be trapped in stalled transition. Therefore, the only way out of this situation was an alteration of the pro-Milošević political course of the Montenegrin ruling party.[10]

During the wars in Yugoslavia (in the 1990s) "Montenegro's economy was damaged by economic sanctions, which also gave rise to extensive smuggling and other organized crime".[11] Considering the economy, that change was evidenced by introducing the Euro as Montenegro's currency in 2002. Earlier, in 1999, when Montenegro was still a part of the Federal Republic of Yugoslavia, the state authorities decided to replace the dinar with the Deutsche Mark (in 2000).[12] Furthermore,

> between 2002 and 2008 Montenegro enjoyed the fastest Gross Domestic Product (GDP) growth in the region. Unemployment levels dropped significantly (from 33% in 2002 to 10.8% in 2008), the country had a budget surplus and foreign debt was reduced from 42.6% of GDP in 2005 to just 27% in 2008. [...] *The Observer* had trumpeted Montenegro as 'Europe's New Golden Coast', investors from Ireland, the UK, and (primarily) Russia flocked to the country. As a consequence, Montenegro's development further fed the economy, the country's export market grew and further economic growth was supported by significant expansions in construction, tourism, and the services sector.[13]

---

substantial inflows of aid funding and advisers", Will Bartlett, "International Aid, Policy Transfer and Local Economic Development in North Montenegro", in Transformation and European Integration, ed. Bruno Dallago (London: Palgrave Macmillan, 2006), 148; Vassilis Monastiriotis and Ivan Zilic, "The Economic Effects of Political Disintegration Lessons from Serbia and Montenegro", Radni materijali EIZ-a, no. 3 (2019): 5.

10   Ivan Vuković, "The Post-Communist Political Transition of Montenegro: Democratization prior to Europeanization", Contemporary European Studies, no. 2 (2010): 63; Ivan Vuković, "Political Dynamics of the Post-Communist Montenegro: One-Party Show", Democratization 22, no. 1 (2015): 75.

11   Marijana Trivunovic, Vera Devine and Harald Mathisen, "Corruption in Montenegro 2007: Overview over Main Problems and Status of Reforms", CMI Report R, no. 9 (2007): 10.

12   Dragan Đurić, "The Economic Development of Montenegro", in Montenegro in Transition: Problems of Identity and Statehood, 152.

13   Kenneth Morrison, "Change, Continuity and Consolidation Assessing Five Years of Montenegro's Independence", London School of Economics and Political Science. European Institute, no. 2 (London: LSEE Papers on South Eastern Europe, 2011): 21–22.

When analyzing the changes in Montenegro's economy over the last thirty years, what becomes evident is the decrease in the number of people employed in such sectors as agriculture[14] and industry. The lower level of employment in agriculture can be explained by migrations from villages to towns (as well as by emigration) and the shutdown of agricultural *zadrugas* [village cooperatives] in 1991.[15] In 2017, only 1.2% (2,178 of 182,368) of those employed worked in agriculture, forestry, and the fishing industry.[16] What is more, the number of people employed in this branch of Montenegro's economy has been gradually falling since 2013.

In turn, the changes that affected industry resulted mainly from the poor condition of Montenegro's economy in the 1990s and from the need to restructure it. In 1990, there were still 55,274 people employed in industry, but by 2015 this number had dropped more than twofold, to 20,973 people.[17] Due to the crisis in this sector, people started to look for employment mainly in trade and in the public sector.

It should be also said that after the crisis period, at the beginning of the 21st century, the construction and real estate industry in Montenegro started to develop, which was caused mainly by the significant development of tourism in the country.[18] What is more, this development of tourism resulted in the greater number of people being employed in the service sector (in 2017 around 3/4 of employed Montenegrins). This result was the highest among the Western Balkan states.[19]

Since Montenegro declared independence in 2006, tourism has been the main branch of the state's economy.[20] Year by year, the number of tourists visiting

---

14 More about agriculture: Aleksandra Martinovic, et al., "Trends of Agricultural Policy in Montenegro", Journal of Hygienic Engineering and Design, no. 18 (2017): 63–70; Goran Rajović and Jelisavka Bulatović, "Some Aspects of Agricultural and Rural Development in Montenegro: Overview", World Scientific News 61, no. 2 (2017): 56–68.

15 Milorad Katnić, (Ne)zaposlenost mladih u Crnoj Gori. Politike za povećanje zaposlenosti mladih (Podgorica: UNDP, 2017), 36.

16 Monstat 2017. Zaposleni po sektorima djelatnosti, https://bit.ly/3GNqaQh (accessed October 18, 2019).

17 Milorad Katnić, (Ne)zaposlenost mladih u Crnoj Gori. Politike za povećanje zaposlenosti mladih, 37.

18 Ibid., 37.

19 Eurostat 2019. Key figures on Enlargement Countries – 2019 edition, Luxembourg: Publications Office of the European Union, 2019: 54, https://ec.europa.eu/eurostat/documents/3217494/9799207/KS-GO-19-001-EN-N.pdf/e8fbd16c-c342-41f7-aaed-6ca38e6f709e (accessed November 12, 2019).

20 More about tourism: Slavica Adžić and Silvana Duraševvić, "The Influence of Structural Changes to the Tourist Industry in Montenegro", Turističko poslovanje 19 (2017): 15–26;

this Balkan country has been growing. In 2010, there were nearly 600 thousand tourists and in 2018 – over one million (Figure 8.1). In 2019, another record was

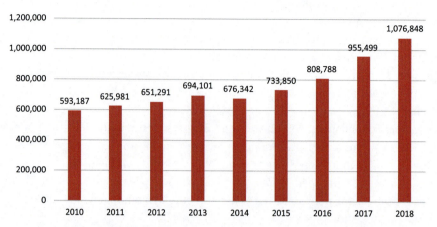

FIGURE 8.1 Tourist arrivals in collective accommodation in Montenegro, 2010–2018
SOURCE: MONSTAT, TOURIST ARRIVALS IN COLLECTIVE ACCOMMODATION IN MONTENEGRO, 2010–2018, 2019, HTTPS://BIT.LY/3CBAAP8 (ACCESSED NOVEMBER 8, 2019).

broken in the number of visitors to Montenegro. Moreover, as the Minister of Sustainable Development and Tourism, Damir Davidović, informed, from January to September 2019, the direct and indirect income from tourism was between 1.1 to 1.15 bn euro.[21] The greatest number of visitors to Montenegro have been from such countries as Serbia, Russia, Germany, France and Great Britain.[22] So far, Montenegro has been considered an ideal place for summer holidays, but the authorities of Montenegro are trying to attract tourists also during wintertime as it is a mountainous country. Thus, by 2022 the government intends to spend around 140 bn euro on building ski slopes, as they believe that modernization of winter facilities will attract a greater number of tourists during winter holidays.[23]

  Silvana Đurašević, "Tourism in Montenegro: A Destination Management Perspective", Turizam: međunarodniz nanstveno-stručni časopis 63, no. 1 (2015): 81–96.
21 "Crna Gora očekuje rekordnih 2,5 miliona turista ove godine", Investitor, https://investitor.me/2019/09/29/crna-gora-ocekuje-rekordnih-25-miliona-turista-ove-godine/ (accessed November 8, 2019).
22 "U hotelima već boravilo više turista nego cijele prošle godine", MINA, https://mina.news/mina-business/u-hotelima-vec-boravilo-vise-turista-nego-cijele-prosle-godine/ (accessed November 18, 2019).
23 Radomir Kračković, Crna Gora Ski-Centar Regiona?, https://www.dw.com/sr/crna-gora-ski-centar-regiona/a-51164001 (accessed November 15, 2019).

Establishing adequate infrastructure in the north of the country now seems to be the greatest challenge for the winter tourism industry.

After the 2008 financial crisis,[24] the Montenegrin economy started to accelerate, and in 2018 Montenegro's economic growth was 4.9%. However, in 2019 it started to slow down. In the coming years (2019–2021), the state's economy is expected to grow at 2.8%[25] or 2.9% (Table 8.1). Due to global recession and insecurity, the forecast does not take into account the investment boom, which was a factor in the previous years.

TABLE 8.1   Montenegro: Macroeconomic projections (2018–2021), low-growth scenario

	2017	2018	2019	2020	2021
Nominal GDP in € millions	4,299.1	4,604.5	4,737.7	4,888.8	5,041.5
Nominal growth	8.7	7.1	2.9	3.2	3.1
Real growth	4.7	4.1	1.4	1.9	1.9
Inflation (average)	2.4	2.9	2.2	1.8	1.6
(in %)					
GDP deflator	3.8	2.9	1.5	1.3	1.2
(as % of GDP)					
Current account deficit	-16.1	-18.1	-12.6	-8.5	-5.2
(real growth rates in %)					
Real GDP growth	4.7	4.1	1.4	1.9	1.9
Domestic demand	7.6	5.4	-3.2	-1.9	-1.3
Household consumption	3.9	1.6	-0.3	-0.4	-0.3

---

24   As Kenneth Morrison stated "[t]he economic boom and the growing consumer and commercial confidence which existed in 2006–2007 began to evaporate by 2008, as the economy began to feel the impact of the global economic downturn. The property market slumped, and businesses struggled to stay afloat as banks ceased lending", Kenneth Morrison, "Change, Continuity and Consolidation Assessing Five Years of Montenegro's Independence", London School of Economics and Political Science. European Institute, no. 2 (London: LSEE Papers on South Eastern Europe, 2011), 22.

25   World Bank, Europe and Central Asia Economic Update, Fall 2019. Migration and Brain Drain, (Washington, DC: World Bank, 2019), 100.

TABLE 8.1 Montenegro: Macroeconomic projections (2018–2021), low-growth scenario (*cont.*)

	2017	2018	2019	2020	2021
Gross investments	25.1	18.2	-10.3	-5.8	-4.0
Gross fixed capital formation	18.7	20.7	-11.3	-6.4	-4.4
Changes in inventories	141.3	-2.1	0.0	0.0	0.0
Government consumption	-1.4	0.3	-1.9	-1.0	-1.0
Exports of goods and services	1.8	6.9	4.3	3.9	3.9
Imports of goods and services	8.4	8.6	-5.4	-3.8	-2.7
Macroeconomic indicators	\multicolumn{5}{Growth in % unless otherwise stated}
Employment growth	2.1	1.3	-1.5	-1.0	0.0
Growth of wages	1.9	0.0	0.0	0.0	0.0
Unemployment rate	16.1	14.8	15.2	15.8	15.8
FDI as % of GDP	11.0	7.2	8.0	7.2	7.9
Domestic loans (corporate and household)	11.8	7.1	2.9	3.2	3.1

SOURCE: GOVERNMENT OF MONTENEGRO: MONTENEGRO ECONOMIC REFORM PROGRAM 2019–2021 (PODGORICA: GOVERNMENT OF MONTENEGRO, 2019), 23.

Still, it should be emphasized that according to World Bank experts, recession is expected to affect the whole Western Balkans region (Table 8.2) and Montenegro will be no exception here.

Due to the implementation of great infrastructural reforms, the Montenegrin government managed to maintain actual economic growth until 2019. The project which still can positively influence development of Montenegro is the Bar-Boljare motorway, connecting Serbia with the Montenegrin coast. Currently, it is under construction and in the future, it is to be a part of Bar-Belgrade motorway. This investment is significant for the authorities in Podgorica, but at the same time, it is a high-cost project.[26] In order to complete it, the Montenegrin government had to take a loan from Exim Bank of China. When the plans for the motorway were announced in 2014, the planned costs amounted to 809.6 million Euro.[27] Today, it is known that the cost will be higher. Thus, the

---

[26] IMF, Montenegro 2019. Article IV Consultation – Press Release, Staff Report, and Statement by the Executive Director for Montenegro, IMF Country Report no. 19/293; Djordje Daskalovic, Works on Bar-Boljare motorway in Montenegro formally get underway - report, 2015, https://seenews.com/news/works-on-barboljare-motorway-in-montenegro-formally-get-underway-report-475943 (accessed November 8, 2019).

[27] Djordje Daskalovic, Works on Bar-Boljare motorway in Montenegro formally get underway - report, 2015, https://seenews.com/news/works-on-barboljare-motorway-in-montenegro-formally-get-underway-report-475943 (accessed November 8, 2019).

TABLE 8.2   Growth rate in the Western Balkans (%)

Year	2017	2018	2019ᵉ	2020ᶠ	2021ᶠ
Albania	3.8	4.1	2.9	3.4	3.6
Bosnia and Herzegovina	3.2	3.6	3.1	3.4	3.9
Kosovo	4.2	3.8	4.0	4.2	4.1
North Macedonia	0.2	2.7	3.1	3.2	3.3
Montenegro	4.7	4.9	3.0	2.8	2.7
Serbia	2.0	4.2	3.3	3.9	4.0
Western Balkans	2.6	3.9	3.2	3.6	3.8
EU28	2.5	2.0	1.4	1.3	1.4

e   estimation
f   forecast

SOURCE: WORLD BANK, "UNEMPLOYMENT DROPS WHILE GROWTH SLOWS IN WESTERN BALKANS", 2019, HTTPS://WWW.WORLDBANK.ORG/EN/NEWS/PRESS-RELEASE/2019/10/08/UNEMPLOYMENT-DROPS-WHILE-GROWTH-SLOWS-IN-WESTERN-BALKANS (ACCESSED NOVEMBER 15, 2019).

International Monetary Fund has warned the Montenegrin authorities against the threat which the project can pose to the state's finances, i.e., it may disturb the budgetary stability of Montenegro. That is why the Fund recommends putting the project on hold for the near future.[28]

In turn, in 2019 in all Western Balkan states, including Montenegro, it has been consumption which has driven the growth in GDP. This does not change the fact that tourism is now and will be in the future the branch of the economy to drive the development of Montenegro.[29] As Piotr Żuk notices, due to the lack of possibilities to run monetary policy, the main tool that is used to stabilize the economic situation is fiscal policy. However, the high level of public debt, related to the expansionary fiscal policy that has been followed for many years, leaves Montenegro with limited possibilities to stimulate the economy

---

28   "MMF: Zaustavite gradnju auto-puta do 2023", Investitor, https://investitor.me/2019/09/17/mmf-zaustavite-gradnju-auto-puta-do-2023/ (accessed November 18, 2019).
29   World Bank Group, Western Balkans Regular Economic Report. Rising Uncertainties, no. 16, International Bank for Reconstruction and Development/The World Bank, 2019: 6, https://documents1.worldbank.org/curated/en/643781570478210132/pdf/Rising-Uncertainties.pdf (accessed November 15, 2019); Srđan Milošević, „Analiza objektivnih pokazatelja razvijenosti turizma u Crnoj Gori", TIMS Acta 11, no. 1 (2017): 31–43.

TABLE 8.3 General government finances (% of GDP)

	2015	2016	2017	2018	2019 (proj.)	2020 (proj.)
General government gross debt	69.0	66.6	66.3	72.6	81.1	74.8
General gov't gross debt (authorities' definition)[a]	66.3	64.6	64.4	70.8	79.4	73.1
General gov't debt, including loan guarantees	76.4	74.1	73.6	78.8	88.8	82.2

a The authorities do not include the arrears of local governments in their definition of general government gross debt.

SOURCE: IMF, "IMF EXECUTIVE BOARD CONCLUDES 2019 ARTICLE IV CONSULTATION WITH MONTENEGRO", 10.09.2019, HTTPS://WWW.IMF.ORG/EN/NEWS/ARTICLES/2019/09/09/PR19329-MONTENEGRO-IMF-EXECUTIVE-BOARD-CONCLUDES-2019-ARTICLE-IV-CONSULTATION (ACCESSED NOVEMBER 19, 2019); INCLUDES EXTRA-BUDGETARY FUNDS AND LOCAL GOVERNMENTS, BUT NOT PUBLIC ENTERPRISES.

in an economic slowdown.[30] According to the International Monetary Fund (2019), the Montenegrin public debt has been increasing since 2017 (Table 8.3). On the other hand, professor of the Faculty of Economics and President of the Association of Economists of Montenegro, Božo Mihailović highlights that "it's important to notice that public debt increase happened due to increased investments, not current expenditure".[31]

The development of Montenegro's economy faces at least two more key challenges, which the government must address – the informal economy and corruption. As the Montenegrin Prime Minister Duško Marković said, the problems of informal labor and the black market should be solved through cooperation between the government and the business sector. Dealing with these issues is impossible without also changing the society's approach to this problem.[32] As the Montenegrin Employers Federation emphasizes, in the absence of rule of

30   Piotr Żuk, Doświadczenia Czarnogóry z jednostronną euroizacją, 2019, https://www.obserwatorfinansowy.pl/tematyka/makroekonomia/trendy-gospodarcze/doswiadczenia-czarnogory-z-jednostronna-euroizacja/ (accessed November 15, 2019).
31   „Mihailović: Montenegro's Economy has Passed the Exam", CdM, 30.12.2019, https://www.cdm.me/english/mihailovic-montenegros-economy-has-passed-the-exam/ (accessed January 28, 2020).
32   Problem of Informal Economy Needs to Be Addressed, 2018, https://mina.news/english-news/problem-of-informal-economy-needs-to-be-addressed/ (accessed November 9, 2019).

law and inefficient law implementation, high business costs have contributed to widespread unofficial work in Montenegro. In the early 2000s, almost 40% of workers employed in hospitality, trade and construction were working informally.[33] This number dropped only after 2005. According to the data presented by UNDP, in 2016 the scope of the informal economy was similar to that in the previous years and remained at the level of 25% of GDP in 2014.[34] It is estimated that one in three jobs in Montenegro are informal.[35] Other Western Balkan states also face the issue of the informal economy. The largest groups among the informally employed are people aged 15–24 and 55–64, i.e., those just entering the labor market and those in their pre-retirement years, as well as agricultural workers.[36]

Although Montenegro has already undertaken activities aimed at eliminating corruption, this problem still needs to be solved before the country joins the EU, as today around 3/4 of Montenegro's citizens consider corruption an important issue which has to be solved.[37] The annual Corruption Perception Index, published by Transparency International, also reveals the problem of corruption in Montenegro – in 2018 the country was in 67th place (on the list of 180), with a score of 45 out of 100.[38]

3   Unemployment in Montenegro Compared with Other Western Balkan States

Since Montenegro declared independence (2006), unemployment in this country has been falling. The most challenging time was during the global crisis, which negatively influenced the Montenegrin economy. As a result, in 2009–2013 unemployment was around 19% (Table 8.4).

---

33   Predrag Bejaković and Ruslan Stefanov, "Characteristics of Undeclared Work in Service Sector in Countries of South East Europe", Zagreb International Review of Economics & Business 22, no. 1 (2019): 122.
34   Ibid.
35   Idris Iffat and Anna Strachan, "Economic Drivers of Conflict in the Western Balkans", K4D Helpdesk Report, (Brighton: Institute of Development Studies, 2017): 13, https://gsdrc.org/publications/economic-drivers-of-conflict-in-the-western-balkans/ (accessed November 9, 2019).
36   Nermin Oruč and Will Bartlett, Labour Markets in the Western Balkans: Performance, Causes and Policy Options (Sarajevo: Regional Cooperation Council, Sarajevo, 2018), 14, https://www.rcc.int/pubs/58/labour-markets-in-the-western-balkans-performance-causes-and-policy-options (accessed November 5, 2019).
37   Nations in Transit, "Montenegro", 2018, https://freedomhouse.org/country/montenegro/nations-transit/2018 (accessed October 18, 2019).
38   Transparency International. Corruption Perceptions Index, "Montenegro", 2018 https://www.transparency.org/en/countries/montenegro (accessed October 18, 2019).

TABLE 8.4 Number of unemployed persons and unemployment rates by sex in Montenegro

Year, quarter	Unemployment rate [%]		
	Total	Men	Women
2005	30.3	26.2	35.5
2006	29.6	29.1	30.1
2007	19.4	18.1	20.9
2008	16.8	15.9	17.9
2009	19.1	18.0	20.4
2010	19.7	18.9	20.7
2011	19.7	19.5	20.0
2012	19.7	19.3	20.3
2013	19.5	20.0	18.8
2014	18.0	17.8	18.2
2015	17.6	17.7	17.3
2016	17.7	18.2	17.1
2017	16.1	15.4	17.0
2018	15.2	15.2	15.1
2019, first quarter	15.0	13.6	16.7
2019, second quarter	14.3	13.0	16.1

SOURCE: MONSTAT, "NUMBER OF UNEMPLOYED PERSONS AND UNEMPLOYMENT RATES BY SEX IN MONTENEGRO (2005 – 2019)", 2019, HTTPS://WWW.MONSTAT.ORG/CG/PAGE.PHP?ID=22&PAGEID=22 (ACCESSED NOVEMBER 15, 2019).

It was higher among women, except for 2013 when more men than women were unemployed (20% to 18.8%). However, the difference was not so significant. Unemployment started to decrease in the subsequent years. In 2018 it was 15.2%.[39] Interestingly, the levels of unemployment among men and women were comparable. Improvement in the labor market was connected with the improvement of the country (Figure 8.2). It should be also said that there has

---

39 It is worth adding that according to the data published by the Ministry of Labor of Montenegro, on 31 December 2018 the unemployment rate in this country was 17.83% – more than 3 p.p. lower compared to the previous year. Moreover, on 31 December 2018 there were 41,378 people registered unemployed (of which 23,944 women), Ministarstvo rada i socijalnog staranja: Izveštaj Ministarstva Rada i Socijalnog Staranja o Radu i Stanju u Upravnim Oblastima za 2018 godinu, (Podgorica: Ministarstvo rada i socijalnog staranja, 2019), 100.

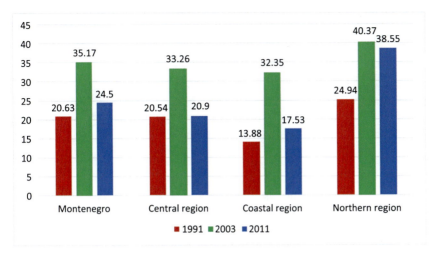

FIGURE 8.2 Unemployment in Montenegro's regions (%)
SOURCE: MONSTAT, „PROJEKCIJE STANOVNIŠTVA CRNE GORE DO 2060. GODINE SA STRUKTURNOM ANALIZOM STANOVNIŠTVA CRNE GORE", (PODGORICA: MONSTAT, 2014), 110.

been a growth in the level of employment mainly in the construction, manufacturing, transport, and hospitality industries.[40]

The largest number of the unemployed in 2018 in Montenegro lived in the north of the country, in the municipalities of Berane, Plav, Andrijevica, Rožaje, Gusinje and Petnjica, as well as in the central region, in the municipalities of Podgorica, Kolašin, Danilovgrad, Cetinje, Tuzi and Golubovce. The lowest unemployment rate – below 5%[41] – was recorded in Novi, Kotor and Tivat, which are coastal municipalities, i.e., the area benefiting from tourism.[42]

According to the data collected and published by the World Bank, Montenegro's unemployment rate is now similar to those in Albania (13.96%) and Serbia (13.51%) (Figure 8.3). It is also much lower than in North Macedonia (21.58%) and Bosnia and Herzegovina (21.22%). However, all these countries have seen a decline in the level of unemployment. Despite these data (in

---

40 Government of Montenegro: Montenegro Economic Reform Programme 2019–2021 (Podgorica: Government of Montenegro, 2019), 9–10.
41 Ministarstvo rada i socijalnog staranja, „Izveštaj Ministarstva Rada i Socijalnog Staranja o Radu i Stanju u Upravnim Oblastima za 2018 godinu", 2019, 101.
42 Ibid.

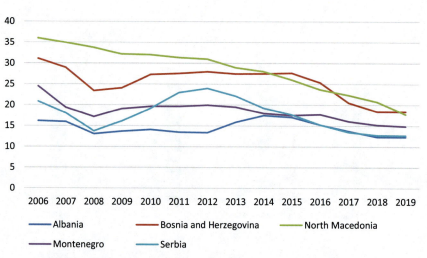

FIGURE 8.3 Unemployment rate in the Western Balkan states (2006–2019)
SOURCE: OWN ELABORATION BASED ON THE WORLD BANK DATA (2019)

2011 – 1.5 mln unemployed, and in the second quarter of 2018 – 776 thousand),[43] it must be emphasized that unemployment still remains the key challenge for the Balkan states.

Attention should be paid to the disturbing issue of long-term unemployment. In the Western Balkans, the level is highest among people aged 25–54, but in Montenegro this group constitutes 82% of the long-term unemployed. In turn, long-term unemployment among young people in Montenegro is 11%, and the highest level is in Kosovo (22%).[44] However, this does not change the fact that youth unemployment is still an important issue. In 2018, 29.4% of young people in Montenegro remained unemployed, in Albania – 28.3%, and in Kosovo – 55.4%.[45] Consequently, a great number of young people look for employment abroad.

---

43 World Bank, "Western Balkans Show Improved Labor Market Performance, but Challenges Remain for Women, Youth and Less Educated Workers", 2019, https://bit.ly/2ZE1wRj (accessed November 15, 2019).

44 World Bank Group, "Western Balkans Labor Market Trends 2019", 2019, 27, https://www.worldbank.org/en/region/eca/publication/labor-trends-in-wb (accessed November 15, 2019).

45 The Delegation of the European Union to the Republic of Serbia, "EU Support to Combating Youth Unemployment", https://europa.rs/eu-support-to-combating-youth-unemployment/?lang=en (accessed November 15, 2019).

In 2018, the average gross monthly salary in Montenegro was 766 euro (520 euro net), and it is estimated that as a result of dynamic nominal prices and wages, real wages dropped by 3%.[46] According to the data published by MONSTAT, between 2012 and 2017 the highest salaries were paid in the sector officially described as "electricity, gas, steam and air conditioning supply" sector – around 1,300 euro, while the lowest were in "administrative and support service activities" as well as in "wholesale and retail trade, repair of motor vehicles and motor recycle" – around 500 euro.[47]

Following the recommendations of the European Commission, the government is trying to support the unemployed by introducing programs facilitating self-employment and development of entrepreneurship. The Labor Office is implementing loan programs for the unemployed, and this form of support has helped create 96 new job openings.[48] With the intention of increasing the scope and effectiveness of active employment policy, new programs are being prepared, in which subsidies will be granted to the unemployed who want to start their own business activity. Active employment programs are being developed in cooperation with the International Labor Organization, and their implementation is scheduled for 2019. Activities included in the project on supporting local initiatives for employment will be initiated as well.

In 2018, a national committee on informal economy was established; however, the results of its activity are yet to be seen. A monitoring system will be necessary to supervise its functioning and influence. The Employment Agency of Montenegro participates in training based on the experiences of the European network of Public Employment Services; however, the Agency's IT system still requires updating.[49]

4 Unemployment versus Emigration in Montenegro

When analyzing emigration among Montenegrins, it should be noted first that there are no official statistics collected by the Montenegrin authorities, which

---

46 Government of Montenegro: Montenegro Economic Reform Programme 2019–2021 (Podgorica: Government of Montenegro, 2019), 10.
47 Monstat, "Prosječne zarade (bruto) po sektorima djelatnosti/Average gross wages by activity sectors", 2018, https://www.monstat.org/cg/page.php?id=1317&pageid=24 (accessed October 18, 2019).
48 Government of Montenegro: Montenegro Economic Reform Programme 2019–2021, 91.
49 European Commission: Montenegro 2019 Report, (Brussels: European Commission, 2019), 78.

would describe this issue.[50] MONSTAT only publishes data on internal migration, showing which municipalities are being abandoned by its citizens and in which the number of citizens is growing. Therefore, when analyzing emigration of Montenegrins, the data published by various international organizations and think-tanks are particularly useful. The data from available sources suggest that the whole region of the Western Balkans is threatened with population outflow, mainly to Western Europe, the US, and Canada. Due to the sparse population of Montenegro, when compared with other Balkan states, the number of emigrants alone will not fully depict the phenomena. According to CIA data, as many as five of 1000 citizens of Montenegro decide to leave their homeland (Table 8.5), which is the highest rate in the Balkans.

TABLE 8.5 Net migration rate in the Western Balkan states

State	Net migration rate
Albania	-3.3
Bosnia and Hercegovina	-0.4
Montenegro	-4.9
Kosovo	-2.6
North Macedonia	0.7
Serbia	0

SOURCE: THE WORLD FACTBOOK, NET MIGRATION RATE, 2018, HTTPS://RELIEF.UNBOUNDMEDICINE.COM/RELIEF/VIEW/THE-WORLD-FACTBOOK/563803/ALL/NET_MIGRATION_RATE (ACCESSED NOVEMBER 8, 2019).

The survey conducted by the Westminster Foundation for Democracy offers further evidence:

> As the smallest Balkan state, with a population of 622,000, Montenegro cannot be compared to other countries in the region in terms of the number of emigrants. However, the share of emigration to total population ranks it among the countries most emigrated from. The average number of working-age migrants leaving Montenegro is around 3,320 persons per year. The losses that Montenegro faces annually due to emigration

---

50 Detailed data come from Petnica municipality, which has noted increasing emigration, mainly of young people, Momčilo Radulović and Mila Brnović, "Ekonomske migracije iz Crne Gore u Evropsku uniju", Evropski pokret u Crnoj Gori (EPuCG), (Podgorica 2016), 16.

amount to €70 million, meaning that every work-capable person who leaves Montenegro takes approximately €21,561 of some potential future annual GDP with them.[51]

What seems particularly striking is the emigration of young, educated people. The results of the survey "The Costs of Youth Emigration" (*Troškovi emigracije mladih*) on the phenomenon in Serbia, Montenegro, North Macedonia, and Albania point to the consequences brought by emigration of the young. These results are losses in the GDP of a given state (young people contribute to the income of other states instead of their homeland). In this respect, it is Montenegro and Serbia which lose most among the Balkan states, followed by North Macedonia and Albania (whose figures are only slightly lower).[52]

Currently, as many as half of young people intend to emigrate from Montenegro, mainly due to the unfavorable situation in the country.[53] They are seeking an improved standard of living and job opportunities which are not sufficient in the country. In the first seven months of 2019 alone, around six thousand young people emigrated to work abroad.[54] The state should therefore first improve the living and working conditions for young people to enable them to find employment in their country and start families.[55] The issue of brain drain is another current problem – those who emigrate are the best educated, yet abroad they often do manual labor and do not use their full potential.

To reverse this negative emigration trend, some students initiated a campaign "Neću da idem" [I do not want to leave], whose aim is to convince young people not to emigrate. The initiative originated in Bosnia and Herzegovina, and then it reached Montenegro, where its representative Vuk Vujsić says that the problem lies also in the Montenegrin system of education, which does not

---

51 WFD, Youth Emigration is Damaging Western Balkan Economies, 2019, https://www.wfd.org/2019/10/24/youth-emigration-is-damaging-for-western-balkan-economies/ (accessed November 18, 2019).

52 Aleksandar Miladinović, "Odliv mozgova": Koliko u evrima košta odlazak mladih iz regiona", 2019, https://www.bbc.com/serbian/lat/balkan-50068685 (accessed November 16, 2019).

53 "Obilježava se Međunarodni Dan mladih: Omladina napušta Crnu Goru jer više ne vjeruje u budućnost države", In4s.net, https://www.in4s.net/dan-mladih-omladina-napusta-crnu-goru-jer-vise-ne-vjeruje-u-buducnost-drzave/?lang=lat (accessed November 15, 2019).

54 "Kampanja "Neću da idem": Mladi hoće da rade, ako su dovoljno plaćeni", Aktuelno, https://www.aktuelno.me/crna-gora/kampanja-necu-da-idem-mladi-hoce-da-rade-ako-su-dovoljno-placeni/ (accessed November 14, 2019).

55 "Obilježava se Međunarodni Dan mladih: Omladina napušta Crnu Goru jer više ne vjeruje u budućnost države", In4s.net, https://www.in4s.net/dan-mladih-omladina-napusta-crnu-goru-jer-vise-ne-vjeruje-u-buducnost-drzave/?lang=lat (accessed November 15, 2019).

match the needs of the changing labor market. The credibility of the system is also undermined by e.g., the practices of purchasing university diplomas.[56] What is more, the Ministry of Education of Montenegro tightens controls on diplomas from rest of the Balkan region. According to the Ministry, about 100 diplomas from the region have been rejected in the last two years.[57]

With regard to regions, the north of the country is most affected by emigration.[58] This is shown by the data collected by MONSTAT[59] (Table 8.6). As shown by the yellow color which marks northern municipalities, all municipalities except one (Cetinje) that are characterized by the negative balance of emigration are located in the north of the country. In that area, only Gusinje and Petnjica have a positive score.

As is presented by one of Montenegrin's NGOs (NVO Euromos), in the last 25 years 50 thousand people emigrated from the region.[60] According to the national census, in 1991 the northern region had a population of 218,592, and twenty years later, only 177,837[61] (Table 8.7). The trend of depopulation of the region results from the negative rate of natural increase as well as from the negative migration balance. It should be emphasized that the region is significantly less developed in terms of the economy and infrastructure than the other two. The poverty and unemployment rates are also higher there.[62] The government is trying to develop this part of the country, which was directly stated in the "Strategy for Regional Development of Montenegro 2014–2020" (*Strategija regionalnog razvoja Crne Gore*).[63] However, this goal has not been achieved.[64]

---

56   „Za dvije godine otišlo više stotina studenata", CdM, https://www.cdm.me/drustvo/za-dvije-godine-otislo-vise-stotina-studenata/ (accessed November 17, 2019).

57   "Crna Gora pooštrila kontrolu diploma iz zemalja regije", Aljazeera, https://balkans.aljazeera.net/news/balkan/2019/10/3/crna-gora-poostrila-kontrolu-diploma-iz-zemalja-regije (accessed November 19, 2019).

58   Monstat, "Projekcije stanovništva Crne Gore do 2060. Godine sa strukturnom analizom stanovništva Crne Gore" (Podgorica: MONSTAT, 2014), 46.

59   Ibid.

60   "Sever Crne Gore za 25 godina iż gubio 50.000 stanovnika", Novosti.rs, https://www.novosti.rs/vesti/planeta.300.html:663417-Sever-Crne-Gore-za-25-godina-izgubio-50000-stanovnika (accessed November 14, 2019); Rade Šarović, "Migracije poljoprivrednika u Crnoj Gori (1948.-2011.)", Sociologija i prostor: časopis za istraživanje prostornoga i sociokulturnog razvoja 50, no. 3 (2012): 379–393.

61   Monstat, „Projekcije stanovništva Crne Gore do 2060. Godine sa strukturnom analizom stanovništva Crne Gore" (Podgorica: MONSTAT, 2014), 47.

62   "Sever Crne Gore za 25 godinai zgubio 50.000 stanovnika", Novosti.rs, https://www.novosti.rs/vesti/planeta.300.html:663417-Sever-Crne-Gore-za-25-godina-izgubio-50000-stanovnika (accessed November 14, 2019).

63   Momčilo Radulović and Mila Brnović, Ekonomske migracije iz Crne Gore u Evropsku uniju (Podgorica 2016), 13.

64   Ibid.

TABLE 8.6   Net migration in Montenegrin municipalities, 2018

Municipalities	Moving in	Moving out	Net migrations
Total	6,631	6,631	0
Andrijevica	72	121	-49
Bar	632	457	175
Berane	170	432	-262
Bijelo polje	200	780	-580
Budva	758	350	408
Cetinje	96	256	-160
Danilovgrad	263	241	22
Gusinje	28	6	22
Hercegnovi	254	218	36
Kolašin	44	142	-98
Kotor	342	292	50
Mojkovac	48	188	-140
Nikšić	419	709	-290
Petnjica	85	53	32
Plav	40	162	-122
Pljevlja	94	379	-285
Plužine	21	81	-60
Podgorica	2,421	1,003	1,418
Rožaje	94	304	-210
Šavnik	22	109	-87
Tivat	264	142	122
Ulcinj	218	117	101
Žabljak	46	89	-43

SOURCE: MONSTAT, NET MIGRATION IN MONTENEGRIN MUNICIPALITIES, 2018, HTTPS:// WWW.MONSTAT.ORG/ENG/PAGE.PHP?ID=113&6PAGEID=53 (ACCESSED NOVEMBER 14, 2019).

TABLE 8.7 Elements of migration with regard to the whole society in 1991–2011

Region	Increase in the number of citizens 1991–2003	Rate of natural increase	Migration balance	Increase in the number of citizens 2003–2011	Rate of natural increase	Migration balance
Montenegro	26,641	50,013	-23,372	-116	16,326	-16,442
Coastal	19,580	6,915	12,665	2,836	2,889	-53
Central	24,559	25,090	-531	14,090	10,255	3,836
Northern	-17,498	18,008	-35,506	-17,042	3,182	-20,224
	Per 1000 inhabitants					
Montenegro	3.5	6.5	-3.1	0.0	3.5	-3.6
Coastal	11.4	4.0	7.4	2.6	2.6	0.0
Central	7.3	7.5	-0.2	6.6	4.8	1.8
Northern	-6.8	7.0	-13.9	-12.3	2.3	-14.6

SOURCE: MONSTAT, „PROJEKCIJE STANOVNIŠTVA CRNE GORE DO 2060. GODINE SA STRUKTURNOM ANALIZOM STANOVNIŠTVA CRNE GORE" (PODGORICA: MONSTAT, 2014), 45.

5 Conclusions

As a country that has undergone significant transformational changes in the last thirty years, Montenegro is an extremely interesting research case from the point of view of analyzing challenges for the social security system of a state. These challenges include both unemployment and emigration, which are particularly high among young people. After the global financial crisis, Montenegro managed to accelerate economic development and reduce the level of unemployment. However, as current forecasts show (e.g., those by the World Bank), economic growth will slow down in the coming years. Therefore, it should be assumed that the scale of emigration will continue to grow. This is an extremely serious problem that this small Balkan state must face.

Further research on Montenegro's social security system is necessary to make a deeper analysis of these two issues, not only with regard to the regional diversity of the country in terms of economic development, but also considering its ethnic diversity. For this purpose, however, it is necessary to conduct qualitative sociological research. The results of this kind of research could contribute to broadening the knowledge about emigration among various nationalities living in Montenegro. As noted, the Montenegrin authorities unfortunately do not keep accurate records that would demonstrate the scale of emigration in general as well as the scale of this problem for individual nationalities or ethnic minorities. Bearing in mind the multinational and multicultural structure of the Montenegrin society, answers to these questions seem particularly important as this situation has an impact on building an effective social security system in Montenegro.

Bibliography

Adžić, Slavica, and Silvana Đurašević. "The Influence of Structural Changes to the Tourist Industry in Montenegro". Turističko poslovanje 19 (2017): 15–26.

Aktuelno, "Kampanja "Neću da idem": Mladi hoće da rade, ako su dovoljno plaćeni", 2019. Accessed November 14, 2019. https://www.aktuelno.me/crna-gora/kampanja-necu-da-idem-mladi-hoce-da-rade-ako-su-dovoljno-placeni/.

Aljazeera, "Crna Gora pooštrila kontrolu diploma iz zemalja regije", Accessed November 19, 2019. https://balkans.aljazeera.net/news/balkan/2019/10/3/crna-gora-poostrila-kontrolu-diploma-iz-zemalja-regije.

Bartlett, Will. "International Aid, Policy, Transfer and Local Economic Development in North Montenegro". In Transformation and European Integration, edited by Bruno Dallago, 142–157. London: Palgrave Macmillan, 2006.

Bejaković, Predrag and Ruslan Stefanov. "Characteristics of Undeclared Work in Service Sector in Countries of South East Europe", Zagreb International Review of Economics & Business 22, no. 1 (2019): 107–131.

Bieber, Florian. "Montenegrin Politics since the Desintegration of Yugoslavia". In Montenegro in Transition: Problems of Identity and Statehood, edited by Florian Bieber, 11–42. Baden-Baden: Nomos Verlagsgesellschaft, 2003.

CdM. Mihailović: Montenegro's Economy has Passed the Exam, 30.12.2019. Accessed January 28, 2020. https://www.cdm.me/english/mihailovic-montenegros-economy-has-passed-the-exam/.

CdM. Za dvije godine otišlo više stotina studenata, 2019. Accessed November 17, 2019. https://www.cdm.me/drustvo/za-dvije-godine-otislo-vise-stotina-studenata/.

Djordje Daskalovic, Works on Bar-Boljare motorway in Montenegro formally get underway - report, 2015, https://seenews.com/news/works-on-barboljare-motorway-in-montenegro-formally-get-underway-report-475943 (accessed November 8, 2019).

Drakic, Maja, Frederic Sautet and Kyle McKenzie. Montenegro: The Challenges of a Newborn State. Mercatus Policy Series Country Brief, no. 2. Arlington: Mercatus Center at George Mason University, 2007.

Đurašević, Silvana. "Tourism in Montenegro: A Destination Management Perspective". Turizam: međunarodni znanstveno-stručni časopis 63, no. 1 (2015): 81–96.

Đurić, Dragan. "Montenegro's Prospects for European Integration: on a Twin Track." SEER-South-East Europe Review for Labour and Social Affairs, no. 4 (2004): 79–105.

Đurić, Dragan. "The Economic Development of Montenegro". In Montenegro in Transition: Problems of Identity and Statehood, edited by Florian Bieber, 139–158. Baden-Baden: Nomos Verlagsgesellschaft.

European Commission: Montenegro 2019 Report. Brussels: European Commission, 2019.

Eurostat 2019. Key Figures Enlargement Countries – 2019 edition, Luxembourg: Publications Office of the European Union, 2019. Accessed November 12, 2019. https://ec.europa.eu/eurostat/documents/3217494/9799207/KS-GO-19-001-EN-N.pdf/e8fbd16c-c342-41f7-aaed-6ca38e6f709e.

Government of Montenegro. Montenegro Economic Reform Programme 2019–2021. Podgorica: Government of Montenegro, 2019.

Homoncik, Tomasz, Klaudia Pujer, and Iwona Wolańska. Ekonomiczno-Społeczne Aspekty Migracji. Wybrane Problemy. Wrocław: Exante, 2017.

Iffat, Idris and Anna Strachan. Economic Drivers of Conflict in the Western Balkans, 2017. K4D Helpdesk Report. Brighton: Institute of Development Studies, 2017. Accessed November 09, 2019. https://gsdrc.org/publications/economic-drivers-of-conflict-in-the-western-balkans/.

IMF. IMF Executive Board Concludes 2019 Article IV Consultation with Montenegro. 10.09.2019. Accessed November 19, 2019. https://www.imf.org/en/News/Articles/2019/09/09/pr19329-montenegro-imf-executive-board-concludes-2019-article-iv-consultation.

IMF. Montenegro 2019. Article IV Consultation – Press Release, Staff Report, and Statement by the Executive Director for Montenegro, IMF Country Report no. 19/293, 2019.

In4s.net, "Obilježava se Međunarodni Dan mladih: Omladina napušta Crnu Goru jer više ne vjeruje u budućnost države", 2019. Accessed November 15, 2019. https://www.in4s.net/dan-mladih-omladina-napusta-crnu-goru-jer-vise-ne-vjeruje-u-buducnost-drzave/?lang=lat.

Investitor. "Crna Gora očekuje rekordnih 2.5 miliona turista ove godine". Accessed November 8, 2019. https://investitor.me/2019/09/29/crna-gora-ocekuje-rekordnih-25-miliona-turista-ove-godine/.

Investitor. "MMF. Zaustavite gradnju auto-puta do 2023". Accessed November 18, 2019. https://investitor.me/2019/09/17/mmf-zaustavite-gradnju-auto-puta-do-2023/.

Katnić, Milorad. (Ne)zaposlenost mladih u Crnoj Gori. Politike za povećanje zaposlenosti mladih. Podgorica: UNDP, 2017.

Kračković, Radomir. „Crna Gora ski-centar regiona?". Accessed November 15, 2019. https://www.dw.com/sr/crna-gora-ski-centar-regiona/a-51164001.

Martinovic, Aleksandra, Darko Konjevic, Jovana Drobnjak, Vesna Boljevic. "Trends of Agricultural Policy in Montenegro". Journal of Hygienic Engineering and Design, no. 18 (2017): 63–70.

Miladinović, Aleksandar. "Odliv mozgova": Koliko u evrima košta odlazak mladih iz regiona". Octobar 17, 2019. https://www.bbc.com/serbian/lat/balkan-50068685.

Milošević, Srđan. "Analiza objektivnih pokazatelja razvijenosti turizma u Crnoj Gori". TIMS Acta 11, no. 1 (2017): 31–43.

MINA. "Problem of Informal Economy Needs to Be Addressed". Accessed November 9, 2019. https://mina.news/english-news/problem-of-informal-economy-needs-to-be-addressed/.

MINA. U hotelima već boravilo više turista nego cijele prošle godine. 2019. Accessed November 18, 2019. https://mina.news/mina-business/u-hotelima-vec-boravilo-vise-turista-nego-cijele-prosle-godine/.

Ministarstvo rada i socijalnog staranja: Izveštaj Ministarstva Rada i Socijalnog Staranja o Radu i Stanju u Upravnim Oblastima za 2018 godinu. Podgorica: Ministarstvo rada i socijalnog staranja, 2019.

Ministry of Foreign Affairs and European Integration of Montenegro, 2019. Accessed November 15, 2019. https://www.eu.me/wp-content/uploads/2021/02/Tabela_poglavlja_MNE-verzija-EU4ME.png.

Mirecki, Nataša. "Country Study Montenegro". In Study of the Organic and Safety Agriculture in the Adriatic Cross-Border Region and of Training Needs, edited by M. El Moujabber, L. El Bitar, M. Raeli, 73–96. Bari: CIHEAM.

Monastiriotis, Vassilis, and Ivan Zilic. "The Economic Effects of Political Disintegration: Lessons from Serbia and Montenegro". Radni materijali EIZ-a, no. 3 (2019): 2–29.

Monstat 2017. „Zaposleni po sektorima djelatnosti". Accessed October 18, 2019. https://bit.ly/3GNqaQh.

Monstat. "Net Migration in Montenegrin Municipalities". Accessed November 14, 2019. http://www.monstat.org/eng/page.php?id=1130%26pageid=53.

Monstat. Number of Unemployed Persons and Unemployment Rates by Sex in Montenegro (2005–2019). Accessed November 15, 2019. https://freedomhouse.org/country/montenegro/freedom-world/2021.

Monstat. Projekcije stanovništva Crne Gore do 2060. Godine sa strukturnom analizom stanovništva Crne Gore. Podgorica: Monstat, 2014.

Monstat. "Prosječne zarade (bruto) po sektorima djelatnosti/Average gross wages by activity sectors". 2018. Accessed October 18, 2019. https://www.monstat.org/cg/page.php?id=1164&pageid=23.

Monstat. Tourist Arrivals in Collective Accommodation in Montenegro, 2010–2018, 2019. Accessed November 8, 2019. http://99.80.44.13/bg/dataset/number-of-employees-by-activity-sectors-in-montenegro-2010-2016-monstat-2017.

Morrison, Kenneth. "Change, Continuity and Consolidation Assessing Five Years of Montenegro's Independence", no. 2, London: LSEE Papers on South Eastern Europe, 2011.

Nations in Transit. Montenegro, 2018. Accessed October 16, 2019. https://freedomhouse.org/country/montenegro/nations-transit/2018.

Novosti.rs. "Sever Crne Gore za 25 godina izgubio 50.000 stanovnika." Accessed November 14, 2019. https://www.novosti.rs/vesti/planeta.300.html:663417-Sever-Crne-Gore-za-25-godina-izgubio-50000-stanovnika.

Oruč, Nermin and Will Bartlett. Labour Markets in the Western Balkans: Performance, Causes and Policy Options, Regional Cooperation Council, Sarajevo, 2018. Accessed November 5, 2019. https://www.rcc.int/pubs/58/labour-markets-in-the-western-balkans-performance-causes-and-policy-options.

Radulović, Momčilo and Mila Brnović. "Ekonomske migracije iz Crne Gore u Evropsku uniju". Evropski pokret u Crnoj Gori (EPuCG), Podgorica, 2016.

Rajović, Goran, and Jelisavka Bulatović. "Some Aspects of Agricultural and Rural Development in Montenegro: Overview". World Scientific News 61, no. 2 (2017): 56–68.

Šarović, Rade. "Migracije poljoprivrednika u Crnoj Gori (1948.-2011.)". Sociologija i prostor: časopis za istraživanje prostornoga i sociokulturnog razvoja 50, no. 3 (2012): 379–393.

Škuflić, Lorena and Valentina Vučković. "The Effect of Emigration on Unemployment Rates: The Case of EU Emigrant Countries", Economic Research-Ekonomska istraživanja 31, no. 1, (2018): 1826–1836, DOI: 10.1080/1331677 X.2018. 1516154.

The Delegation of the European Union to the Republic of Serbia. "EU Support to Combating Youth Unemployment". Accessed November 15, 2019. https://europa.rs/eu-support-to-combating-youth-unemployment/?lang=en.

The World Factbook, "Net Migration Rate", 2018. Accessed November 16, 2019. https://relief.unboundmedicine.com/relief/view/The-World-Factbook/563803/all/Net_migration_rate.

Transparency International. Corruption Perceptions Index, "Montenegro", 2018. Accessed October 18, 2019. https://www.transparency.org/en/countries/montenegro

Trivunovic, Marijana, Vera Devine, and Harald Mathisen. "Corruption in Montenegro 2007: Overview Over Main Problems and Status of Reforms". CMI Report R, no. 9 (2007).

Vuković, Ivan. "Political Dynamics of the Post-Communist Montenegro: One-Party Show". Democratization 22, no. 1 (2015): 73–91.

Vuković, Ivan. "The Post-Communist Political Transition of Montenegro: Democratization prior to Europeanization". Contemporary European Studies, no. 2 (2010): 59–77.

WFD. "Youth Emigration is Damaging Western Balkan Economies, 2019". Accessed November 18, 2019. https://www.wfd.org/2019/10/24/youth-emigration-is-damaging-for-western-balkan-economies/.

World Bank. "Europe and Central Asia Economic Update, Fall 2019: Migration and Brain Drain". (Washington, DC: World Bank, 2019).

World Bank. "Unemployment Drops While Growth Slows in Western Balkans, 2019". Accessed November 15, 2019. https://www.worldbank.org/en/news/press-release/2019/10/08/unemployment-drops-while-growth-slows-in-western-balkans.

World Bank. "Western Balkans Show Improved Labor Market Performance, but Challenges Remain for Women, Youth and Less Educated Workers, 2019". Accessed November 15, 2019. https://bit.ly/2ZE1wRj.

World Bank Group. "Western Balkans Regular Economic Report. Rising Uncertainties, no. 16, International Bank for Reconstruction and Development / The World Bank, 2019". Accessed November 15, 2019. https://documents1.worldbank.org/curated/en/643781570478210132/pdf/Rising-Uncertainties.pdf.

World Bank Group. "Western Balkans Labor Market Trends 2019". Accessed November 15, 2019. https://www.worldbank.org/en/region/eca/publication/labor-trends-in-wb

WTO. Montenegro, 2019. Accessed November 15, 2019. https://www.wto.org/english/thewto_e/acc_e/a1_montenegro_e.htm.

Żuk, Piotr. "Doświadczenia Czarnogóry z jednostronną euroizacją". Accessed November 15, 2019. https://www.obserwatorfinansowy.pl/tematyka/makroekonomia/trendy-gospodarcze/doswiadczenia-czarnogory-z-jednostronna-euroizacja/.

Index

absolute poverty   64
active labor market policy   4, 25, 91, 99–101
aging   47, 110–112, 131–132
agricultural pension   52–53
allowance   179–187
   birth allowance   180, 182, 187
   care and support allowance   184–186
   child allowance   181, 187
   disability allowance   183–184, 187
   education allowance   80–81
   foster care allowance   16
arduous and unhealthy (hazardous) occupations   122

benefits   179–187
Beveridge model   46
birth grant   180, 182, 187
birth rate   47–48, 130–131
Bismarck model   40, 46, 58

centers for social work   17, 26, 27–28, 177, 179
corruption   206–207

decentralization   22, 30
deinstitutionalization   22–23
demographic policy   16
demographic structure   72, 131–132
depopulation   214
disability insurance   2, 6, 39, 45–46, 49, 50–57, 58, 175
disability pension   52–53, 55–56, 115

early retirement   49, 115, 118, 122, 140–141
economic crisis   95, 201–204
economic growth   205–206
education   4, 75
emigration   212–216
employment policy   211
European integration   1, 4, 191, 197
European Union   30, 37, 65, 68
extreme poverty   63

family material support   179, 184
family pension   52–53, 55, 115, 117

Federal Republic of Yugoslavia   36, 69, 171, 197
financial crisis   95, 201–204

grey economy   90, 111, 191, 206–207, 211

healthcare   2–3, 157–167
health insurance   39–45, 59, 159–160, 165–166, 175
Health Insurance Fund   3, 42, 44, 178
healthcare reforms   157–160

independence   36, 88, 103, 197
inequality   5, 68, 70
informal economy   90, 111, 191, 206–207, 211
insurance
   health insurance   39–45, 59, 159–160, 165–166, 175
   insurance companies   165
   insurance fund   159
   insurance system   38–39, 178–181
   pension and disability insurance   39, 45–46, 49, 50–57, 58, 175
   pension insurance   45–46, 115
   social insurance   35, 36, 58, 115, 122, 175

labor law   175
labor market   3–4, 7, 25, 37, 77, 84, 87
labor market policies   4, 98–101
life expectancy   49, 50, 57, 116, 163
long-term unemployment   25, 95, 210

mandatory capitalized pension system   109, 117
material deprivation   70–71
maternity leave   183
minimum wage   67, 183

neo-liberalization   13
net migration   129–130, 212, 215

old-age pension   50, 52–54, 58

parental leave   182
Pay-as-you-go system   2, 58, 109–110, 113–114

pension
    agricultural pension   52–53
    disability pension   52–53, 55–56, 115
    family pension   52–53, 55, 115, 117
    old-age pension   50, 52–54, 58
    war pension   52–53
pension and disability insurance   39, 45–46, 49, 50–57, 58, 175
pension reform   2, 115–118
pension system   2, 46–47, 112–113, 115–123
population projections   124–131
poverty   5, 14, 63–82
poverty reduction   74–75, 77–81
poverty threshold   14, 68
private healthcare   45, 157–158
Private Pension Fund   115, 117
private pension system   21
privatization   89, 103
public pension fund   109

recession   95, 201–204
reform
    healthcare reform   157–160
    pension reform   2, 115–118
    social protection reform   189–191
regional differences   162
relative poverty   64–65, 74–75
retirement policy   140
retirement system   50, 140
revenues and expenditures of the pension system   141–143

social assistance   18, 184, 188
social exclusion   15–17, 21–22, 70–71, 78
social insurance   35, 115, 122, 173, 175, 178–179
social insurance system   35, 115, 178
social pension   81
social protection   13–14, 15–21, 173–192
social protection system   13–14, 15–21, 174–187
Social Security   13–15, 23–28, 34–39
social state   13, 18, 31, 40
social work   17, 22–24, 27–30, 177
Socialist Republic of Yugoslavia   36, 69, 171, 197
sustainability of healthcare   165–167

three-pillar system   2, 49–58, 109, 115–117
transition   90, 103–104, 110, 130

unemployment   3, 24, 72–73, 84–103, 207–214
    long-term unemployment   25, 95, 210
    unemployment benefits   182–183
    unemployment insurance   18, 38
    unemployment rate   3, 24, 52, 65, 73, 84–86, 88–96
    youth unemployment   14, 93–94, 210

Voluntary Pension Fund   54, 56
voluntary pension scheme   54, 56, 109, 115
vulnerable social groups   25–26, 76, 99–100, 162

war pension   52–53
welfare state   18, 19, 102
workers to retirees ratio   120–121

youth unemployment   14, 93–94, 210
Yugoslavia   36, 69, 171, 197